Generation Z

Chloe Combi is a consultant on youth issues and a former school teacher. She has written for the *TES*, *Guardian*, *Independent*, *Daily Mail* and *Marie Claire*. She is a regular on Sky News and Channel 4 News and has also appeared on Newsnight, Woman's Hour, LBC, Radio 5 Live and Radio 2. She has been quoted by David Cameron in the House of Commons and is involved in the Mayor of London's ongoing campaign against youth crime and gangland culture. In 2010 she founded Write Club, a project which aims to raise aspirations of state-educated students by promoting literature, debate, art, film, theatre, music and philosophy.

Generation Z

Their Voices, Their Lives

CHLOE COMBI

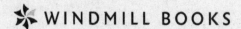

WINDMILL BOOKS

5 7 9 10 8 6 4

Windmill Books
20 Vauxhall Bridge Road
London SW1V 2SA

Windmill Books is part of the Penguin Random House group of companies whose addresses can be found at global.penguinrandomhouse.com.

Penguin Random House UK

The names, locations and some identifying details of the people and events in this book have been changed to protect the privacy of those involved.

First published by Hutchinson in 2015
First published in paperback by Windmill Books in 2015

www.windmill-books.co.uk

A CIP catalogue record for this book is available from the British Library.

ISBN 9780099592075

Typeset by SX Composing DTP, Rayleigh Essex
Printed and bound in Great Britain by Clays Ltd, St Ives Plc

FSC www.fsc.org MIX Paper from responsible sources FSC® C018179

Penguin Random House is committed to a sustainable future for our business, our readers and our planet. This book is made from Forest Stewardship Council® certified paper.

To all of Generation Z, particularly the many, many I interviewed for the book. But all adults must have their favourites, so especially for:

Isabel Combi, Rhiannon Combi, Sam Deanus and George Deanus.

Contents

Foreword

The teenagers and children of Generation Z were born between 1995 and 2001. They are the first generation who have never saved their pocket money to buy an album. They are astonished when you tell them there used to be only four channels on TV.

They've never known a world without the internet. They've grown up with violence and porn at their fingertips via an object unknown just one generation before: a smartphone. Not many of them have grandparents who fought in a war. They invented sexting, One Direction, slutting, braining, texting, butters, bae, boo and they like big butts (particularly Kim Kardashian's, currently).

Generation Z are growing up in a world shadowed with economic uncertainty, shrinking job prospects, widening social inequality and political apathy. They made London burn in 2011, they hang out on street corners, join gangs, are obese, claim the dole, have underage sex, commit crime, watch porn, fight, litter, swear and are a menace to society. Or so the government, the media and much of society would have you believe.

But is this a fair representation? Prior to researching and writing this book, I had worked with teenagers in various capacities for years and I thought I knew a lot about them. I had written about teenage gangs, violence, homelessness, pornography, education, bullying, sex and underage sex, dogfighting rings, grooming and a number of school-based pieces from around the world. Nothing, however, could have prepared me for the experience of writing this book. I revisited some of those situations and characters – finding two now dead and at least three in prison.

I travelled all around the UK finding every type of teenager I could. I visited schools, homes, hospitals, mental institutions, young offenders' institutions, prisons, parties, churches, mosques, synagogues, festivals, youth clubs, gay clubs, under-eighteen nightclubs, festivals and forests – all with the sole intention of interviewing Generation Z. I made friends, made a fool out of myself, got a skin disease, was nearly arrested twice, got hit on, nearly got hit (twice), was cried on, cried a lot, got yelled at, felt up, confessed to, cursed at, prayed for, prayed with, and invited to join various teen cults and groups.

I talked to rich kids and poor kids. I talked to kids who want to save the world and kids who want to blow it up. I talked to kids whose parents should be given awards and kids whose parents, in my opinion, should never have had kids. I talked to religious kids and kids who could explain with exactitude why God doesn't exist. I met kids whose lives are so achingly normal that they worry if it rains too much, and kids whose lives are so chaotic that – in one case – their reaction to finding their drug-addled prostitute mother dead on the floor was just to call the police and head off to school.

There was a temptation to string together all the most shocking and affecting vignettes, but this would have been disingenuous. The mundane is as much a feature of being a teenager as the fantastic. And *Generation Z* was only going to work as a window onto this generation if the whole gamut of teenage experience was represented.

Some topics came up again and again. These emerged as the natural chapters of the book. They are: family, relationships, the body, sex, school, race, gender, technology, class, crime, and what became a chapter entitled 'Looking to the Future and Advice for the Next Generation.'

The sheer number of interviews I conducted made detailed exposition of each subject impossible but the interviews were mostly so powerful and entertaining that they needed little explanation. It was enough to let the subjects tell their stories in their voices. All the stories are in the first person with very little editing or prompting from me.

One of the things that may surprise the reader is how candid the interviews are – it surprised me at times. Teenagers are so used to be spoken at, or to or about, that when they get the opportunity to speak for themselves, they really seize it. Quite often there was something cathartic and perhaps therapeutic in the interviews. They went down paths that were intimate and highly revealing, and I feel honoured to be able to give them a voice. There are, of course, standout stars for me but there is a story in here for everyone, whether it is because you can identify with it, remember it, are horrified or delighted by it, or it just makes you laugh or cry.

Generation Z will doubtless raise many questions and provoke reactions. One of the problems teenagers face is that they feel that they are living in a world that doesn't understand them. Many feel ignored, unheard and disenfranchised. Some parents feel that they barely know their teenager or the world they live in. This book is an accurate snapshot of teenage life today in all its grimness and glory and I hope it will be a conversation starter between teenagers and adults.

One question I have been asked a lot, whilst writing this book, is how, based on my experience, I would label this generation. Are they the Internet Generation, the Sex-Mad Generation, the Social-Media Generation, the Celebrity-Obsessed Generation or the Not-Much-to-See-Here Generation? Technology, the media, sex, celebrity and apathy are certainly features of this generation. But there is so much more to Generation Z. In the past year, there hasn't been a subject that I've discussed with them about which they haven't been interested and interesting and many of those opinions or experiences are contained herein.

I'll leave the last word on Generation Z to a member of it. As Kurt, 16, said to me before he went on stage with his jazz band: 'I can't wait to read it because it's going to be sick and I'm in it, and then I can give it to my mum so she can stop fucking asking me what I'm thinking all the time.'

Family

TOM, 15, CARDIFF

Currently studying for his GCSEs. His interests are Xbox, gaming, YouTube, fast cars and girls. He says he has no role models because 'most people are totally whack' but he would quite like to take over Jeremy Clarkson's job at Top Gear. *He would also like to sleep with Kim Kardashian but wouldn't choose a night with her in exchange for a year of gaming.*

My parents are whack. I don't hate them. Definitely not. They're just a bit lame. There's not much to tell you about them, really. My mum works in a school, I think. My dad has a job, but I'm not really sure what it is. He fixes things and something to do with trains. I dunno. They're just really boring.

My dad is sort of going bald and he doesn't say all that much, which is fine by me. He watches the TV a lot and goes fishing. He sometimes tries to get me to, but that's so boring. Have I ever been? No. Once, maybe when I was younger, but I hate the outdoors. I don't know why people get so excited about the summer. It's whack.

My mum winds me up. She's always in my business and trying to get me to do shit. Like tidy my room, or go outside. And she's always asking me about my business. About girls and stuff. She tidies up my room *every day* but I just think it's a good reason to snoop. Luckily she knows shit about computers and stuff, so I have everything passworded up to the max.

She once heard me gaming. There's a lot of banter, like cussing each other out, and she got really pissed off with me and told me I couldn't do it any more, but I told her to piss off and mind her own business.

She once tried to impose this rule about laptops all being kept in the lounge and no internet after 10 p.m., but I went fucking mental and she caved after a while. Dad didn't really have an opinion on it. I know he's had a crafty look at some internet stuff because I've looked at his search history after he's been on it. I don't think he knows you can do that. They're both a bit thick, to be honest.

The one time I do get into fights with my family is over my little brother. He's a little shit and I like to fuck around with him. But then he always tells on me, and Mum changes the WiFi code in the house until I apologise.

Parents should just stay out of their kids' business and rooms, pay the bills and give us the money we need. You ask any kid. That's what they really want.

MARK, 17, BERKSHIRE

Currently studying for his A levels. He lives with his mum and younger brother. He wants to be an ethical banker because he believes it is a highly corrupt sector that 'needs to be fixed from the inside out'.

My mum is awesome. My dad left when I was five and my brother was two, so I've never known him at all, and I don't want to. He tried to get in touch a couple of times, recently, via Facebook, but I told him to fuck off. I've just won a really good internship at this company that will pay my whole way through university and a really decent salary when I work in the holidays and somehow I think he heard about that. He was all like, 'I'm so proud of you,' but Mum told me to be careful. Apparently he always pops up when he smells money. When she inherited a bit of money when my granddad died, he tried to come back to her, but she told him to piss off.

I've always felt a bit like the man about the house, because of not really having a dad, and I worry about my mum all the time. We're really close and talk about everything, which some of my mates find weird. But when they meet my mum, they understand. She's really cool. Which is a good thing, considering she had to do all the things a dad is supposed to do. You'd think the whole sex conversation would have been difficult, but it wasn't. I mean, what real difference does it make a woman talking to you about boners, than a man?

I definitely think having such a strong mother has made me respect women more, and has also made me more comfortable around them. Because I see Mum as a whole person and not just this person who puts food on the table, gives me money and is married to someone I call Dad, I have a far greater understanding of what women are, and what they are capable of.

There was a time when I was little when I'd have been really jealous if my mum got a boyfriend and I think Mum didn't because of this, but now I'd really like her to. Kids find it impossible to see their parents as human beings with needs and I worry about her being lonely. We don't discuss her romantic life that much, but the other day, me and my mates were teasing her and telling her to get online and get internet dating. Of course I worry about her meeting weirdos, but it's so common now, everybody is at it. Not just old people in their thirties and forties.

I'd like my mum to maybe meet a cool, progressive head teacher of a school. Or perhaps someone who runs a successful charity. And why shouldn't she? She's really smart, pretty and cool. I'd like her to be with someone by the time I leave for university. Me and my mate Toby are going to set her up a dating profile on the Guardian Singles website. I don't think too many axe-murderers read the *Guardian*. They would probably read the *Express* or the *Telegraph*.

LINDSAY, 16, NORFOLK

Studying for her GCSEs at an all-girls' grammar school. She says she 'used to' have lots of interests and hobbies, but since her brother's death she feels guilty about socialising and having fun. She spends most of her time doing school work and washes her hands exactly 100 times a day. Her parents haven't noticed.

I think it started with a football injury. Jason, who was exactly nineteen months older than me, was a really gifted sports player. He was good at all sports, but in particular football. He wasn't good enough to go pro or anything. He always made me promise that after he was dead, nobody would exaggerate who he was and I've always tried to uphold that.

He wasn't a saint and he wasn't a martyr and he could be a real pain in the arse. He wanted to be a doctor when we were younger, although he quickly realised he wasn't strong enough at science to go into medicine. He worried about that. Just before he got sick, he was talking about joining the Navy, and he would have been good at that, I think. He was just the kind of boy who they probably would have wanted.

A team player with a mind of his own. And he was really kind.

Anyway, he'd been hurt in football – or so we thought – a knee injury. But it wouldn't heal. And Jason just seemed generally out of sorts. Mum has always mollycoddled Jason. There is no doubt he was her secret favourite, although she'd never admit it in a million years. We were eating dinner and Jason, who was feeling unwell again, came downstairs in his boxer shorts. We were never the kind of family that worried about that. Locked bathroom doors aren't a big thing in our house. They still aren't much except when I know Dad is in there crying with the shower on. Mum doesn't really try to hide it. The crying, that is.

Jason appeared, I don't know, just really out of sorts. Confused. He was really sweating and was muttering about Fanta. He got really, really angry when Mum said there was no Fanta left. He'd drunk it all, because that was all he'd really wanted the last couple of days. Previously, Jason had been a real pig and would eat everything in sight without gaining an ounce. I hated him for that! His knee was so swollen and he'd lost so much weight. Mum was staring at him and I knew there was a real problem when I looked at Dad. He'd just gone pale, like he was seeing Jase for the first time. In just five days, he'd deteriorated that much. The week before, he'd been bombing about and going to school and now he seemed like this weird, sweaty shadow of himself.

It sounds awful but I just looked away. I didn't know what to do.

Mum and Dad took him straight to the hospital. We'd been given, like, private medical insurance when we were born as a present from my grandma and she paid it every year for our birthdays. We used to think it was the shittiest present ever, but now I think it might have been the greatest. He was seen and admitted that night. Mum and Dad left me all by myself until really late that night, and I was really upset. Eventually Dad came home and I could tell he'd been crying. He also smelt of cigarettes. He had given up when I was seven. I asked him if he'd been smoking and he just got really angry with me, so I started crying. He hugged me and said sorry and I asked what was wrong with Jason and he wouldn't say anything, he just hugged me really tightly.

The next day, Mum made me go to school. I was really angry and confused. I felt like I was being punished. I kept asking what was going on and Mum just *snapped* at me, like, 'For fuck's sake, Lindsay, stop making things worse,' and I've never heard Mum swear. That day they forgot to give me lunch money. I didn't have any lunch that day. Or the next day. They kept forgetting and I was too scared to remind them in case it made Jason worse.

On the Wednesday of that week – he'd been admitted on the Sunday – my parents picked me up from school. They hadn't done that in years because school was so close to home. They picked me up at lunchtime and the head teacher walked me out. He was being really nice to me even though he's usually a bit odd. Mum and Dad were taking me to see Jason. He'd been begging to see me. They explained in the car he had cancer in his bones. I was completely shocked. I kept asking if he was going to be OK. Mum kept pulling up and pushing down the lock on the car door and because it was a central lock it kept making this really annoying 'thwonk' sound. Dad kept telling her to stop and she would stop and then start again. Dad asked me about school and I knew it was bad.

Jason looked much better although he was attached to these machines and Mum started arranging his flowers and that. I felt weird. I felt shy, like I was intruding on someone else's family. Jason started to laugh and said something like, 'Well, this is awkward,' which made me laugh. He asked Mum and Dad to go and get some lunch from the canteen and bring him some more Fanta. I think they were relieved.

When they were gone, he gave me a hug and I started to cry. He told me not to be upset, that this was an excellent excuse to bunk off school and he was going to be fine. I asked him to be honest with me, was he really going to be OK, and he looked me in the eye and said, 'Maybe not.' It was a funny thing to hear. I can't really describe it, so I asked if he wanted to watch the Glastonbury highlights on the BBC iPlayer. He let me lie next to him and when Mum came back she yelled at me for not taking my shoes off. Jason said, 'Don't yell at her, it's not her fault, you know,' and Mum's eyes just filled up with tears and she ran out the room. Dad sat down with us and watched Kasabian – they were *so* good that year. She came back later and apologised. We all had dinner together that night on Jason's bed.

They didn't do chemotherapy on him for very long. It had gone too far and it made him so ill, he begged them to stop. He said he'd rather leave it to chance than choose to make himself that ill. I was so angry with him about that decision. I still am. I feel like he was choosing to give up, and that so wasn't him. He wasn't a macho boy, but he was definitely strong in his own way.

But Dad told me a little bit later about the physical things that were happening to him and the risks. I don't really want to talk about that, because the pain he was in and the fact that I didn't know makes me feel sick. He died less than two weeks later. It was quite a peaceful slipping away. I think he was in pain but was also on a lot of medication.

No one was sleeping very much those last two weeks. It was like a hotel. People up and down and checking on Jason. Mum and Dad in the living room either crying and holding each other or arguing in a way I'd never seen. Not like shouting, but kind of asking 'why' over and over again and batting the blame back and forth.

But I woke up really early on the day before he died. Like 5 a.m. It was light because it was the summer and for the first time in ages, the house was completely quiet. I thought everyone was asleep for once and I just wanted to go downstairs and have a drink of water and sit there by myself.

Jason was sitting there on the couch next to the French windows watching a fox sort of potter about on the lawn with what I guess was the baby fox. He was smiling. Not just happy smiling, but sort of ... I can't think of the word. Peaceful. I didn't say anything. I just put my head on his lap and watched the foxes with him too and he stroked my hair.

He died the next day. I still get up at 5 a.m. There is often a fox in our garden just snaffling about. I like to think it's the baby one that got to grow up.

LEROY, 15, SOUTH LONDON

Currently studying for GCSEs. Attends three drama clubs. Wants to rule the universe, because 'any other job is a bit shit in comparison'. He will, however, settle for being a Hollywood actor because 'a lot of black actors in Hollywood are wankers, especially

Will Smith'. His role models are Sidney Poitier, Forest Whitaker and Samuel L. Jackson because they are 'definitely not wankers'.

I know it's not cool to say this, but I fucking love my parents. They are jokes. Mum says we are the London estate Obamas because my dad is this quiet guy who just wants to walk his dog and she is scary and bosses him around. That's true of them, isn't it? He might be the President, but you get this idea he just wants to chill with a beer and let her run the country.

My mum runs everything she can get her hands on. She is on the committee for our church, my brother's nursery, she's a school governor at my school and she runs a book club. And she has a job. Dad says it's a good thing because otherwise she'd be at home driving us all mad instead.

My dad is doing a PhD in political science, I think, so you never know. Maybe we will actually become the Obamas. But Dad says Mum is more fly than Michelle. My mum is the breadwinner but Dad says she wore the trousers from day one, anyway, so what's new?

My mum says I have a talent. She drives me to all my acting classes, but she says I can't do any proper auditions until I've finished my GCSEs, as everybody needs options.

I don't think I will, but you don't argue with Mum.

MICKY, 18, MANCHESTER

Unemployed and not in education, Micky was put into care when he was two. He had two foster families growing up, both of whom were unable to deal with him and 'put him back in the system'.

He has a criminal record for stealing and has been to youth detention twice. He was homeless for weeks at a time throughout his teens.

I never knew my dad. Didn't meet him. Didn't know him. To be honest, I don't think my mum did really. He took off way before I was born. My mum was seventeen when she had me and didn't even know she was pregnant till about six months in. She was using all sorts of drugs, but luckily not heroin then, so I was all right.

I don't know Mum at all, really. She'd turn up occasionally when she was a bit cleaner once in a while and I'd sit in a room with a care worker and her and she'd try to chat and she'd usually cry. Occasionally we went to McDonald's and I'd get a Happy Meal. That's the only thing I ever got from her, and the care worker would buy it anyway. I kept those toys for a long time, but they are long since gone. I don't know where.

I was in and out of foster homes when I wasn't running away. But you know the thing that really fucks that system up? It's not the parents, because obviously they are do-gooders who want to help. It's if they have kids. Those kids – period, point blank – do not want you in their fucking house, under their fucking roof. Every time I got kicked out it was because I lost it with my so-called foster brother and sister.

The first time I beat the shit out of the oldest boy. He deserved it. He was a nasty little shit and just did anything he could to get on my case. I hit him with a chair and knocked him cold out. The parents – I remember their names – Sue and Gregg – acted all sad and said it was a last resort, but you could tell they were relieved to have an excuse to get rid of me. I was nine then, I think.

Second time, it was this really nice house. Really nice. I don't remember much of what happened. Sometimes I don't remember the past that well. But it didn't last long. I probably did something to deserve it.

So, it was back to care homes. They're not unlike prisons. A lot of drugs, a lot of violence, a lot of watching your back. They're just bleak. I started smoking weed, drinking. Anything I could get my hands on. You would think because of my mum, I'd have learnt to stay away from heroin, but I didn't. Everything just goes very, very quiet on that, you know? When you don't belong anywhere, things are never quiet or still and you need that. I get that.

I didn't make it through school. I was expelled three times and I think they just gave up. I'm in temporary accommodation right now and hoping to get a council house. I have a girlfriend, but when you both use, it's like three of you are in the relationship and it's always causing trouble between you.

She found out last week she is pregnant, so we have been referred to a clinic and I want to get off heroin and do it right. I'd like a family.

FAROOD, 17, LEEDS

Completed GCSEs last summer and is now studying for A levels in maths, engineering and physics. He has only spoken English for four years. He was originally from Iran but had to flee in 2010 after the previous year's governmental elections.

We had a very nice life in Iran before things went terribly wrong. My father was quite high up in government and my mother stayed at home to raise us. I went to a very good school because I was academically quite gifted and hard-working. My father says education is the most important thing for both boys and girls. He and my mother are very encouraging of my younger sisters' education. He believes women should be educated and allowed to do the same jobs as men. He thinks it is a grave mistake what some Islamic countries do to women and thinks equality is the key to progress. My father is not a very religious man, but you have to keep that fairly secret. Actually, Iran was a very progressive country before the government changed, especially in comparison to a place like, for example, Afghanistan.

My mother was not formally educated because that was not what was expected then, but her father was quite progressive and let her be educated at home. My mother is brilliant. She speaks nine languages fluently and probably about six more reasonably. I think she gets sad sometimes at the opportunities she missed. She would have been a great academic, I think. My father says not letting women learn is like cutting off half the possibility of the human race. Imagine how many brilliant women have been wasted in history? I think both of my sisters will be brilliant. They are cleverer than me, for sure. I am the stupid one, which is a funny joke in its own way (*laughs*).

Apart from my father, I think my sisters were the biggest reason we had to leave our country. A lot of Islamic countries are not safe places for anyone really, but especially girls. I hear terrible things from people at home that make me very scared for our future. I don't know what is happening to the world.

My father opposed Ahmadinejad very passionately and was working very hard to stop him being voted in. He was a big supporter of Mousavi. Nothing in Iranian politics is perfect, but Mousavi is much more progressive. He believes in reform. Under Ahmadinejad things have gone severely backwards. It is a much more totalitarian regime again.

I was quite young then, but I was very, very frightened before that election. I remember hearing many conversations late at night between my father and his colleagues and there was so much worry. It's not like here where if the person you don't like gets in nothing much changes. We knew that if Ahmadinejad were to win, our whole family and many, many of our friends would be in serious danger. They have different attitudes there, as I'm sure you know from the BBC. People disappear, get put in prison, tortured.

My mother was very worried, but she told me not to worry. That the right people would win and we would be safe. It was what was expected, but again it's not like here. We didn't see my father very much during the campaigns but he would come home and see us when he could and bring sweets. He would check my work and ask me questions about it. He was very affectionate in those last few weeks and would hug me more than usual. I would protest and my mother would laugh at us and tell me these were precious moments.

The day after the election results, the country was in turmoil. It wasn't like in the movies where you are hidden in the backs of cars, but I think my mother hid a lot of the terror from us. We learnt my father had been arrested and that we had to leave immediately. I suppose my father had good connections because we stayed with friends of his for a couple of days and then flew to Germany the same week. The worst thing was nobody knew what had happened to my father. Or maybe they did, but they didn't want to tell me. But I'm not stupid. I kept dreaming for many weeks of seeing my father in a room full of water through a glass window, not being able to get to him and screaming his name. I kept waking up shouting and my mother begged me to calm down because she didn't want my sisters to be more frightened than they already were. She told me I had to act like a man until my father came back and I told her I would do that for her.

I had to leave the country without my father, not knowing what had happened to him. That definitely makes you a man.

CRESSIDA, 16, CAMBRIDGE

Completed her GCSEs this summer and will be studying for her A levels next year. She would like to work in fashion. Her family is worth in excess of £50 million.

To be honest, it never really occurred to me how wealthy my family was until I was well into my childhood. I think a big part of that is if you are surrounded by wealthy people, it normalises it and it didn't really occur to me that most people don't grow up with swimming pools, horses and several houses in different countries.

I don't think rich people should be made to feel bad about having money. I mean most of them have worked really hard for it. But at the same time, I find those kinds of *Made in Chelsea* programmes really embarrassing. It implies we are all spoilt airheads who just shop and drink for a living. The school I go to *is* really expensive, but it's not some ridiculous finishing school. They expect you to work really hard. My older brother got into Oxford and they don't just give those places away.

But at the same time, I do know some people who laugh at poor people and think their money gives them entitlement. I was at a nightclub a couple of weeks ago and there was a group of boys who were working out how many hours someone on the minimum wage would have to work for a glass of the champagne they were drinking. These were £6,000 bottles of champagne. Lots of people were laughing and putting it on Instagram, which I thought was a bit tasteless.

My family, despite the money, is fairly normal. We do normal things. My dad is rarely home. He runs a hedge fund and is mostly in New York or Hong Kong. Sometimes he takes us during the school holidays but I've become a bit bored of those places. Once you've seen a few top hotels, you've pretty much seen them all. I'm quite fond of our beach houses. We have one in the South of France and one on Muscat. My mum hates the beach, so Dad is constantly teasing us about the fact that it's a nightmare to get us all together to go on a holiday. My brother has this weird hippyish streak and has reached a stage where he's embarrassed by our wealth and went off on some tiny budget to India or somewhere. He got all inspired after watching that film *Into the Wild*. I thought that boy was an idiot. Idealism is one thing, but he had so much guilt, he couldn't even enjoy life or the journey. It's not a crime to have money.

I don't see my dad that much and Mum is really busy. But they do provide me with a really good life. I have my own credit card, which Dad pays off for me. He gets mock-annoyed at the bill and only put his foot down once when I spent £31,000 in one day at Gucci. Quite a bit of it was on a coat. He said I had to work off the bill, but then went away the next day and forgot. Mum is pretty spendy, so she wasn't too worried and we have people to do chores for us.

I love shopping with Mum and so do all my girlfriends. My mum was quite a successful model in her day – like back in the Eighties – so a long time ago. She still looks really good and takes really good care of her appearance, which all my friends' mothers do. Ageing in our circles just isn't acceptable or necessary any more. Even my grandmother is still beautiful. But Mum has an amazing eye for style and has this really inherent knack for working the latest fashions and trends. She is very good friends with a lot of the top designers and attends all the fashion shows. She took me and my best friend to all the best shows at London Fashion Week and we got to go to some of the after-parties with the properly A-list crowd. It was amazing.

She is currently arranging an internship at a top fashion magazine for me, which I am super excited about. To be honest, I'm rather bored with school and would like to start my fashion career. Mum absolutely agrees with this, but Dad says having spent all this money on my education, he'd like me to see it through until the end.

LOTTIE, 15, EXETER

Currently beginning her GCSEs. She hopes one day to be a doctor. She and her three siblings are raised by her father. Her mother is in long-term care in a psychiatric hospital.

My dad worked his whole life until about eight years ago at Kodak. When smartphones and digital cameras really took off, there was less and less for him to do. He did something with film, which isn't really used except by a few people. Eventually he got made redundant. The redundancy money lasted for a while – quite a long time. He thought he would get another job easily. He told me a few weeks ago, when he was drunk, that he has applied for about 4,000 jobs in the last eight years but eventually stopped when he got rejected to be a bin man. I felt so upset when he told me that. He was drunk but he took my hand and there were tears in his eyes and he said, 'I'm sorry I'm not even good enough to be a bin man, Lottie.'

I think because I'm the eldest and help him out a lot, I'm the closest thing he has to a wife at the moment, so he tells me more things than some dads would tell their kids. I gave him a hug and told him I was proud of him anyway. I am proud of him. There's not a lot of dads that would cope as well as he has. We have no money, and my mum isn't showing any signs of getting better. She hasn't for a while now. She has never been well since I was born, but had good times and bad times. She has been having her bad time for about four years now. She went out on her own, which she never would do, because I was out at school and so were my brothers Robert and John. Dad was at the job centre, I think, because he doesn't really go anywhere else, except to the pub, because we can't really afford it. He didn't like leaving her especially with the baby, but sometimes he had to. When he got back, Mum had just disappeared with baby George. He's nearly a year now, but was newly born, then.

At first, Dad thought she had gone for a walk, even though she doesn't like to go outside much. But then he realised the buggy was still there and started to worry and went out to look for her. Only Dad has a mobile phone, which we all share and borrow when we go out, but that was at home too, so Dad couldn't call her.

Eventually she was found on the top level of a multi-storey car park just walking around and around it with George in her arms, crying. She goes all sort of glassy-eyed and sometimes doesn't respond when she's really bad. Someone called the police. They were worried that she was a suicide risk, even though I don't think it's true. After that she got worse and worse. She was talking to people that weren't there and would suddenly start screaming in the middle of the night. It really scared us all. We have a lovely lady doctor – Dr Patel – and she worked really hard to get Mum a place at the hospital, which I know was hard. I really miss my mum and I just want her to get well. I know the hospital is the best place, but sometimes she doesn't really seem to recognise us. Dad has stopped taking the boys there. He says we can't really afford the bus fare, which is true, but I think he mostly worries how it affects them.

I have had to do a lot of stuff that mums do, but because I am good at school and want to be a doctor, Dad won't let me do any chores after dinner. He says that's my time for school work and he won't let the boys bother me unless it's really serious. I have to help him wash John's hair though, because John will headbutt you if you don't watch it.

The boys have stopped asking about Mum so much. It's weird how kids seem to adapt to things. In all honesty, I think they find the lack of money the hardest. We rent a television and sometimes I wish we didn't because it just shows kids what they are missing. Every single advert is like an advert for food we can't afford, or TVs, mobiles, holidays, places to go. Robert asked Dad the other day if we could go to Disneyland. He might as well be asking if we could ever go to the moon.

We don't have a car any more, because something went wrong with it and Dad couldn't afford to get it fixed. Things have got a bit better because of the food banks. We get a lot of stuff from there and since we have been saving on food, we managed to pay off part of three bills that were threatening to send bailiffs.

We have had the bailiffs before, but actually they haven't been too bad. They mostly agree on a payment plan. I mean, what can they take? George? Everybody around here is on a payment plan with collection people. Everyone here uses food banks.

Things aren't too bad. I'm doing well at school; the boys seem to be happy now we have enough food. There were times the winter before last we had to cut down because it was so cold and we couldn't afford to have three meals each and put money on the electricity meter. But food banks have helped.

I mostly want my mum to come home, though. I'm doing my best, but I wish she'd get better.

AISHA, 17, NORTH LONDON

Failed most of her GCSEs 'because I was crap at school'. Is currently a junior at a top hair-styling salon. It is her ambition, when she qualifies, to be a celebrity hair stylist. She has worked backstage at several major television talent shows, assisting the more senior stylists. She has been to the homes of some of the most famous people in the world as an assistant to a highly sought-after celebrity hairdresser.

When my boss met me, he thought I was going to be a 'typical Indian princess' type. I have proved him wrong. I'm really hard-working and good at what I do – he thinks I'll be an amazing hairdresser one day – but I know what he means. I have an amazing family life. Not just because I want for absolutely nothing, but because my family are very, very close and have a brilliant time together. Family life is very important to a lot of Hindus, but my family are close even for Hindus.

We will all go out together possibly three times a week, normally to some fabulous restaurant. People assume just because you are brown, you only eat curries in a sari with other Indians, but we go for cocktails at the Sanderson Hotel or maybe Claridge's and then on to a very, very nice restaurant – and usually not an Indian or any kind of curry!

We aren't particularly religious although we do go to the temple. But it's to socialise as much as anything. Recently my dada (*her grandfather*) has started talking about me meeting a nice Hindu boy and he arranged these kind of chaperoned meetings with some boys. They were so moist. They all looked like they had been dredged up from the 1970s and had acne and thick glasses – and a few of them were wearing turbans, which we only wear on formal occasions. One was so nervous, he just sat there sweating and stammering. My dad's back was to me, standing by the door, and I could see his shoulders shaking with laughter. Once we were in the car again, I hit him and made him swear not to do that to me again. He said OK. I can choose my own boy providing he is a Hindu.

It's my older sister I feel sorry for. It's the one dark spot in our family. It's like an elephant in the room – is that what it means when everyone knows something and no one will talk about it? She has been dating a Muslim boy – well, man now – for nearly twelve years. They were high-school sweethearts. He's such a great guy and they love each other so much. When my parents found out, about seven years ago, there was a huge – and I mean *huge* – fight. They told her that she had to choose between him or us. My dad usually rolls over in fights, but there is no room for argument here. She just can't. If she wants to marry him, she'll lose us forever. Even I wouldn't be allowed to see or speak with her any more – but I would.

They know she still sneaks out to see him, but the clock is ticking. In our culture, marriage is the only acceptable route. You stay as girls with your parents until you are married and then you go to your husband. It's frowned upon to live with your girlfriends like in white culture. Even going away to uni can be a problem. Unless you are studying medicine (*laughs*).

My sister is waaaay older than a girl should be to get married. She's getting on for thirty and is made to go and meet all these guys in a really aggressive way. Like 'GET MARRIED NOW'. I feel sorry for her. She's trying to buy herself time but she's going to have to make a decision soon. And she knows it. I'm frightened of what might happen to my lovely family because of it. If he were Hindu, everything would be fine.

JASON, 17, BURY ST EDMUNDS

Completed his GCSEs this summer. Has a younger brother who is autistic.

When I tell people my story, they never think it could be possible. I mean, it happens to people on housing estates. Not people with six-bedroom houses, a pool and stockbroker father. We have moved since, which was hard. It's been a bad few years.

My dad has been violent with my mum ever since I remember. She used to hide it well when I was a little kid, but it got so much worse since my brother was born, seven years ago, that it was impossible to hide. I think I've noticed it more since I was about twelve. What do you notice when you are a kid, but when the next cartoon is on, or when the next Wii game is coming?

I remember the first time I really saw Dad hit Mum. I was stunned. I knew they argued quite badly. I'd hear my mum screaming and then crying and my dad shouting. But it was only ever at night. The next day Mum would be really shaky and red-eyed and she always wore this bathrobe afterwards. Mum is quite glamorous and wears these white, pretty pyjamas usually but after arguments it was always this ugly bathrobe and she'd have a tissue screwed up in her hands.

I knew from a really young age, when she wore the bathrobe, it was a really bad sign and I'd be extra nice to her and make her tea. I never wanted to leave for school on those days and I never wanted to come home either. When I was eleven, Dad started talking about me going to boarding school. I knew, deep down, that I didn't want to leave Mum alone so I begged not to go. Dad agreed in the end. He wasn't all that interested in us anyway and by that time we had worse problems. My baby brother had been diagnosed with severe autism and needed serious care.

It was like Dad blamed Mum for both my brother and the fact they couldn't hide it. Image was big with my dad. You can hide bruises. You can't hide a brother with a mental disability. He was bad and getting worse and the reason, I think, was because of Dad.

By this time, Dad would openly hit, kick and punch Mum in front of us. Once he held her head in the pool. He would call her a cunt, bitch and slag and say it was her fault they had had a 'mong'. My brother was such a calm thing, usually. Just in his own little world. I was one of the few people he would really respond to. From a fairly young age, when Dad started hitting Mum, he would throw these absolute fits. Like terrible, terrible scary ones. He would start to shriek in this long, high-pitched wail and would thrash and spit. Or he'd ball up and moan and I'd try to comfort him. I begged my mum to leave. But she said where? With an autistic little boy, no money, no friends.

It happened on March 10th, I remember it so clearly. The weather was so cold. I was on my way home, almost at the bottom of my drive, and I could already hear the screaming. I ran up the drive and they were in the kitchen. There was blood everywhere and I didn't even recognise my mum. She was absolutely covered in blood and was holding a knife in a really shaky hand and Dad was just laughing at her. Laughing. He hadn't seen me, because his back was to me, so I hit him as hard as I could around the back of the head. He went down like a sack of shit. It was almost funny. One moment he was standing and then he just dropped flat on his face. I kept hitting him and hitting him until Mum pulled me off. I didn't even realize that I was crying or what I was doing. I'd smashed the side of his face, broken ribs and was about to smash his head again, which probably could have killed him. I wish I had.

Luckily, almost straight away, the police arrived. The neighbours had made a call. When they saw the scene, they called an ambulance straight away and two turned up. They took Dad away in one and us in the next. I held my brother, who had been up in his room the whole time. They kept Mum in for two nights and Dad for ten days. On top of his injuries, he went into alcohol detox. That's how much he'd been drinking.

Dad's sentence was bullshit. Mum actually did press charges. He got a suspended sentence and ordered to stay away from us. His solicitor went massively to town on his whole addiction problems and the fact he was 'acting' the way he did due to massive coke and booze problems. He basically got out of jail free if he promised to get treatment. He didn't even lose his job. I'm guessing this happens a lot more than you might think in those kind of worlds. We are so much better off without him, and he won't change. He was beating up Mum long before all the drink and drugs. And my brother is so much better now. He'll never be fine, but he's like a different boy. I've sometimes wondered how much the stress of Dad affected Mum during pregnancy. I blame everything on him.

I'm not scared of him. I'll kill him if he comes near us again. But I am scared of turning out like him. I keep reading that boys who see domestic violence often turn to it. But I'd never hit a girl, ever.

Relationships

JESSICA, 16, HAMPSHIRE

Attends an all-girls' school and has become an active anti-bullying campaigner. Thinks the legal rights of schoolchildren are under-represented and wants to become a barrister specialising in legal cases for under eighteen-year-olds.

One of the most complicated, weird things ever is girls' friendships with other girls. It's something guys will never understand. My dad has spent the last ten years, practically, quizzing me and my sisters on the subject. He is so confused by them and says with friends like the friends we have, why do we need enemies? We're always like, 'Oh Dad, shut up,' but I can sort of see where he is coming from. My friends are the most important thing to me, but have definitely caused me the most problems over the years. Like, when I think about all the mean things we've all done to each other, I suppose it is a bit *shocking*. But I would literally die without my best girls. It's the most important thing in the world.

If I had to give an age where things are the worst for girls' friendships, it would definitely be Year 9. My little sister is in that year and it is a good reminder of how hellish it can be. As we speak, three of her best friends aren't talking to her because she said she didn't like tattoos. One of them decided that was an insult to her mum, who I guess has tattoos, and the whole thing has blown up. She's devastated and won't eat, so on top of that, she's now arguing loads with Mum, too. It's soooo stressful being at home at the moment with a half-anorexic sister and a stressy mother.

Really, honestly, you *do* compare yourself to your friends. Like, I'm not the prettiest in our friendship group, but I'm quirky looking. Aliana, my friend, says I have the kind of prettiness that other girls aren't threatened by, which is why I haven't had too many fallings out. There's this girl in our school called Rain and she's absolutely gorgeous, but loads of other girls bitch behind her back, because I think mostly they're jealous. And boys won't talk to her because she's soooo pretty, she's quite intimidating. I actually think she might be kind of a bitch, but I don't talk to her, so I don't actually care.

The funny thing is, it's sooooo hard to remember what you argued over from a couple of months ago, let alone a year or two years ago, but it seems so important at the time. Like last summer a friend of ours, Jazzy, posted all these pictures on Facebook that were like, sooooo inappropriate. Like, so slutty. All these selfies of her in her underwear and stuff. And the trouble is, she doesn't have a good, *good* body. Like you'd give her a six, maybe seven. There's definite back fat and her legs aren't great. And she's always talking about her amazing arse, because it's kinda big, but it's not good big. Do you know what I mean? So we had to sit her down and tell her like, 'You not only look like a bit of a slut in these pictures, but you look a little chunky, too.' We didn't tell her she looked fat, because that would have been nasty. She cried a lot, but I think she appreciated the pointers in the end. It's hard sometimes drawing the line between mean and honest, because you don't want to upset your friends, but at the same time, it's your duty to be honest. That's what a good friend does. Like, one time I kind of got into a ghetto girl image for a while. And Ali had to sit me down and tell me I just couldn't pull it off. It was kind of like a fashion intervention. I was so upset at the time. This was in Year 10. But now I'm grateful for the honesty. They didn't want me walking around looking like a skank. And that's real friendship.

LISA, 14, BRISTOL

Attends a large and oversubscribed comprehensive school. She has just chosen her GCSE options and feels so uncomfortable with some of her peers, she based her options on what they didn't choose. She says the school 'haven't noticed' her predicament and she feels too scared to ask for help.

I don't have any friends at all. I've tried and tried and nobody seems to like me and I don't know why. It's not really like I get terribly bullied. It's just that everybody ignores me and thinks that I'm weird. It makes me really sad and I cry myself to sleep at night. Nobody picks me in games or lets me hang out with them in the playground or talk to them. They say I 'won't understand' their conversations and when I come over, they all go quiet and sometimes they giggle.

It was OK in primary school. I had quite a lot of good friends, but it all changed when I went to secondary school. My parents say it is very important for young people to enjoy childhood and they think everyone is growing up too fast now. I look quite young for my age. I haven't started my period yet and I'm one of the last. But my mum makes it worse. She won't let me wear make-up or jewellery or trainers or any really nice clothes. She says it's 'completely unnecessary' for me to have an iPhone, iPad or even a laptop. So I can't be on Facebook, Instagram, Ask FM, Snapchat. I can't even play Candy Crush Saga. Everyone at school is *obsessed* by it. Me and my brother aren't really allowed to watch TV, so we read a lot and do our school work very well. But I feel like I have nothing I can talk to the other girls about. The boys don't notice me at all. This big boy the other day, maybe in Year 11, told me to 'get the fuck back to nursery'. I cried in the toilets because everyone in the corridor laughed at me.

What was the worst thing was, all the popular girls went to see a film a couple of months ago. It was a '15' rated so they were all boasting about it. I so wished I could go, but they never talk to me. It was this film called *Carrie* (*the remake of the Brian Palma classic starring Chloë Moretz*). On Monday all the girls started calling me 'Carrie'. I didn't understand it at all, but I knew it wasn't good because everyone was laughing really bitchily. I went and asked the librarian who is really kind to me and she got really angry when I told her. I think she had a massive go at the girls for me, because they backed off, but I know they are still whispering it when I pass.

I went and looked it up on the school computer and I cried. It's so horrible. I don't understand why everyone hates me so much. I have never done anything wrong or bad to anyone.

SKYE, THOMAS, HOPE, ARIANE, ALL 15, AND RICHARD, 14, MILTON KEYNES

They have all been friends since primary school and attend secondary school together. They are united by their love for music, skating and 'hating chavvy bullies'. There has, on occasion, been romance in their friendship group but they made a collective decision to all 'just be friends'. They think this will mean the friendship group will remain forever intact, as getting off with each other 'messes things up'.

THOMAS: We get called everything. EMO, goth, faggot, punk, grunger, metaller, gay, gaylord. We've had so much shit said to us. We've had things thrown at us. We nearly got jumped about three times in the last year by these fucking wanker hooligans. Ariane got put into hospital by these girls just because she was wearing the clothes she was and had some piercings. I hate putting labels on things. If anything I'd identify myself as a skater. That's my life. That and my friends. We might not be one of the cool crowd, but our crowd is wicked. There's none of the shit everyone else puts up with, with their friends. No comparing trainers or being called a fag, or a slut if you're a girl. We just like our music and we like to skate.

ARIANE: And smoke.

THOMAS: Yeah, we're big into our smoking. It's probably the only thing we've got in common with all those Rihanna clones. But I hate it here. Absolutely loathe it. I just want to be in London. Camden is our spiritual home.

ARIANE: I LOVE CAMDEN! After I got assaulted by these girls walking home, I had real difficulty going out again. I was having panic attacks. These guys were the *best*. They did shifts in hospital with me. I was in for nearly a week. They went everywhere with me, but I was too scared to go anywhere. So Thomas organised this secret trip for me. His older brother has this really wicked camper-type van. I agreed to go if he promised I didn't have to get out the van. So Eliot – Tom's older brother – drove us to Camden. I'd never been there before. Everybody looked like us and I felt safe. I managed to get out and walk around all day. I got much better after that.

HOPE: The thing that makes it so hard is another life is so close. It's *horrible* at our school being like us. Like, it's OK to discriminate against us but you couldn't do that for other reasons. Everyone in our school is the same. They love Chris Brown, One Direction, Miley Virus ... whatever. I get slammed into the lockers. Called a lesbian. Everything. Just because I dye my hair red and listen to Panic! at the Disco. It's disgusting. And the teachers let it slide. Like they'll do all these lessons on homophobia and racism. But if someone wears black and pierces their nose, it's all right to call them a 'fat, goth dyke'.

THOMAS: Which you're not, by the way.

RICHARD: I get called gay all the time, too. I wouldn't even care, except it's causing me real hassle. I got punched in the face in PE. This kid said it was an accident. But he's a fucking bully. I hate him. I wish he was dead.

HOPE: Me too. Justin. All Justins are wankers. He's said some awful things to me too. I'm so glad we can all be together at lunchtime. Luckily Skye is in all my classes. We just avoid everyone else.

SKYE: I feel the same. Like, sometimes you sort of wish you could fit in and be like the 'mainstream' and then you see how they treat each other, not just us. I don't understand how being a bully and total bitch is a ticket to making you popular, but it seems to work. The absolute worst kids in the school, everyone virtually worships. It just doesn't seem right. There is only one girl called Evie, who is super popular, but is really nice to us, because she likes the same kind of music as us.

RICHARD: Music is so important. It tells you everything you need to know about a person. The music we listen to is, er …
SKYE: Inclusive. You can be white, black, Asian, gay, straight, fat, thin, pretty, ugly. There's no abuse. I love that. We try to live by that. Of course we argue, but I'd rather be like that than shopping at Topshop and being called a slag behind your back by your best friend. I trust all my friends.
ARIANE: Me too.
THOMAS: Me three.

JONAH AND MIKEY, BOTH 17, SOUTH LONDON

Both attend a large academy school. They have been close friends for over a year. Jonah is openly gay and Mikey likes girls. Jonah is currently living at Mikey's parental home due to 'impossible' relations with his parents.

JONAH: I wasn't in the greatest state when I first spoke to Mikey. He found me in the locker room of our school. I'd just had the shit beaten out of me by six other guys. They'd taken all my clothes and were making all these 'jokes' about gang rape. I was crying and I felt so humiliated. I couldn't breathe properly because I was having an asthma attack from the panic.
MIKEY (*quietly*): Bullying is a big problem in our school.
JONAH (*cheerfully*): Not for you!
MIKEY: Nah. Not really. But it's horrible to watch. I've always had this policy. Y'know. Live and let live. But mind my own business. It's better that way. Less shit to deal with. To be honest, I can't fucking stand all that popularity bullshit at school. I wanna do my work and get a scholarship to the States

so I can play pro basketball. I was raised to respect people, but keep my head down. My dad had a lot of trouble with the law back in the day, and so his advice was be strong and quiet. It's good advice. But yeah, it's weird. The more you try to resist, the more people try to pull you in. Like, if you're good at sports, it's a ticket to popularity. It's that way in a lot of schools. But I hate all that bullshit. I can't be bothered with all the locker-room stuff. You know, chatting about all the girls you've fucked, or all the guys you're going to fuck up. I keep my head down. I've been accused of being up myself loads of times. I stay out of other people's business and they stay out of mine. But it was late and I'd been practising alone. I like to do that. I do lots of stuff alone. I went in to get my stuff and I saw this fool, and it's not really the type of thing you can look away from, y'know? And it's a tough situation, man. Because you don't want to humiliate someone. Like, man who has just been beat often wants to be left alone. Y'know. To lick wounds and shit. Allow it. But that was beyond something where you can just mumble, 'You all right mate?' and walk away from.

JONAH: It was a bad night. Mikey helped me get dressed and walked me home. No one was at home, because no one ever really is. Mum's usually out getting pissed and Dad . . . God knows what. We sat and talked for a while.

MIKEY: Jonah's fucking funny. Like, he just had the shit beat out of him and he's going through this stand-up routine about queer bashing, and hockey sticks and I don't know whether to laugh or run away. I thought maybe he'd had a massive blow to the head and gone a bit mad. And I didn't know any gay people really, except some of my parents' friends. But I never really knew anyone gay my age. I sort of thought it happened later.

JONAH: It happened to me about age six. Unfortunately. I've been hit with hockey sticks ever since. My dad hates me. But anyway, I expected Mikey to never come near me again, but he came round the next morning and asked if I wanted to walk to school with him. I was so shaky I was seriously thinking of not going in, but if you don't go back, it gets worse. We walked to school in this sort of weird silence and Mikey kept talking about basketball and I didn't know what the hell he was talking about. I kept wondering if I was concussed and imagining it all. He walked me to my first class and everything. And he came and ate lunch with me. I don't think I've ever had so much attention. I felt bad, because there were some really nasty things said about us fucking each other and being 'Oreo queers' but comments just seem to roll off Mikey. He doesn't care. It helps that he's about nine foot tall and looks like a model, I guess. Lucky bastard. I didn't seem to lessen his appeal. Maybe I added to it. (*They both laugh.*)

MIKEY: I do care what people think of me. But I'm not going to be told who I can and can't be friends with. Fuck that. Jonah's gay. Why do I give a shit, man? He's not trying to have sex with me. He's just cool. We just chat about shit. Get a little high sometimes. My girlfriend really likes him. My mum *loves* him. She babies him, enough. Feeds up his skinny ass. It was jokes. She gave him some jerk chicken. Like proper hair-on-your-chest shit. It virtually have Jonah sunburn. He practically lives with us now, and he's helped Mum do all this nice stuff with the house. Like all this decorating stuff. I better watch it or she'll give him my room next and I'll have to sleep in the box room.

HARRY, BRIAN, KURT AND AMIL, ALL 16, PETERBOROUGH

All attend a very oversubscribed mixed grammar school and have been friends for 'far too long'; Kurt and Harry have known each other since they were five. They all say they 'can't remember' how they became friends but spend a lot of time together. They all have girlfriends although only Brian spends a significant amount of time with his.

BRIAN: I don't think boys have friendships like girls, at all. It's not as complicated. It's like, you hang out together and banter, and that's it. I *like* my mates, but I don't analyse it like girls do. If, say, Amil had a bit of a face on or didn't text me back, I wouldn't run home crying and spend the whole night talking about it with my other mates. My girlfriend does that. And it's like, maybe she didn't get the text? Maybe she was just in a bad mood? Girls *obsess* over their friends.

KURT: Girls obsess over everything.

AMIL: Innit. Same as arguments. Boys have beef. And shit gets said all the time. But you just brush it off. Girls hold grudges longer than elephants.

HARRY: Elephants have long memories. Not grudges.

AMIL: Shut up. You know what I mean. Like, I was seeing this girl who was fiiiit. And her mate was fit too. And when they saw each other, they were all, 'Oh hey boo, love you,' and it'd be kiss, kiss, hug, hug. And the second the other girl was out the room, my girl would be all, 'I hate that fucking bitch, she's so up herself.' And I'd be raar man, that's cold! You just told her you loved her to her face. And then when I broke up with her, the other one would come and tell me how much she hated my ex. And I'm thinking *why* would you pretend to be friends with someone you properly hate? Life is too short. Like, I hate Kurt but he comes with these other two, unfortunately.

KURT: I hate you too. But Amil is right. And if you have a group of friends, you ain't bothered if one person likes someone else more. With girls it has to be a pecking order. I've known Harry much longer, so I'd call him more of a close friend but Brian wouldn't cry about it and write all these posts on Facebook like, 'I guess I should have realised I'm not that important to *some* people.'

AMIL: YEAH! Girls do that, *enough*. What's the word for something when you are saying one thing but are really saying something else?

HARRY: Girl-speak?

AMIL: YES! And girls are always saying to other girls, 'Do I look fat?' and their friend will all be like, 'Not fat, *exactly*. But have you thought of wearing the blue one which covers you a bit more?' It's cold. If I asked my friend that, they'd be, 'What the fuck? Are you gay?'

HARRY: That is sort of true. One of my friends – she's a girl – she admitted to me, she'll try and get her friend to wear the outfit which makes her look *worse*.

KURT: Really? Girls are evil. Or maybe they're not. There must be something that makes them act like that to each other.

AMIL: It's us, man. They're all competing for us.

BRIAN: Yeah, but we're all trying to get girls. And we don't try to cock-block each other. I'd say we help each other.

HARRY: Bullshit. If some girl asked me about you, especially if she was good-looking, I'd tell her you had AIDS. And a small dick.

AMIL: Believe. But the difference is, you wouldn't come and tell me, 'Oh, I just saw Charlotte and told her you were the greatest guy ever.' You'd tell me, 'I just saw Charlotte and I told her you had AIDS. And you shit the bed.'

KURT: Girls are sneaky. Girls are really nice too. But they feel so much more. I get pissed off with my mates and I get on with my mates. But between that, there's not much else. But with girls, I don't know, there's loads more. If I said to Brian I was having a shit day and wanted to be by myself, he'd be like, 'All right mate, take it easy.' If a girl says that, it would be, well . . . my sort-of girlfriend spends *hours* obsessing over what her girlfriends have said or done. It's so boring. And pointless.

HARRY: Yeah, but if girls have a serious problem, they pick up on it straight away. I have this second cousin called Terence. I didn't know him well but he was all right. Nice bloke. Always seemed cheerful. He was really into the weird comic books. Obsessed with them. And he had this whole group of mates, all boys because what girl is into comics books and superheroes and shit? His mum came home one day and found him in the bath, wrists slit. He had fucked it up, of course, because he's a bit of a muppet and it hadn't worked. But it was still pretty horrible. He had to go to a mental institution for a while. I think he was clinically depressed or something. But that's sort of the point. No one knew. If he'd been a girl, her mates would have been on that shit.

AMIL: To be honest, anyone into comics at our age should probably kill themselves. It's a comic, you sad wankers.

HARRY: That's cold, man. Comics are all right.

AMIL: Yeah, well, you're a wanker too. But you're all right. You can read comics and cry alone if you want to. You can still be my mate.

HARRY: Fuck off.

CHERRY, 19, BIRMINGHAM

Is 'unsure' of what she wants to do with her life. She didn't pass her A levels, doesn't want to attend university, and can't find a career path that appeals. Works at a local bar in the evenings, which she says is 'all right'. Would like to travel. Says her best friend's suicide 'definitely isn't the reason for drifting' but did 'mess her head up a bit'.

I can still remember that day like it was a second ago. It's weird to think it was two years ago. It's all just really clear. The date, the time, what I was wearing, what I was doing. It's like people tell you, they can remember the exact moment when they found out Princess Diana died. I was a baby then and can't remember that. But I remember when Abbie died.

She was my best friend from the age of eleven. She moved near to me when she got adopted by her adoptive parents. She seemed really different to everyone else. She came from London and I remember thinking she talked really funny. She had two different voices. Sometimes she spoke sort of posh and sometimes she spoke really cockney. I think people should have paid more attention to that, because I think it was important. There were two definite sides to Abbie. There was the good, happy side. And there was this *other* side. It didn't come up all that much, but when it did, it was really hard to deal with. She wouldn't do that much to anyone else. But she'd do the worst stuff to herself. Really dark, destructive stuff. And she suffered with pretty much everything imaginable. She dabbled heavily in drugs; she suffered from bouts of anorexia and bulimia. She'd self-harm. She'd sleep sometimes with the most dodgy, random people and couldn't remember it. I had to physically stop her leaving a party once with these two totally random guys who looked as sketchy as fuck and were both about thirty-five. Seriously. She drank heavily. And then sometimes – a lot of the time, she'd be all sweetness and light. Like, perfect and funny and smart. She was so fucking smart. And so pretty. What a waste.

I tried sometimes to get her to talk about her childhood, but she'd laugh it off or get defensive unless she was really drunk or high. Then some stuff would come out. The most appalling stuff about childhood abuse . . . and much, much worse. Like, really weird stuff. But it was all so garbled, it was difficult to tell what was real and what wasn't. I mean, she was obviously so disturbed, but this veneer of being normal was really effective and she kept that in place a lot of the time. If I said she was a good actress, that's just really horrible, because it makes her sound like a liar or a fake. She wasn't. I think she was just trying to survive and be OK and it was too much for her. She couldn't quite bring herself back from whatever had happened.

My mum came into my room and she was as white as a sheet. I was watching *Hollyoaks* even though it's total shit. It's sort of always on in that bit in the day when you are trying to work up to doing school work. You know, along with *Come Dine with Me*. You can't help it, can you? Mum pulled me onto my feet and held really tightly onto my shoulders and just said, 'Look, Abbie is dead. She killed herself.' I just felt everything wobble and then I started to laugh and I kept laughing, but this really creepy high-pitched laugh, and there wasn't even a second where I didn't believe it, where I couldn't take it in, because the awful thing is, I almost expected this moment. It was like that bit in *Romeo and Juliet* where he foresees all the awfulness and I sometimes wondered if I had that a bit with Abbie.

And then I had this thing where I absolutely had to see her. I wanted to see her so badly, and I sort of pushed Mum off and I ran downstairs and I guess I was crying now and shouting, because I could see my little brother standing there with his fingers in his ears and he might have been crying too. I went to go out the front door, and my dad was just coming up the path. My mum had called him and he came home early. I'm closer to Dad than Mum. Still am. He pulled me really close, so close I could hardly breathe, and was like, 'I know, I know,' and I cried and cried on him. He was covered in snot.

The funeral was the worst. Although Abs had been difficult and sometimes strange, people liked her. They were sort of fascinated by her, too. She'd hanged herself, which was a detail that was always going to come out, but it haunted me for ages. It still does. There's something so awful and final and I don't know ... medieval about it. What a thing to do. How lonely and painful were those last minutes? Did it hurt her? What was she thinking of? And could I have done anything? I mean for fuck's sake, we *saw* each other that day. She was fine. Or I thought she was.

I miss my friend so much. She was my best friend. But I'm so fucking angry with her. She had so much to live for and I know there was worse stuff for her than I think any of us realised, but it feels like a big puzzle was left behind. A mystery. I just wish she had told me more.

KATIE, 15, AND ROCKY, 16, SOUTHAMPTON

Have been in a relationship for two years. Rocky was already in a wheelchair when he met Katie. She says his disability 'makes no difference to her at all'. Rocky's greatest dream is to carry Katie across the threshold if they get married, but he'll probably just have to have her on his lap.

KATIE: The thing I can't stand is the way people talk to Rocky. Like he's thick. Or mentally disabled. Or deaf. He's in a bloody wheelchair, not stupid. They worst is when they bend down and talk very slowly to him like you do with a dumb kid. It pisses me off so much. And when I tell them we're going out together, they give you this *look*. Like sort of a cross between 'Aaaah, aren't you sweet' and 'Do you really know what you're doing there?' Rocky is awesome. He just can't walk and do a lot of other things physically. But he *isn't* stupid.

ROCKY: The best one was when this sort of counsellor at school – they make me see people like that all the time – asked me if I wanted to change my name. I asked why. I couldn't even work it out for the life of me. She got all embarrassed and said something about it being an 'athletic name' because of the film. That stupid film with that actor who seems more of a cripple than I am! I mean, what the fuck? Are all people called David supposed to rename themselves if they're not as good-looking as David Beckham? But the point is, I know people usually mean well, but it's the patronising I can't stand. I also can't stand people who refer to it as 'my condition'. I have muscular dystrophy. There's no way of making it nicer. It sucks.

KATIE: And actually, this country is *not* good for wheelchair access. I mean, it's OK some places, but so many places, it's sort of a big deal, and Rocky gets embarrassed. He just wants to go about his life. Did you know loads of stations in London don't have any wheelchair access at all? He wanted to go on this tourist trip to London, especially to the London Eye. The people who run the London Eye were super cool. I emailed them first. They couldn't have been nicer or more helpful, but the journey was so awful and difficult by train, Rocky just got frustrated and upset and decided he didn't want to go.

ROCKY: I know it sounds a bit wet. But everyone stares. And it's a nightmare for Katie because she's not very physically strong. Not enough to push up train ramps and all the other things you don't think of. This is electric. But it doesn't work everywhere. And people just sort of look away and get embarrassed when you are struggling. It makes everything a bit ... well, you wonder whether you can be bothered. You end up going to 'safe' places you know are OK, which pisses me off. And England is a pretty good country. I'm not going to live until I'm old. My real dream is to travel to faraway places and I've been told a lot of them are almost impossible to get around if you are disabled. At least I have Katie, though.

KATIE: And I have you. Rocky is always saying sorry, but I wouldn't change anything about him. I hope we can get married. I think he's so brave. But I don't really like thinking about it too much. It makes me really sad.

ROCKY: I was sad for a long time. Especially before Katie. And I was so angry. But I got diagnosed very young and had to go in a wheelchair full-time by the time I was twelve. I'm not ever going to walk again. I dream about it all the time, though. And you wake up, and for a split second, you think you can again. I've tried to jump out of bed *loads* of times. I've done it loads of times. My older brother is wicked. Mum and Dad get really upset at things like that. Even still. But he just comes and has a laugh and helps me out. That's the other two things that really piss me off. People assume, when you're disabled, it disables your sense of humour too. Like you can't have a laugh. Some kid was telling this rude joke in form the other day and I came in and he just stopped! Even said sorry! Like, I'm not going to understand or be offended or something. Stuff like that really bugs me. But the thing that bugs me the *most* are these disgusting people, especially in America, who are making themselves wheelchair-bound and disabling themselves through obesity. I would give anything, other than maybe Katie, to walk again. Anything. And these fucking – can I say fucking – these people are doing it to themselves because they want to eat twenty doughnuts a day. It makes most other people laugh at them in disgust. It makes me so angry I want to scream at them. How could they abuse something like that? It's sick.

KATIE: I couldn't agree more. Nothing is fair in the world.

SIMON, 19, AND DAVID, 18, NORTH LONDON

Have been in a relationship for over a year. Simon's family are wealthy and he inherited a significant amount of money in his early teens, which means he was in the unusual position of being able to move into his own place at age eighteen which he shares with David. They are about to launch their own business, which is 'a big secret until it happens'.

SIMON: I'm going to come out and say this. I don't believe in bisexuals. You can't be both. Bisexuals are either kidding themselves, as Phoebe in *Friends* said, or just attention seekers.

If you like dick, there isn't a chance you like fanny too. Not. A. Chance. And the only bisexual women are the ones who want to turn men on or are like wannabe models or TV presenters. Like, 'Oh, ya, I'm bisexual,' and bingo, you've made it into the *X Factor* top ten, even though you sound like an anorexic cat being force-fed.

DAVID: But isn't River bisexual?

SIMON: River is no more bisexual than his birth certificate says River. Mind you, people like River need to be bisexual. Increases his chances by 50 per cent. Major, major issues.

DAVID: Really?

SIMON: Oh yes. So you want to know about our relationship? Well, I was *very* keen to discuss this matter. Because David and I, and just about all of our friends who are in the gay way, would like to explode a few myths. Gay relationships, especially young ones, are always shown to be so bloody tragic. And I'm not denying there is a lot of tragedy surrounding gay people historically, but *hello,* what about the good stuff? We're never going to have to work on a building site; we're genetically predisposed to careers in fashion and interior design or starting cool magazines or fabulous businesses; gay people are rich; we live longer because we're all so vain we eat well and work out. We tend to live fairly fabulous lives. It's revenge for years of homophobia. And to make things even *better*, I'm Jewish too! I'm practically destined to be rich and successful in everything I do. Both my peoples were persecuted. That makes us resourceful.

DAVID: Actually, Simon is right. I mean, I knew I was gay from about the time I could remember. School was awful for me. Absolutely terrible. I was bullied to the brink of suicide. I was sort of forced out. If I hadn't met Simon, I don't think I'd be here. I not only completely love him, but he's just so proud to be gay, it's made me feel that way about it too. It's infectious. He introduced me to this whole new world, which was just great. Before him, I'd never even been to Soho, except when we'd got lost on a school trip to Madame Tussauds.

SIMON: Gays definitely had *nothing* to do with Madame Tussauds. Vile. Utterly vile. I'd rather sleep with River again than go there. So much of London is just vile now. It's because they are catering for rich Russians who are the most homophobic people in the world. I mean, ugh, have you *seen* Putin? I mean no wonder he's so angry. If I looked like that, I'd probably want to take it out on fabulous gay people too. I hope he gets a gay pride float dropped on him. But yes, anyway, David was a mess when I met him. I'm not going to tell you where, because it's just too tragic (*they later admit it was Waitrose*). But I was just like, darling, no one is ever going to have sex with you if you don't bloody cheer up. And shave. He had one of those *ridiculous* beards every straight man in London is running around with at the moment. Awful. It's like a bloody plague. It's like being at Glastonbury Day Three permanently at the moment. Vile. So we got him cheered up, spruced up and then I realised he was just lovely. He's been lovely every day since. We have so many plans together. Work plans. We have a *brilliant* business idea, but we can't tell you, because you'll put it in your book and someone will steal it. Life is just *fabulous*. So please do put us in your book, so all the little gays can realise that as soon as you come out, life gets wonderful. Don't waste your time trying to date the wrong sex. Just be who you are.

Body

MAYA, 15, NORTH LONDON

Had a 'fairly comfortable upbringing with a normal family'. Attended a well-performing comprehensive school until six months ago when anorexia nervosa forced her into full-time hospital treatment. Has always academically excelled, though describes herself as a bit of a loner and misfit. Didn't really pay attention to body issues until the age of ten and then became 'obsessed'.

I don't really remember how it happened, but it happened really quickly. I think it started with breakfast. One day I ate it and the next day, I didn't. I remember everyone in primary school was really worried about being thin; it was all we talked about and even then we would worry about eating biscuits and stuff. There were even these two girls who would make themselves sick after lunch, and they were only in Year 6, but I just thought they were really silly. And then when I got to high school, maybe I shouldn't say this because it sounds racist, I don't mean it to, but there were a lot more black kids there. The girls have a really different attitude to their bodies, like they don't care so much about being skinny, and me and my best friend were really confused.

A few weeks after term started in Year 9, my best friend went off with all the popular girls and they all started being really nasty about me. Making up stuff about me not being a virgin and how I'd let all these boys see me naked, which wasn't even true at all. And then some of the girls started saying I was fat. Even some boys said it. My mum used to say I had puppy fat, but who wants to look like a puppy? Puppies are fat.

So it started with breakfast. I would put a bit of muesli and milk in a bowl and leave it in the sink. Or sometimes I'd put the toaster down with no bread in it, so it smelt like someone had been cooking toast. No one was up at that time anyway. I'd leave the house earlier and earlier to walk around the block and I'd always have this little rhyme in my head. This is embarrassing but it was that nursery rhyme, '100 Green Bottles'. I didn't want to stop walking until I reached no green bottles, but the hundred got more and more. By February, I was on '5000 Green Bottles'. I had to leave the house very early, which got more difficult as my parents started to watch me more closely after Christmas. And I'd run, not walk.

I think all my troubles began that September. Like the skipping breakfast. By October I was skipping lunch too. By Christmas things were terrible. But not eating seemed to block all that out. The sense of accomplishment put me in a bubble that no one could get near and it didn't matter what people said or how mean they were to me, I could deal with it. All the weird headaches and the strange feelings became like my friends. If I didn't feel them, I knew something was wrong. Maybe I'd eaten too much. But anyway, in a weird sense I think the fact that I was losing weight stopped a lot of the meanness. I think a lot of the girls were impressed, jealous even. Some of the girls who had been horrible to me before complimented me. Said I was looking good. And I think a lot of the others realised there wasn't much point in saying things to me because I barely noticed. I didn't notice a lot of things by then. So not eating saved me from a lot of my troubles. But then by Christmas it began to cause a lot of trouble, too.

But by then I was so scared of eating food, I'd begun to avoid it in every way possible and I was terrified of getting fat again. But by then my parents had begun to try to get involved and ruin everything I'd worked so hard for.

I wasn't that hungry by December – I felt like I'd beaten it. Got past the urge to eat. But I was always thinking about food. I was obsessed with it. Not just about me, but about what other people were eating. I'd spend a lot of time just watching people with food. To me, it was like those programmes where people put insects in their mouths. I would shudder and feel sick and add up the calories. I kept having these things where stars would creep up in my vision and then big black blobs and then I'd have to sit down and I'd be covered in this cold sweat. And I think people began to stare more. But they said less about me looking good. Even at school. People would stare at me in shops. Some girls tried to talk to me a couple of times. Even the ones who had been horrible to me, but I'd blank them out and then one day, everything in art class went really bad. Normally I could breathe my way through the black blobs but I couldn't and I fainted and that was the stupidest thing I ever did.

Suddenly everyone got involved. The school, my mum and dad and sister. All the people at school who all suddenly said they were my friends, they all got together and they all suddenly were trying to make me eat. Mum would get up with me in the morning. Teachers and some girls would sit with me at lunch. I'd suddenly be made to go home for dinner and I couldn't say I was staying late for music practice or homework club. And the thing is, no one can actually make you eat. Physically force you. So rather than pretend everything was OK, I'd just refuse and suddenly everyone was crying or on my back. It was like being at war with everyone and though everyone was all around me, I've never felt so alone. By April, my mum couldn't cope any more, because I wouldn't drink water and my kidneys were not working very well, so I was sent here to hospital. Where I am now. Everyone keeps telling me I could die if I don't try to get better.

Are you afraid of dying?

Not really. I'm just afraid of putting on weight. Why can't everyone accept me for who I am and let me be me? I have days when I want to get better, but I just don't want to eat.

JAWAD, OMAR, RICHIE, 16, JT, AND SUNNY, 15, EAST LONDON

JT *would like it mentioned for the record he is an 'international playa and gangster'. None of the others concurs with this. They all attend a fitness and rehabilitation club particularly aimed at young men with prison convictions and criminal records.*

OMAR: Being in prison is the worst as far as your own body is concerned. I don't care what nobody says. You are in charge of no part of your own body. You're told when to piss, when to shit, when to shower, how often, when to eat, what to eat. And sex is of course non-existent because there are no girls around, which makes everyone think of sex 24/7. It's excruciating. The gym saved me in there.

JT: Believe. When I came here, I'd just been in for six months and I was heading back. All I wanted to do was fuck, fight and make up, which in the end adds up to the same thing. Or leads you there. And I was getting high all the time. Colin (*who runs the club*) taught me that when you're high all the time, it's like, er, having a phone without a signal. It's there, but it doesn't work really. You can't get it to do what you wanted to do.

What kind of drugs were you taking?

RICHIE: Weed.
JT: Weed. A lot of weed. And sometimes coke.
SUNNY: Weed and coke.
JAWAD: Most of the weed in South America. And cocaine. Cocaine – yaa-baby! And crack, a few times. That stuff fucks you up. And biscuits. Colin says sugar is the drug of this generation and all the kids are getting hiiiiigh. (*They all laugh.*) But, no word of a lie, drugs are OK. To put it another way, on a scale of one to ten, I was about four, maybe five, with drugs. I was doing a lot, any that I could get my hands on. But hard drugs are an older person's game. About nineteen, maybe, I see a lot of people start with those. Some schoolkid can't be smoking crack, you know what I'm saying? Or just a rock he bought with his lunch money. You can't get that fucked up on sandwich and juice money. But a lot of boys take drugs to show that they've made it, you know what I'm saying? Like they start to show the world they have some money in their back pocket, and then the drugs take over and there's no money in your back pocket, so you need to do something to get the money back in your back pocket. It's a fucked-up cycle that so many walk into. In truth, the smart ones, the *rich* ones, don't take a thing ... the scariest guy I ever met, you know who I mean, is like this vegan. He does yoga and stuff. Talks about the universe all the time. Gives people a look if they're even smoking weed. No such thing as a rich junkie.
JT: Trust.

OMAR: It probably sounds simple to you, but I've never had no discipline in my life. I dropped out of school pretty much at twelve – I just wouldn't go – and have been doing what I need to do to get by ever since. I don't think I've ever sat down for a meal in my life with my family. On a good day, my mum would give me money to go to the chicken shop when I was younger, when she was together or hadn't spent it all. Mostly I fended for myself. I knew nothing about exercise or food or sleep or health. I'd stay up to four in the morning and play PlayStation or Xbox and smoke weed and keep myself pepped up with Monster (*an energy drink*). I'd wake up at one, start smoking and taking care of business, maybe have a little drink. I never even showered regularly. It was weird. Prison was the first time I was made to think about routine of any sort. Made to have one. It was shit in there. One day, I was talking to one of the counsellors in there and I just started to properly cry because I realised how bad things had got and I didn't know how to change it, so he hooked me up with Colin. When I left prison I was nearly two stone heavier because I'd been exercising and had proper food. And it was the first time I didn't have really bad acne and shit.

JT: Nigger, that's true. Before you went in you looked like Domino's were going to hire you as a model.

OMAR: Didn't stop your mum from fucking me.

SUNNY: Basically, that's what Colin does. He teaches us boxing, but we talk a lot about other stuff too like future and responsibilities. And if you turn up high or drunk or you try to sling you get kicked out. Plus we all have to give him some money – what we would have spent on food – and he makes us go in turns on a food run for like, health food.

JT: Yeah, man. Before all this, I'd never even heard of ... what's that green ectoplasm shit he's always getting? Something with mould in it?

SUNNY: Oh, yeah. It sounds Spanish.

OMAR: Yeah, yeah! Guacamole. I honestly thought he was having us on at first. It's fucking rank.

JAWAD: But then you sort of start getting used to it and I quite like that chicken with beans thing. And the salad. Sooo much salad. But with the vinegary stuff, it's all right.

JT: No, it's not. It's rank. And eggs too. Did you know an egg is a chicken's period?

OMAR: That's not true, is it? Is it?

JT: Yes it is! Your toast is like the maxi-pad!

SUNNY: That's disgusting.

JT: It's better, though. I've found I'm not hungry like ten minutes later, which you feel like after a Maccy D's.

SUNNY: My tongue feels better. It always used to hurt.

OMAR: That's because you have an STD from hos.

JT: I've had 'nuff sex. I've had more sex than Sunny's had hot dinners.

OMAR: That's because Sunny is a Muslim, you fucking idiot. It's against his religion. I used to be sort of religious but couldn't be bothered any more. I smoke too much weed and have too many girls. But anyway, Colin is always telling us to wait for sex and respect girls. Says a boy shouldn't have sex until he's a real man. I used to think it meant just getting pussy. I don't know. I used to think about it 24/7, but now maybe it might be better to wait for a nice girl. I think that might be ... better. More filling. Did you know Colin has been with the same girl since he was seventeen? He says if I do my training and wait for the right girl, and use my head rather than my dick to think, I'll become a man.

JAWAD: If you stay with the same girl your whole life, I think your dick falls off.

OMAR: You don't have a dick anyway, so what's the diff?

SUNNY: Can we stop the dick talk, it's making me feel nasty. Besides, we've got to go get some guacamole and fish.

JT: Oh my days, I hate fish.

RACHEL, 16, AND HAYLEY, 14, CAMBRIDGESHIRE

Sisters. Both are doing their GCSEs. Their mum died from breast cancer twenty months ago.

RACHEL: I'd say I've got a fairly normal relationship with my body. There are things I'd change about it, of course. I'd like longer legs – mine are really stumpy – and I'd like sometimes to be a bit thinner. I'm a size twelve or thereabouts. I might have become more like my friends are now – obsessed with everything to do with it – but Mum got diagnosed just before my twelfth birthday, which puts things massively into perspective. It started out as breast cancer and wasn't diagnosed fast enough, so she had a double mastectomy. The cancer was in remission for a while, but then came back. When your mum is going through that, you stop worrying so much about a bit of belly fat or cellulite. You realise a good body is a healthy body. Mum was really positive about her chances right up until the last six months, when it was fairly obvious she wasn't going to make it. Then she made it her mission to equip us with all the stuff your mum does. Obviously we already knew about periods and sex by then, but the last year of her life we spent a lot of time talking about relationships, our bodies and the future. She taught me so much. Everything from a good way to decide about having sex for the first time to cooking a lasagne from scratch. She was really glad to have made it for my first period. She missed Hayley's by about six months. She was really sad about that and we visited her grave on the day it came to tell her. It was that really shit summer where it rained every single day. Do you remember that? On that day it was really hot. The sun shined all day. Mum loved the sun. Before she got sick, she was always in the garden. Dad would make her wear a hat, which she hated.

HAYLEY: I forgot about that hat (*laughs*).

RACHEL: Mum organised for us to have all this testing, to check if we've inherited the genes that make cancer more likely. Me and Hayley call it the BRA genes. But Dad really, really doesn't want us to. It's really upsetting him and I keep having big fights with him about it. Now I'm sixteen, I can, but I don't think he should wait with Hayley.

What do you want to do, Hayley?

HAYLEY: I don't know. I get scared sometimes, because I'm not as brave as Rachel. She says she would have a full mastectomy if she needed to, but I'm not sure I could do that. Breasts are considered so important as part of a girl. I don't want to be deformed.

RACHEL: Deformed is better than dead. One thing Mum taught me is to let go of your boobs as a vanity thing. They aren't there for boys, at the end of the day. I know I might be being a bit gloomy in preparing for the worst. But I lost my mum. Nothing will ever be worse than that.

Tell me your favourite thing about your mum.

HAYLEY: How she felt. She was really hard-working. She

worked for the government. And she often got home late. But she would always have time for a cuddle. She'd lie across my knees in bed. When she got sick, she lost a lot of weight almost straight away and it scared me.

RACHEL: Mum was really beautiful. Really beautiful. But she didn't care about her looks at all. She didn't even own a lipstick, I don't think. She said a woman had much, much more important things to worry about than her looks all the time. That it was more important to work on your mind and personality. One time Dad bought her all these expensive cosmetics at Christmas and Mum made him take them all back and swap them for some gardening tools for her. He was so upset, but then she built him this really cool shed. He used to say she was the only wife who'd be able to build a shed better than her husband. He goes there when he misses her the most.

HAYLEY: I love make-up and dressing up. Unlike Rachel. A week before Mum died, she left a little make-up bag with some make-up under my pillow. Dad went out and bought exactly the same things the day after she died, just so I'll never have to use the stuff she bought me. I'll keep those forever.

RHONA, 17, NOTTINGHAM

Rhona was born Nigel. She is currently studying for her A levels. She is planning to have a total sex change as soon as she is legally able.

My dad's in anti-Rhona mode at the moment. He does that occasionally and he kicks me out, so I'm staying with a friend. It's a fairly periodical thing and then my mum will talk some sense into him and I'll be allowed back. I'm desperate to move out, which doesn't exactly make me unique for someone my age, I know. But most of my friends are rowing over curfews and money, not having your bits permanently altered.

I've known there was a problem with who I was ever since I could remember. I absolutely hated everything about my body and I did all the classic things you can imagine. Starvation, self-harm. I even tried fucking religion at one point. Didn't do me any good.

It was a good friend of mine, a girl who I tried to tell myself I fancied, who got me talking. She thought I was probably gay and we realised it went much deeper than that I talked to my mum. I even talked to the school, who were really great and they got me some help. I expect they probably thought I was going to come out as gay – I am attracted to men, mostly, actually. I think they could have coped with that fine. But the more I talked about it, the more I realised who I was and what had to be done.

The first year was the worst. The school didn't know how to cope with the issue of a transitional pupil and I think were genuinely worried about me being bullied, but also their reputation. They were right on both counts. I was spat at, hit, ostracised, called names, inappropriately touched, even kicked down the stairs once after PE. It was agreed it would be better for me if I finished off my GCSEs at home. But really I think it was better for them. A day after I left school, I went out because I couldn't stand being around my dad and this group of lads in the park threatened to gang rape me. And then said I couldn't even be properly gang raped because I was a chick with a dick.

I didn't leave my room for three months and I just sat there crying and having all these awful thoughts about suicide and self-mutilation. A teacher from the school came to see me. She'd taught history and had been fairly open about the fact she was gay. She put me in touch with all sorts of help groups and social organisations, who helped me get more confident about becoming female. I know it's hard enough getting a sympathetic doctor for gender reassignment when you're an adult. They'll barely touch you as a minor. They think it's a phase you'll grow out of, or not a decision you can make at such a young age, but I know myself really, really well. I know I am a woman – I always have been.

It's been hard to get the help I need here – the best clinics for dealing with underage cases are in London and neither of my parents would give me the money to go to London on the train or drive me. I've also found it really, really hard to get a part-time job. Places say they have strict equality policies, but you can't legalise against natural, secret prejudice. Luckily I got a job in a really nice indie record shop and am now able to go to a clinic in London and have found a brilliant case worker who is going to support me through gender reassignment once I'm over eighteen.

I'm also applying to all the London universities, as I think in London all sorts of lifestyles are celebrated and supported. If you are changing so much about yourself, sometimes you want to get as far away as possible from where the old you was.

Everybody has a rocky relationship with their body. You're too fat, you're too skinny, you're too ugly, you're too black, you're too white. You need bigger boobs, you need smaller boobs, you need more muscles, you need a bigger dick. Being born the wrong gender is like every body anxiety you can imagine to the power of ten million. You don't feel like you fit in anywhere. You think no one will ever want you. Especially if your own parents are horrified by you. But sometimes the greatest prejudice is towards yourself. I don't – and never did – work as a man. I lie awake at night sometimes wondering what will happen when I am properly a woman. Whether I will find my place in the world. It's really hard not having a place in the world. Besides, who the fuck can blame me wanting to change sex when I was christened Nigel?

MELISSA, 18, BIRMINGHAM

Currently a stripper at a popular establishment in the heart of the city. She describes the club as 'pretty OK relatively speaking'. She has been stripping since she was fifteen at clubs in various cities using false ID. She does what she describes as 'stripper tourism', which means she travels from city to city picking up work at different clubs in an attempt to keep the work varied and maximise her earnings. According to her, it also prevents anyone getting to know her too well. She has so far avoided prostitution despite 'hundreds' of offers of cash for sex. She would like to go back to school and go to university and 'maybe become a teacher'.

I get it, you know; I use my body to make a living or specifically I use my body for sort of sex, which as far as some people are concerned leaves me somewhere below trash. I sort of block it out. What do they know, you know? I have more or less been stripping and things since I was fifteen. This place is fairly above board, it's got a pretty good reputation as far as the girls are concerned, about checking ages, you know? But some places barely require ID. They hardly check. Really young-looking girls bring in customers, which brings in money, so what do they care, you know? The bloody problem is, all this night working really ages you. All the booze, the fags, the worry and the uncertainty. There isn't really much in the way of employment rights here, you know? I probably look twenty-five by now.

There are a lot of upsides. The money can be good, obviously. It's social if you like that kind of thing. A lot of the girls are well all right. The boss here is really nice, he doesn't mess with any of the girls, which is pretty unusual. You get to sleep in. Lots of booze, although I had to cut that out a bit as I was drinking so much, I was having black-outs. Drugs, if that's your thing. It's frowned on, but (*she whispers*) all stripping clubs are awash with drugs, you know? Loads of the girls take drugs, especially coke. It keeps you awake and is sort of numbing, you know?

To be honest, I used to be really involved in the lifestyle, but now I just want to get in and get out. I'm starting to think about other things. Going back to school, you know? I guess it's not always a good feeling being on display in the way that we are. It sometimes feels like when you get to work, your body isn't your own. You sort of leave that part of you at the door. I mean, I know a lot of girls who do a lot more than strip. Anyone who tells you that stripping doesn't lead to other sex work is a fucking liar. It doesn't have to, of course, but it often does. I know places where it's actively encouraged, not just blind-eyed by the managers. Here it isn't. You could lose your job. But that doesn't mean it doesn't happen. Everyone knows from dumb films about hookers having, like, professional names they use and that's a big part of the reason. You want to keep a part of yourself for yourself. I mean, I don't feel like I ever had much in the way of that. I was in care at four and raped by a person I trusted at eleven, but I don't care what anyone says about what I do, my body is still my own and I still get to say what happens to it, you know? On a good day you might tell yourself your body is like art. But mostly here, it's just something for clients to get off on.

JONI, 17, BELLA, PRITI, BLOSSOM AND ANNABELLE, ALL 16, WEST LONDON

All attend a top-performing grammar school in West London. They have just started A-level and International Baccalaureate courses and would all like to attend Oxbridge, except Bella who wants to be an architect and wants to study in Germany.

BELLA: There has never been more focus on the bodies of girls and it's really hard-going sometimes. Like, every time you open a paper or magazine or go on the internet, there's, like, a million pictures of famous girls' bodies either being praised or torn apart. You can't help but reflect on your own.

ANNABELLE: I agree. Like, my mum was saying that in her day, if you wanted to look at the pictures of celebrity bodies, you had to seek it out. Like buy actual fashion magazines and all that. Now, it's inescapable and it can make you feel like total shit. Sorry, I shouldn't swear. But it's true.

JONI: It used to be, like, having to see all these gorgeous and skinny women and models in bikinis and everywhere. But now, the responses to them are even worse. I saw these pictures on the *Daily Mail* website a few days ago and there were all these pictures of a supermodel. I can't remember her name. She's Brazilian, I think. And there were all these comments saying things like she had fat ankles and a mannish face or a face like a horse and I was thinking, she's a supermodel! What hope do we all have, if she is getting torn to shreds?

ANNABELLE: They have some girl who's put on a ton of weight and they have all these faux-sincere platitudes calling her 'curvy' or saying 'she looks smashing in her two-piece' or whatever and then everyone piles in saying the worst things imaginable. I don't even quite know what the point is, really.

BLOSSOM: Basically they're making money out of women's misery and people saying terrible things about them.

ANNABELLE: Yeah, but they're famous. They chose to be famous. They know what goes with it.

BELLA: I don't think that's true or fair, really. Like if you're a model or model underwear or a Page 3 girl, you're pretty much asking to be judged for your body. It's like your livelihood. But why should women in politics or writers or even actresses, really, have to constantly be under that kind of scrutiny? It shouldn't matter what they look like. Like, what difference does it make if Michelle Obama has gained some weight?

BLOSSOM: Yeah, like no one comments on Barack Obama's booty in his grey trousers!

ANNABELLE: But that's just the way of the world now. Looks are the most important thing. Everything else is second. And have you noticed everyone gets way hotter after they become famous? Even women who don't have to be. Everyone is in on it. And if they weren't, they'd stay the same. But the second someone is famous, boom. They get skinnier and their breasts get mysteriously bigger. All their wrinkles disappear. They get that sheeny skin. Like, some older women in the spotlight look younger now than they did when they were famous before we were even born. That shows how much things have changed.

PRITI: Yeah, women aren't allowed to get old now. I feel sorry for older women. They're treated like they're committing a crime.
BLOSSOM: Yeah, but it's the same for all women. No fat, no ugly, no ageing, no body hair. It's why I choose to be a fat, hairy lesbian. It's my protest. (*They all laugh.*)
BELLA: You're not fat!
BLOSSOM: Yeah, I am. And I'm OK with it. Like I'd like to lose a bit to be healthier, but not to look good in a bikini to please the *Daily Mail* or some shit. But I think if everyone could laugh a bit more about it, it would debunk all this fear. Like when black comedians started to laugh at racism and racists, it actually made things better for black people. Like I know there are some really good women flying this big-girl flag, but I think they sometimes become clown-like figures. Everyone should be more open.
ANNABELLE: I don't disagree. But I totally buy into it. If I was famous and being photographed all the time, I'd want to look good. And thin.

I ask them what they think of the 'selfies' phenomenon. They all groan.

JONI: I *hate* them. And they've caught on so much with everyone. Endless photos of girls with duck faces in soft-lensing. The whole world looks like a bad Seventies porn film again. And the weird thing is, they never look like the actual person. (*She lowers her voice.*) There are girls in this very school that have selfie nights where they sit around and just take endless pictures of themselves or each other for hours on end and then post all the good ones on Twitter and Instagram or whatever.
BLOSSOM: Have you noticed the more selfies people put up, the less she has to say? It's like a formula or something. Except

our Annabelle here. But then if I looked like Annabelle, I'd selfie my entire life.

PRITI: My mum would kill me if I selfied. They look suggestive. No one really selfies in a bathrobe looking fat. It's always at your best angle wearing something sexy.

BLOSSOM: I think the Photoshop thing is well out of order. I mean it's bad enough having to deal with supermodels, but airbrushed supermodels? That's nuts!

ANNABELLE: But it is having an effect. Like when you see Kate Moss un-airbrushed, she gets crucified.

BLOSSOM: I love Kate Moss. She's one celebrity who doesn't give a fuck. Sort of ironic, really, that the original waif supermodel is one of the ones who will go around with a bit of a belly, chugging on beer, now.

JONI: Yeah, but can you imagine how you'd feel reading the comments and things people will say on the internet about you? The language is plain scary. Like girls aren't just insulted for their looks, they're called ugly whores and told to get gang raped and die.

PRITI: Yeah, like some celebrities – especially girls – get targeted for their looks.

BLOSSOM: What I don't understand is, if you were a bit famous, like in a reality show, why you'd even bother with social media and all that. Like the girls in that show *TOWIE* or *Geordie Shore* are all so gross – that's sort of the point of them – but they almost seem to have a love/hate relationship with their followers. They get called gorgeous and fat, ugly slags in equal measure due to all the selfies they put up.

ANNABELLE: Yeah! Or Kim Kardashian. I mean she's annoying and all but what she gets called, you'd think she was as bad as

Hitler. Especially when she was pregnant. What's a woman supposed to do? Not get bigger?

BELLA: I think so. It's like if you put on a bit of weight, or haven't fully waxed or get pregnant, or get a few spots, you better hide away and not show your face unless you're perfect again.

Do you think this message – that physical perfection is the only acceptable standard – is trickling down to normal, not famous teenage girls?

(*All together*) YES!

RYAN, 14, BLACKPOOL

Has just started his GCSE courses. Currently weighs nearly seventeen stone and has been told by his doctors he is in critical danger of developing Type 2 diabetes.

I don't think I was ever a skinny thing. After me dad left – I was well young – there was no money and mum had to work nights and leave me and my little brother. So we didn't get upset, she'd leave us all our favourite foods and we'd sit up well late and play Xbox and eat. And because everyone on this street knows each other, the neighbours would come and check on us and bring us food, and the lady who owns the chippie is Mum's best friend, so she'd let us have chip suppers all the time for nothing.

I just really liked the feeling of being full. So I'd eat loads and loads and then you don't think about eating when you're gaming, so at the end of the night I'd sometimes be surprised by all the wrappers and boxes and like and I'd take half of them outside to the bins on the street. I'm not sure why, because Mum didn't mind us eating.

I love chips and battered sausages. Funnily enough, I've not got much of a sweet tooth – except pop; I love fizzy pop. But I love savoury stuff: crisps, white bread with loads and loads of butter, chips, pizza, curry sauce, bacon butties. I love it. Especially salty stuff.

My brother – Tom – he loves his sweets. And he used to cry all the time when she left, so she'd treat him with these big bags of penny sweets. They're wicked. So when the penny sweets came out, he stopped crying.

My mum used to cry on Saturday mornings looking at all the bills, so I'd make her this big bowl of Frosties, like half of the packet, in her favourite bowl that I think is supposed to be a fruit bowl. And we'd all sit together and finish off the bowl and she'd cheer up and then she'd let us choose some DVDs to watch.

Her friends would come over on Saturday night and they'd all put their money together and we'd get different takeouts and eat and watch films and have games tournaments. She and her friends would sometimes get a bit drunk and then they'd either be happy and make a lot of noise or cry over our dads, or their weight, or the fact there was no good men around here. And then once I was getting some food from the fridge and she was in the garden having a fag with her mate. She was really upset and talking about weight again. I knew she had got bigger and it was depressing her. But I didn't care because she's fine how she is 'cos she's me mum. But then I realised she was talking about me and her friend was agreeing and saying, 'You've gotta do something about him,' and she was just crying and crying. I just got me food and went back to the living room and pretended I hadn't heard anything. She didn't say nothing more about it.

But then the bullying started at school. These girls asked if I needed me own postcode and all these lads in the years above me were making, like, pig noises and calling me a fat little shit. And then once in assembly my chair broke. It just pure cracked. And the whole school was laughing and I was so embarrassed. But it's not too bad here, because there's a lot of bigger girls and lads at my school, and we all clubbed together. But then these lads called us the 'Weigh Team' – you know, like the A-Team – and they'd all sing the music when we passed. But I'd let them come to mine after school – me mates, I mean – so I do have a lot of friends, and I don't let it worry me too much. But then this girl, she's a right bitch called Hazel, went and grassed on us. Well, she lied about us. Said we were having like eating sessions in my house and I was like this food pusher or something, y'know, like a drug dealer.

So the school started asking me questions about what I eat and stuff and then the nurse weighs me. And I remember this – she actually gasped, and then she calls me mum and my mum had to not sleep that afternoon and come into school, and she were proper crying and they said I had some weight problems.

They said I was obese, which is worse than fat. But no way. Like, I know I weigh too much, but there's all this stuff about how my weight could kill me, which I don't believe.

I'm not as good at sports as I want to be. And sometimes I run out of breath climbing up the stairs. But mostly I'm all right. I feel upset because they upset Mum and now we can't have as much fun as we did. Food is so much fun. Everything was OK before all the trouble at school.

What do you think of your reflection in the mirror?

I don't know. I don't look that much except in the shaving mirror.

NICHOLAS, 18, AND APRIL, 16, BRISTOL

Nicholas is starting Cambridge in September and will be studying theology. April is about to start her A levels. They have been dating for four years. They are both devout Christians and are getting married next summer, with her parents' full blessing.

NICHOLAS: April moans about her body all the time. And then I have to remind her that it's the body she was blessed with by God and that she is healthy and happy and just generally blessed. I think she's completely beautiful. Perfect as she is.
APRIL: I do get a little self-conscious. I've won a scholarship to a very competitive girls' school to do my A levels and I can't believe how different all the girls look there. I don't want to sound too reverse discrimination or maybe biting the hand that feeds me, but I found their body obsession a bit odd. It's all they talk about – their looks and figures. I thought there would be loads more debate about philosophy and politics and religion – but they seem mostly to talk about diets, bodies, celebrity bodies, looks, money and fashion. I mean, we talked about that stuff a bit at school. Who doesn't? But it wasn't such a big thing. Maybe the richer and more beautiful you are, the more it matters to you, which seems like an odd equation. After my induction there, I felt like a fat frump and had to work a lot with God to restore how I saw myself. I

guess – I guess the other thing I struggle with is the obsessive association most of my peers have with their bodies and sex. My background and beliefs are able to separate the two.

NICHOLAS: Can I jump in here? Everything now is about sex. Getting sex, getting as many sexual partners as you can, being sexually attractive. And that's true of both genders. But in particular, I think, girls are made to feel worthwhile if they are sexually attractive and boys if they can get sex. But ultimately, because of our faith, we are encouraged to look far beyond the body for attractiveness and the fact that the body should just be about sex. For me, April's soul, goodness, personality and spirit were the things that struck me before anything else. And also, because I absolutely don't believe in sex before marriage, I can let go of the pursuit of sex that plagues so many of my friends, and can see girls in a different light. I don't look at breasts just in a sexual way, but in a way I hope is more profound.

APRIL: Also, because I see Nicholas as a life-long partner, and he sees me that way too, maybe we feel less of a need to compete with others. Like in a race to be the most beautiful to the opposite sex. But, whereas girls are programmed to do pretty much everything so they are attractive—

NICHOLAS (*interrupting*): Exactly! They forget to work on other things. Men and women, girls and boys . . . everything is so geared towards physical attractiveness and being attractive, they forget to work on other much, much more important things. How can anyone be beautiful or healthy if their soul or peace of mind is in such bad shape?

LOUISE AND HANI, BOTH 15, WEST SUSSEX

Both attend a comprehensive in South London. Have been best friends since they were four. Both started their periods at twelve.

HANI: I would love, love to have parents like Louise. Her parents are crazy and so much fun. Mine are so strict. Her mum is an actress and is always doing these crazy, impulsive things and so is her dad. I can't remember what he does. It's a weird job. But anyway, Louise started her period a week before me and her parents threw her a party! I got this text from her mum inviting me around and there was cake and all this crazy New Age food. They said it was a celebration of her womanhood!

LOUISE (*rolling her eyes*): I was so embarrassed! I mean, I like the fact my parents are open, but sometimes they are too open. Like Dad bought me some flowers the day I started, which was nice, but then he started banging on about how my body represented the flowers and I was in bloom now. I nearly died. I wanted to die. I almost wish I had parents like Hani who threw a book and a pack of sanitary towels at her and made her sign a Secrets Act. (*They both giggle.*)

HANI: I'm a Muslim. We're not the strictest family in the world, but women's issues are kept very confidential. When you have your period, you have to conduct yourself really differently, and it affects how you practise your faith and religion. Like you can't pray or fast. (*She lowers her voice.*) Some of my friends don't really mind this all the time, some find it upsetting. But it is the will of Allah. So, there is no way you ever talk of women's issues. I think if I mentioned this to my dad or my brothers, they would probably have a heart attack! And you keep your rituals very private. Like if I have cramps or feel faint, I would tell my father it is from tiredness. And I would never leave, er, sanitary towels in the bathroom. We keep them in a place away from men's eyes. Unlike Louise. (*They both giggle again.*)

LOUISE: My dad built these shelves in the bathroom and he painted two of them with red flowers and we keep all our stuff there. He calls it the red flower shelf. My older sister calls it the 'on the rag' shelf. Her and my dad argue all the time. He wanted her to bring her boyfriends home and said sex was natural and should be celebrated. She says he's mad. He brought up contraception at dinner a few weeks back and she went crazy, threw some broccoli at him and stormed out.

HANI: You didn't tell me that.

LOUISE (*rolling eyes again*): It was so embarrassing. He and my mum have a period dance. When she's about to have her period, they dance around the living room and he puts her hand on her stomach. (*They are now both laughing so much, it takes them a minute to recover.*)

How did you feel when you started your period?

LOUISE: Relieved. Happy. Everyone is so obsessed with it at school; it's all you want to do. And then it comes and you wish it could stop. You feel self-conscious. And then all the boys started making jokes about closing your legs because you smell of fish, and you panic because you wonder if you do smell. And then my skin got spotty, but luckily my mum took me to the doctors really quickly and it cleared up.

HANI: And your dad bought you incense.

LOUISE: Yes. Special incense to clear something.

HANI: And appease the moon goddess. (*They both giggle again.*)

The moon goddess is more intrusive than Allah, I think. I was sort of happy. But there is a lot of pressure to behave in a different way after you start your period. It's quite complicated. There are a lot of different categories. But actually it isn't considered a curse in Islam, like in Christianity. Or a punishment. But you are considered to be unclean. For some of my friends, they are terrified of periods because of that and it is, really, the end of childhood for us. We are women and all that comes with that – that is expected.

LOUISE: That's why my parents are anti-religion. All religions. They say they encourage hatred of women.

HANI: I don't agree with that. I think Islam makes women sacred. It does treat you differently. But we are different.

Sex

KELLY, 15, BRIGHTON

Is about to enter Year 11 for her GCSE courses. She is five months pregnant with her first child. The father also attends the school and has just turned sixteen. The school (with full support of the governors) has agreed to let Kelly remain at school until the birth. She hopes to sit ten GCSEs next summer.

Sex is just everywhere, isn't it? You can't escape it. I mean, we all know it's what all adverts are about. Films, TV, books, clothes, shop signs, the internet. I mean, if you reduce everything down – there's nothing that isn't about sex. Even things that are telling you not to have sex are really obsessed with sex because they're thinking about it enough to tell you not to have it.

Maybe the only place there isn't enough of it is in school. Not people having sex. Because that would be a bit weird and get you expelled but, you know, teaching of it.

I mean, we got the basics, of course, but most of the teaching is stuck in the last century. Everyone knows you can make a baby and that, but no one really teaches about the consequences. And I don't just mean my consequence. But emotionally.

Sex is sold sort of like a designer watch or something. Something you should have, need to have, people will laugh at you if you don't have, and all that. But it's like a lot of things. Once you've got it, you're not quite sure what to do with it.

Like, I think there is too much put on virginity. Or losing your virginity. It's like once you've done it, you have to keep on doing it, or else. Which in a way is more dangerous than the idea of being in a rush to lose it. Say people lost it and then could happily think, 'Whoooo, I've done it and now it's out the way and I can wait for a few years and concentrate on something else.' But sex is like people with alcohol or chips. You keep going once you've started and you think, 'Well, I've started, what's the point of stopping?'

I think that's the point I'm trying to make. It's difficult to give it back once you've got it. I'm not being very clear here, am I?

I lost my virginity when I was thirteen. Not to Josh, my boyfriend now. To a boy called Callum in the park. I really, really wish I hadn't. Not just because I should have waited, but because I got so badly bullied afterwards, I thought about killing myself. The whole school was calling me a 'slag' and a 'dirty whore' and even my mum got abused on Facebook by other mums. Eventually I moved school at the end of Year 9.

When I started at my new school, it was so different. My last school was absolutely massive, but this school is much smaller and people are cleverer. I love this school. They are very learning focused but also have a big policy on well-being and talking about your problems. I was lucky to get a place here.

I met Josh on the first day here and he was really nice to me. He was in my form and offered to show me around. Unlike absolutely every other school I've ever heard of, there aren't that many cliques here. People just seem to get on with each other, which is *so* unusual these days. I was really scared when I started dating Josh that people would turn against me, but they didn't. It just happened gradually. There was some good-natured piss-taking, but that was about it.

It was all quite innocent really. We held hands in school,

and went out after school. One time the deputy head saw us kissing in the playground and gave us a bit of a lecture on appropriate conduct in school. I thought it was funny but Josh was mortified. But that night on the way home from school, it seemed a good time to bring up the issue of sex. I wanted to do it, but he wanted to wait. We agreed we'd wait for three months and see how we felt then and if we were still together.

Three months later and we were still together and so we did it. It was a lot nicer than the first time but it's definitely never how they show you in films. I know it sounds gay, but we were so focused on the relationship aspect of it – how is it going to work? Is it going to be good? Will it change our relationship? – we didn't think enough about the practicalities.

We had tried it a few times and then we went to the family planning clinic and they put me on the pill. It was too late by then. I didn't realise I was pregnant until nearly ten weeks, because I assumed the contraception had messed up my periods.

It was my best friend who noticed first and then my mum. My friend Sarah said my boobs had got much bigger, which I had noticed, but I was pretty happy about! I didn't even know this was a pregnancy symptom. And I was feeling tired, but again I'm always tired. School tires you out. But I was sleeping a lot. Like I'd come home from school and just pass out.

Then on a Sunday, Josh had come round for dinner and Mum was roasting a chicken. I was talking to her about something in the kitchen and she opened the oven door to look at it, and the smell just made me retch and instantly go be sick in the downstairs loo. And I love roast chicken. It's my favourite food. I could happily eat my way through the best part of a chicken by myself.

When I came out, Mum had a really funny look on her face and asked straight out if we were having sex. Neither of us knew where to look. I asked why she was asking and she said, 'Because I think you might be pregnant. I've wondered for a couple of weeks.' We had to admit we had been.

Josh almost went green. She drove down to the local Tesco's and got two test kits and made me do one straight away. It was definitely positive. You know those seconds where you just can't believe something and everything around you just seems to bend? Well, that was one of those moments. I started to cry and Josh just looked like he'd been hit in the face with a brick.

Mum was pretty level-headed. She got mad later, but basically said, 'The damage has been done, what's the point in shouting?' She insisted on calling Josh's parents and they came round. I was mortified. That was the worst bit. They all sat around talking like we were two little kids who had got caught stealing sweets and what best to do about it?

Actually, that was when Josh was brilliant. He was like, 'It's our problem and we want to deal with it, and you will have to deal with our decision.' His dad lost his temper at that point, but Josh stood his ground. I was proud of him.

So here I am. Getting too fat for my school uniform and worrying about GCSEs and how to change a nappy.

The school has been brilliant and most people at school have been really nice. But it's Josh I'm the most amazed by. He's gone from sort of being a bit of an idiot and constantly messing around on Xbox to being this really focused person. He says we *have* to both do well at our GCSEs as it's the baby's future now and not just ours.

We found out it's a girl a few weeks back. We're going to call her Katy because I love Katy Perry and so does Josh.

MICHAEL, 18, WEST LONDON

Studying for A levels. Describes himself as 'an ardent feminist and socialist'. Volunteers for a number of charities and donates a 'good portion' of his wages every month to women's charities.

I was at a mate's house. A good guy. He's still my mate. There were four of us – yeah, I know, a bit like *The Inbetweeners*, right? That programme was spot on about everything.

But anyway, Tom suggested we look at porn for a laugh. I wasn't all that comfortable. I mean I've looked at bits, I'm not a saint, but it just doesn't do that much for me. So we looked at some bits and then my other friend Alex suggests we look at some hardcore sites. So we start looking at these like rape sites. Like simulation gang rape. A woman having knives held up to her throat with, like, two cocks up her and screaming.

I just lost it completely. I ran out the back door. Tom has some woods out the back of his garden and I just sat on a log and cried. Tom and Alex came to find me and I thought they'd take the piss, but they were really nice about it. Tom didn't really know what to say, but Alex was surprisingly helpful. It doesn't surprise me; he is going to study psychology at university. Our other mate Jack just stayed in the kitchen and ordered pizza and when we came back, he was like, 'You all right, mate?' But didn't ask anything else. He's still like that.

But it was from that moment I decided that sex and violence have become too interchangeable. Everything for boys is geared not just towards sex but being sexually dominant and yeah, violating. Footballers raping girls, rape jokes, violent porn, tons of misogynistic language – and there is a subtle encouragement of it. You listen in on any conversation amongst teenage boys and you can spot it. Well, hear it.

So I've made a pledge. I don't want to add to any more of that. I'm not a head banger or a devout Christian. Quite a lot of my friends are having sex and that's just fine. But I'm not interested in having sex. I don't want sex with women and I don't want sex with men because I'm not attracted to them. I do have a girlfriend and she is supportive of my views. I suppose you could argue it is asceticism of a kind, but I don't feel like I'm denying myself at all and actually I feel really liberated. I find sex off-putting, degrading, often violent and can't see anyone getting that much pleasure out of it. On a wider scale, it seems to cause more misery than pleasure.

Do I think I'll change my mind in the future? Maybe. It's not out of the question. But my life is better and freer since I took this stance. I'm a happier person and I think a surprising number of young people would feel the same if they could see what I see.

JAMES, LUKE, HARRIS AND TOBY, ALL 18, DURHAM

All attend a private sixth form. James has a steady girlfriend. Luke and Harris are single and 'pretty desperate at this stage' and Toby is gay and 'in a very happy relationship'. All have been friends since they were five. They live by the moniker 'bros before hos' but would drop this 'in a second if the possibility of sex was on the table'.

LUKE: As irony would have it, and as you can probably see, Toby is by far, far the best-looking out of all of us. He models regularly (*they all jeer*) and so, since we were fourteen, he's been our secret weapon.

HARRIS (*interrupting*): But then the bastard has to come out as gay. And to everyone! We were like human Teflon and he was like this girl magnet and he was *gay*! (*They all laugh.*)

LUKE: But little did we know ...

JAMES: Girls love the gays ... our social cachet went through the roof! (*They all laugh again.*)

That was fairly progressive of you, no? To accept a friend as gay at age fourteen?

TOBY: You would think so, wouldn't you? I mean I was terrified, a long story, but my mum had asked me if I was gay. And she encouraged me to tell my friends. Actually our school has got the best LGBT pride programme. One of the head boys was gay. It was kind of a big deal. And I know some head teachers, still, are funny about the issue because it scares parents off. But ours is very cool. Some of the teachers are openly gay. So it was a really nurturing environment. Someone had written something about me on the toilet wall about taking it up the arse and some real obscenities and someone had written underneath it, 'Stop fucking your sister, you ignorant moron.' And someone else had written underneath it: 'Only homophobes hang out in men's toilets.' So the secret gay-basher got pretty badly bashed. They painted over it but we took loads of pictures of it and I had it as my banner picture on Facebook for quite a long time. The thing is, people who are bothered about gay people are most bothered about sodomy. Like that's all there is to gay sex. And they think about it a *lot*. The same twats who probably think all lesbians would invite them in for a threesome.

JAMES: You mean they *don't*? (*They all laugh.*)

HARRIS: Lesbians are great though, aren't they?

TOBY: You're thinking of porn lesbians. In real life they have no interest in you because you have a cock. In fact for the most part, they tend to find cocks fairly repulsive. Hence the whole lesbian thing.

JAMES: What about bisexuals?

LUKE: I think bisexuals might be just a bit greedy. Like, dude, pick a side.

HARRIS: Maybe they're really smart. But cocks – no offence, mate, but bleurgh!

TOBY: None taken. But you have a cock I'm sure you are pretty fond of. I feel the same way about vaginas. I really like girls. Some of my favourite people are girls. But I had an aborted attempt at sex with one once, aged fifteen . . . and just, no. I ended up in tears. She was really nice about it, though. It was horrible. I desperately *wanted* to be straight. I'd challenge any young gay man to admit they didn't want that at some point. It's what you're supposed to be.

LUKE: My mum tried to teach me how to go down on a woman recently. (*There is a stunned silence.*)

JAMES: *How?*

LUKE: With a piece of fruit. A passion fruit. It was fucking horrible. I'll never eat fruit again. She said a woman's body is a complex thing.

JAMES: She's not wrong.

MARTHA, RACHEL, 18, CHLOE, AND PRITI, 17, SUFFOLK

All attend a sixth-form college. Martha, Rachel and Priti are all heterosexual. Chloe is 'uncertain' about her sexuality. They will all be attending university next year. Martha and Rachel are both in 'fairly serious' relationships and Chloe and Priti are single.

RACHEL: Do you know, I have a theory about the *Twilight* books? You know how all those, like, *Guardian* journalists were saying they were bad because they were a metaphor for Christian conservatism or something and preserving your virginity? I think girls and secretly a lot of boys liked them because they weren't banging on about sex. Like, you know, escapism. When everything is 'he fucked her and she gave him a blowjob and he fingered her' and lesbians and porn and more 'shall I do it, shan't I?' It was total bloody escapism into a world where no one seemed that interested. Like how bored housewives used to read Mills & Boon to escape their boring husbands.

CHLOE: I think Rachel is right. I mean I haven't had sex yet. But it's like being told over and over and over again about, say, a really nice restaurant. By the time you get there, you feel it's sort of ruined because it's impossible to form your own opinion and it's kind of been made up for you anyway.

MARTHA: I don't agree. I love talking about sex. I love having sex. I mean, let's face it, we talk about it a lot so it must be *fairly* interesting. And actually that's kind of the rub, because there *is* a new taboo or judgement about girls doing it. My older sister told me in the Nineties, or the late Nineties, with, you know, *Sex and the City* and a lot of girl bands and things, there was like this sort of wave of freedom. Which is gone now. I think especially social media has brought back this new wave of girl-hating and slut-shaming that is making girls scared of being sexually open or liberated. I mean, I *refuse* to play this good girl. And the shit I get is unbelievable. What's worse is both my sister, who is quite a bit older, and my mum in the late Eighties, went to Cambridge. They said it was brilliant because there was this huge sense of just *acceptance*. I'm going there in the autumn and the shit I hear already is more than disheartening. It's scary. 'Fuck a Fresher' is old news. Still, Oxford sounds like it's much worse. But it's like things are going backwards.

CHLOE: I agree. Twitter and Ask FM are bloody horrible. The things that have happened to girls on them. And in the States. Girls getting sport raped and it's put on social media for a laugh. And then *they* get castigated. (*We all sigh.*)

PRITI: That scares me more than sex. Slut-shaming. That's always been rife in my community although we call it 'honour' – but it's the same thing. Girls have been killed forever for falling in love and having sex.

RACHEL: And it's like the whole world is embracing it. Like, obviously no one is getting stoned to death or strangled by their brothers. But schools are awful. Society is awful. They crucify girls for having sex. It's like you can only flaunt your sexuality if it's socially acceptable. Because Beyoncé has a kid and is happily married, it's fine for her to dress up in a basque. But if Miley Cyrus does or Rihanna does, she's considered a total slag. Like Martha – can I say this, Martha? (*Martha nods.*) Martha had sex pretty early in our year group and was really open about it and all sorts of shit happened. And she's so together, she survived it. But it was like ... she had to grow ...

MARTHA: What Rachel is trying politely to say is I had to grow balls if I wanted to be me. I went off and got a shitload of tattoos and wore a shitload of make-up and told everyone to go fuck themselves. Kind of like Rihanna, though I can't stand her. But yeah, if you're a woman now and want to be sexually liberated, you have to be tough. And thick-skinned. My total role model is Brody Dalle. I wish she did more now. I *love her.* I also like Karen O. (*We all have a brief off-the-record discussion about Josh Homme.*)

CHLOE: Show me a picture of Brody Dalle. (*Martha does.*) Oh my God. I'm definitely a lesbian. She's gorgeous!

MARTHA: Sometimes I wish I was a lesbian. Girls are nicer. But I like willies.

PRITI: Martha! That's disgusting!

RACHEL: I hate willies. They're so funny looking. They look a bit like they're looking at you pitifully. And then they get angry and hard.

MARTHA: And go red in the face. Or purple. (*Much mirth follows.*)

PRITI: I *never* want to see a willy, ever, now!

MARTHA: Actually, that's the pay-off for being a girl after all the shit we get. It must be like having an angry toddler in your trousers all day.

MICHAEL, JAWAD, 17, LUPINE, 16, RASHID, JAVI AND ROBERT, 15, EAST LONDON

All are studying for their GCSEs except Jawad and Michael who are currently doing BTECs. Jawad 'hates his course and rarely goes'. Michael quite likes his and is determined to pass because he is 'going to be a father early next year and wants a real job'. The others all go to the same school and say it is a 'complete waste of time, with shit teachers'. Their collective predicted GCSE results are significantly below the national average, except Lupine who has excellent predicted results, particularly in the context of the school's average results. Due to Lupine's dyslexia, his mum coaches him for five hours a week and makes him read at least two books a month. He will admit, when asked, to enjoying reading.

JAWAD: White girls are the easiest. Afghan girls, forget about it. Asian girls, maybe. Black girls you have to buy enough gold and listen to all their shit and get the approval of all their girls until you can, even.

RASHID: What the fuck do you know about girls? If you saw a pussy you'd cry. Girls are bare difficult to understand. Like sometimes I think they're not even worth it. Some guy I knew fucked this girl and was chatting his shit all over town about her, you know? She heard and she came and broke his ear. Like hit him so hard she broke his ear. I think he might be half deaf or something now.

LUPINE: What the fuck are you talking about? You can't break people's ears. I heard that story too. It was that skinny fool who thinks he's like the Scarface of the chicken shop. Struts around carrying some nasty drumstick. I think he thinks it's a gun or something, he's that dumb. His sister is probably his mum or something (*they all emit a low 'oooohing' sound*). And I don't blame the girl. That was his girl. Your girl gives you head or whatever, that should be between you and her. You call your girl a ho, even to your boys, you deserve to have your earring ripped out. But no one around here seems to think anything is sacred.

ROBERT: I know what you mean. But like, it's hard, man. Like people see you with a girl and everyone's like, 'What happened, what happened?' and you're all like, 'Nothing,' and then everyone starts saying you're batty and then you end up saying shit and the next thing you know she's trying to tear your eyes out. But it's still worth it. I've fucked more girls than all of you.

RASHID: Yeah and you won't use johnnies. Which is so stupid.

ROBERT: Johnnies are for pussies and gays.

MICHAEL: You won't be saying that when you get your girl pregnant.

Are you excited about the pregnancy?

MICHAEL: Yeah, man. Of course. Every man wants to be a dad. My mum had me young and I'm good. I'm going to be there for the birth and everything. It's a boy, you know?

ROBERT: You know when a girl pushes out a baby, there's blood and guts everywhere? Like all over the walls. I saw that shit on TV.

LUPINE: You are so dumb. That's not guts. It's like ... birth stuff.

RASHID: That is nasty, boy.

MICHAEL (*shrugs*): You gotta be a man. It's like my mum said at the time, when I told her: you play, you pay. You want to have sex girls, you have to face the music. Plus her cousin threatened to drop me off a ten-storey car park if I didn't stick by her (*laughs*).

JAWAD: How long were you doing it before she got pregnant?

MICHAEL: What the fuck difference does that make?

LUPINE: It can happen any time, fool. You should always wear a condom. Bitches be crazy. There is so much crazy talk about condoms. I don't understand it. They can save your life.

RASHID: And you a *lot* of money. No man needs more than one baby momma.

MICHAEL: True. I was more scared of telling my mum than I am about the pregnancy. Luckily she just hit me with a spatula with holes in it, which didn't even hurt that much. But she's OK now. She's going to let us move in with her for a bit, which is pretty safe of her. I can't believe how much a baby costs. It's only a tiny little thing and needs more stuff than I do.

RHONDA, SOOKI AND JANE, ALL 15, BRADFORD

Studying for their GCSEs at the same comprehensive. They are fiercely committed to retaining their virginity and eschew any sexual relations although Sooki does have a boyfriend. This commitment is not driven by a religious conviction or parental pressure. They describe themselves as 'anti-ho'. They will admit to imposing these views in particular on other girls and have been spoken to/reprimanded many times for what teachers have described as 'aggressive and bullying tactics'. They continue with their cause.

RHONDA: You know that racist group, the English Defence League? Well, we are the 'Anti-Ho League'. I guess that's not our official title because we have to be careful now with some of the shit we got at school from the teachers. But we are a cause. No doubt.

And what does this cause represent?

RHONDA: Our hatred of hos. It's got nothing to do with colour, looks, nothing. It's not jealousy, though some people will tell you that. We are against hos. All this women's liberation (*makes speech marks with fingers*) stuff is *bullshit*. It's not an excuse to behave like a ho, to dress like a ho, to act like a ho. You wanna walk around with your booty and tits hanging out, sucking on a man's dick? You should be prepared for the consequences.

JANE: We warn girls first. We tell them we don't like the way they dress, their attitudes and shit. We remind them that they are betraying all girls by not having respect for themselves. And if they don't listen . . .

RHONDA: We teach them a lesson. We have this Facebook page with 'Top 10 Dressed Hos of the Week', 'Top 10 Ho Behaviour', 'Top 10 Nasty Hos'. You *do not* want to get on that. One time this sket was like really drunk at a party in our year. We filmed the whole thing and put it online. She had to leave the school. We are popular in school, so people agree with us. It's for everyone's good. I am so sick of all this nasty behaviour from girls and they all be acting like it's fun and their right. They should have some self-respect.

SOOKI: Exactly. Like look at all the teenage pregnancy, STDs, girls becoming strippers and Page 3 girls. There's some girl in the year above and it's her *ambition* to become a Page 3 girl. So skanky. She's a white girl, though. No black girls are seen in those newspapers. And everyone sitting around acting like it's all OK. It isn't. It's time someone made a stand. And I'm sorry but this particularly affects the poorer and ethnic communities. Not like stripping and all, and STDs. But how many rich white girls you know with a baby? There's about thirty girls I can think of who live near me with a baby under eighteen. That is wrong. And they're not getting pregnant falling over a dick in the market or whatever, y'know?

RHONDA: Yeah, and all this is doing is making boys' attitudes worse. They go round expecting all girls to suck their dicks, fuck on the first date. Girls are happy to be passed around groups of boys like dick sport. There was a girl who fucked three boys at her school. On the school grounds! It's no wonder boys have been calling us bitches, hos and that for years now. Boys rape girls *all the time, for fun* and people be wondering why. If they behave like hos, what do they expect?

JANE: It might seem sometimes we are bullying, but it's the opposite. We are anti-ho because we are anti-rape, anti-sexual bullying and we want girls to respect themselves. All change has sometimes been harsh. We can't go round asking girls not to act like hos or pieces of meat for boys, so we have to show them how.

JAY, 17, NORTH LONDON

Currently studying at a prestigious music college. Would like to be a professional concert pianist.

The first time I had sex was terrible. You would think I would know better really, the amount of porn I watched when I was younger, but all my mates became convinced of this sexual technique where you had to, uh ... actually I can't even tell you, it's so horrible. She was like, 'What the fuck are you doing?' Amazingly she let me have another go a bit later. She's still my girlfriend. She's great. I like to think I've improved.

AVI, 18, CARDIFF

Is about to start an engineering course at UCL. Says this 'scares him less than women's bodies'.

The first time I had sex was at camp. It was basically an expensive summer camp for Jewish kids. This girl – Marianne – bless her, was this, to put it nicely, sexually forward girl. Rumour had it, she got off with one of the camp counsellors and got kicked out. Anyway, one night she basically came in, ordered me out of my bunk and told me to follow her. I was wearing these ridiculous striped pyjamas that my mum had bought me. I was a little, er, excited and thought it would look less ridiculous if I tied a towel around my waist. It didn't.

So I followed her into these woods by this lake and she said, 'We're going to have sex now.' I was terrified. Basically, I had no clue as to insertion, so I ended up sort of rubbing my penis between her thighs. I came in about two seconds. She told all her friends and they nicknamed me 'Limp Zebra' and kept singing some horrible song at me. I guess in reference to the pyjamas. I still haven't really lived it down. I can't wait to get to uni and be known as another animal. Hopefully a tiger this time. Grrr.

ELLIE, 19, EDINBURGH

Does a lot of jobs: bartending, waitressing, occasionally temps at a record label and is learning burlesque dancing in the hope she can make a living out of it, because 'that's the dream'.

This first time I had sex was with the singer of a famous band (*she mentions the name of a very famous band*). I was obsessed with him at the time and I went to all their gigs and had his posters all over my wall. I thought he was God (*laughs*). I'd realised by then – because I'm pretty damn hot – that because of that I can get what I wanted. It was like a shot in the arm of power. Guys would give you seats on the bus, buy you drinks, follow you down the street. They're basically dogs on hind legs.

So, anyway, they'd been playing a show in London and I decided to blag my way backstage because I knew some people who knew people. It worked. I chatted up this music journo with all these music laminates. He got me into the proper after-show party and I ditched him as quickly as possible. I made a beeline straight for the singer and he was well up for it. He took me back to the tour bus which was outside the venue and we fucked in his bunk with the tour manager asleep – I think he was asleep – below us.

In terms of sexual prowess, I'd give him a six, which might not be entirely fair because it's hard to get a proper rhythm going in a bunk. But nonetheless, he gave me his hat and kept sending me backstage tickets to his gigs. He still does. I might go, but I've gone off him now. I've got my sights set on someone even better (*another famous singer*). And I'll get him.

JOHN, 18, MANCHESTER

Lives at home with his parents whilst he tries to get his band going. They are starting to enjoy 'some success, but it pays fuck-all money, yet'.

The first time I had sex was a fucking disaster. I was so drunk; I could literally not remember my name. It happened at a party. I was fifteen. I woke up to find I'd pissed the bed, she was gone and I barely knew where I was. I nicked someone's Oyster card to get home and was violently sick on the bus. I was sick seven more times, but decided I'd better try and eat something, so I ordered a pizza. I was sick again and the doorbell rang. Instead of the pizza boy, it was some lad – I didn't have a scoobie who it was. And he just punched me in the face! Just like that. I fell over and was sick again and he ran away yelling, 'Stay away from fucking Lisa or I'll kill you!' It was her brother. Apparently she posted all about it on Facebook, and not in exactly flattering terms. She'd given me a nickname but I'm not telling you what it was.

I could have sworn her name was Sarah. I kept calling her that, apparently. I swore off girls for quite a while after that.

LISA, LUCY, MINNIE AND DONNA, ALL 16, HAMPSHIRE

About to start studying for A levels and work in a stable together. They all want to be involved in horses in their professional lives. Donna is already an award-winning showjumper.

LUCY: All I'm going to say about it is, I wish I hadn't done it. I wish I'd waited. And like everyone else pretty much my age that has, alcohol was involved. I was drunk. I bled a lot afterwards. It really hurt, despite the fact I was pissed out of my head, and the lad barely spoke to me again. And all his friends were *awful* about it. Said all sorts of awful things. He's a bastard. He's in the year above me.
MINNIE: He's a massive cunt. We told you that. I haven't done it. I'm not particularly waiting because I feel I have to, but it just sounds not great. Every one of my mates who has done it says it hurts, you bleed and an orgasm is less likely than the Tooth Fairy.
DONNA: Yeah, definitely. Like you watch *The Notebook* or *Atonement* and they have sex for the first time and it's all wonderful and they have orgasms in the rain. It's not really like that, is it?
MINNIE: It *might* be different if you were shagging Ryan Gosling or James McAvoy though, mightn't it? (*They all laugh.*)
LISA: In all honesty, and this isn't a judgement of anyone else and especially not you, Lucy, but I think you *should* wait for someone you love. It's a pretty special thing, isn't it?
LUCY: It's OK. Judge. I *wish* I hadn't done it. It *is* special. I want every girl reading this to absolutely wait until she's ready.

MINNIE: I think there is too much focus on sex. I wish everyone would stop obsessing.

ANGIE, 19, MIDDLESBROUGH

'Barmaid and a dyke.'

Can't remember the first lad I had sex with, but the second one tried to put it in my bum. So I punched him in the windpipe. I think it caused lasting damage. Now I am a dyke. I hate the word 'lesbian' or 'gay' for women. 'Dyke' sounds out and proud. That should be in modern sex education in schools. Would have saved me an awful lot of hassle.

WAYNE, 15, CREWE

Says he has slept with at least twenty girls, although 'he can't remember all their names'. His pet name for his penis is 'my dawg'.

I get enough pussy. I've been having sex since I was twelve because I've always liked the ladies. I've never had any complaints about my dawg. It's massive. My favourite position is her on top, so I can smoke a blunt (*joint*) at the same time. Good times.

RONITA, 14, ST ALBANS

Is about to enter GCSE courses fully but is doing her maths and science GCSEs a year early due to her exceptional ability. Would like to be a doctor specialising in women's healthcare in places like India 'where women receive very little or quite poor care unless they are rich'.

I am very worried about my generation where sex is concerned. My mum is a doctor and specialises in women's sexual health. She works in a poor part of London and deals a lot with teenage pregnancy, sexual diseases, rape victims and things. She is very open about her work and I find it interesting. We have long discussions about medical ethics at the dinner table.

I am very glad to live in a country where women are considered equal and taken care of, because I spend every summer in India with family and I have seen what it's like and how different it is. I think there is an attitude here that because you can have sex and get out of the consequences then you should, which is wrong. For example, my mum disagrees with me, but I think abortion is used and given too freely. I don't think it is our fault though, really. Everything is sex, sex, sex. People can't stop talking about it. I opened my copy of *Of Mice and Men* the other day in English and someone had drawn a very graphic picture of a man and a woman, you know, *together*! What's that got to do with *Of Mice and Men*? I don't know why, but it upset me.

When I was in London last week, we were in a salad restaurant and there were all these signs like 'How do you like to be tossed?' and 'Squeeze my tomatoes. They're firm.' I do not want to be looking at that standing with my dad. It's what you'd expect in Burger King, with all the Whoppers and things. I bet a man named it that, the amount boys talk about their penises and draw them on everything.

ZUBEID, 15, NORTH LONDON

Moved here three years ago from Afghanistan. Lives with his mother, uncle and seven brothers and sisters. He is the second eldest of the siblings. He is a devout Muslim.

I am extremely worried about the sexual attitudes here. I find it very upsetting and offensive. I do not wish to insult England because it is a very good place, but I'll explain myself. I'll start with my brother, OK? The older one. Since he came here, he has gone crazy. The second he went to school it was like he forgot all his values and beliefs and he started smoking the weed and having sex with girls. Always very pretty girls because he is very good-looking and he has charms. He loves white girls as he says they are the best, and very, very easy in their morals. He especially likes blonde girls. He has a poster of Taylor Swift on his wall, which my younger brother kisses at night until he punches him in the head.

He says he has had sex many times now and he climbs out of the window at night and comes back very early smelling of weed and alcohol. He watches pornography too and has had many fights with my uncle. They are starting to get physical now. The trouble is, where I come from, girls are forbidden. You don't mix with them in any way. If you see them on the street, they are covered up – except in Kabul – but we don't come from there. It is much more conservative.

My religion does not hate women, but it is very strict about resisting temptation and not being distracted in your commitment to Allah. When so many boys from my country here see the girls and how they behave, it is too much of a shock for them. It is like your boys going to school and all the girls turning up naked. Wouldn't that be a shock and cause troubles? I am not saying you are wrong, but I am trying to explain. Many people say we Afghans and Muslims are pigs and hate women. It is a complicated situation. But when you are told to fear something and avert your eyes from when you are small and it is suddenly all around, it is quite difficult for us.

What do you think of the girls here?

I think they are very pretty and very friendly but I am trying very hard not to be like my brother, and so I concentrate on my studies and my prayers very hard.

My brother described his time with a girl to me the other night, and I was very upset and embarrassed. My younger brothers were very interested. I think there will be problems with them, especially my ten-year-old brother. He talks about girls non-stop and listens to all the music about sex on his iPod. Especially Chris Brown, who I do not approve of. He looks so dirty with his blond hair and tattoos.

EDITH, 18, CORNWALL

Currently doing her A levels. Has had three sexual partners and now has a regular boyfriend. He stays overnight at her house with the blessing of her parents. She wants to be a teacher.

Sex is just a thing you do, isn't it? Can you imagine if we talked about anything else like we talk about sex? Like, if I don't get a good game of tennis soon I'm gonna explode? That was the best game of tennis of my life? I'd take her and play her in a game of tennis all over that court. If you aren't playing tennis, you aren't a man. It'd sound pretty daft.

School

ROB, 14, EAST LONDON

Attends a comprehensive school for over 1,500 students. Class sizes are in excess of thirty students even for the core subjects. The school's results are significantly below the national average. There is a rapid teacher turnover due to the school's Ofsted report, which identified 'significant behavioural issues', and the school is reportedly on the brink of going into special measures. The school has a very diverse ethnic make-up and is in one of the poorest boroughs of London.

To say my school is shit would be an understatement. It's awful. I don't think I've learnt anything of value since primary school, which was all right. I liked primary school. When people say that school is the best years of your life, well, that just makes me wanna top myself, or something. But what are you going to do? To be fair, I do get bored at weekends and in the holidays, and then the second you walk back into it, you realise how fucking depressing the place is and you just want to walk out again.

First off, the building should be knocked down. It literally isn't safe to be in, in the least. Last week we were having physics and the teacher was going on about something and suddenly a big chunk of the ceiling fell down and nearly hit him. It was jokes and we pissed ourselves laughing, but I suppose it would have been bad if it hit him. It might have killed him. He's one of the few teachers that have been here a long time, and actually knows our names. He's all right, even though he stinks. The caretaker came and, like, Sellotaped a cardboard tile to the hole and we helped and it wasted a whole lesson. That was a good one. Physics is hard, man.

The toilets stink of piss and worse. The playgrounds aren't playgrounds: they're just these concrete things with fences like you see in prison films. Except you can easily get over the fence in some places because it's broken and I don't think they can afford to fix it. Or don't want to because people go get stoned at lunchtime and then either don't come back or fall asleep in class, which actually makes class better. I don't like to get stoned. It makes me feel sick, so I don't bother. Loads of people come back looking all mashed up and paranoid, and I think, 'What's the point?'

Classes are ... classes, once a month maybe, go well. Like some work gets done or you get to watch a DVD or something. But most teachers in the school have no control over us and we just fuck around 24/7. There are fights, people swear at the teachers and throw stuff. Last week this crazy kid called Omar crawled out the window and walked across the ledge to look into the class next door. It was on the first floor, so pretty high and we all were going fucking mental. The teacher burst into tears and eventually one of the deputies heard the commotion and came in and went absolutely fucking mental. Omar got suspended, which was pointless as he spent the two days hanging around the school gates chatting with us or climbing through the fence into the playground. Actually a lot of people do that when they get suspended, which is funny. You hate school, you get two days off and you spend those days trying to come back.

Look at my English book from last year. (*He shows me his English book. About two pages have some scrappy words on them, the rest is ripped, covered in practice graffiti tags or empty. The cover has an amazing pencil-drawn portrait of Tupac Shakur covering it.*) That's a year's work, there. Bit shit, isn't it? I'm not saying it's *all* the teacher's fault. I hate English. It's so boring. We had this supply teacher for about six weeks and she was OK. And really fit. She taught us *Macbeth* and gave us all one part in groups, which was quite good. We got Macbeth. He was some madman. We hoped she'd stay, but she went back to New Zealand or Australia or some place.

Another teacher we had walked out on the first day. Another teacher had a name that sounded like penis. It was well funny. We cussed him so badly, I think he went mental or something. He locked himself in his classroom one day and wouldn't come out and we had to go to the library and watch *The Incredibles* all day, which was wicked. He never came back.

Sometimes, the head teacher, who is a dickhead, tries to give us lectures in assembly about making the most of our lives and our school years. But he always loses it and starts yelling at someone for laughing or something.

School's good for the jokes and the peng girls and PE is good, though we have to do it on a week-on, week-off timetable, because they sold our sports field so there isn't room for us to do it all at once. I start my GCSEs next year and will try to focus and do well, but I don't even know what my teachers are next term yet and we start in three weeks.

JUSTIN, 15, SURREY

*Attends a highly competitive, £30,000-a-year independent school. He will be taking his GCSEs next year. On top of ten standard GCSEs he will be sitting Latin and Japanese. He also plays the violin and is a first in the cricket team. He says he will be 'thoroughly shocked if he doesn't get all A*s' with the exception of Japanese, where he expects an A. He wants to attend Harvard University when he finishes school, as the American system is 'better suited to his academic needs and intensely competitive streak'. He is also disillusioned with the 'can't do' attitude in the UK, which he thinks is the real reason for unemployment and the economic downturn.*

I love school and always have. The school I attend is very much a family tradition. People say that boarding school is cruel, but that's complete bullshit. People who say that are the type of people who read *Boy* once and somehow have an idea that still represents boarding or private schools. It doesn't. I get that not *everyone* enjoys boarding school, but they've changed so much now, there is something for everyone. Whether you're sporty, academic, musical, political, social, antisocial, gay, straight, conservative, socialist – there is something for you. And not just a cursory nod to it. Something really stimulating. And the whole fagging and buggery thing? Nonsense. That's as antiquated as saying white people are smarter than black people. It just doesn't represent what we think or are. Maybe in my grandfather or great-grandfather's day. But not now.

This might be all boys, but believe it or not, we have loads of contact with girls. There is a stringent anti-bullying programme. All the younger boys are mentored and looked after by older boys. There are lots of female teachers here and we manage not to grope or belittle them – strange but true. There are loads of boys here heavily involved in charitable work, human rights stuff. This isn't a ticket to Oxford and Cambridge. What I'm trying to say is, there seems to be an almost accepted discriminatory view of people attending public schools that just isn't accurate. I'm not about to say it isn't fair. Because my life and position are more than fair. I'm rich, white, heterosexual and male. I understand that. But if I said all kids that attend state schools are poor, thick, diseased plebs, I'd get my arse kicked. And rightly so. But I get called a 'posh twat', 'an inbred posh cunt' and 'Little Lord Fauntleroy' all the time and that somehow seems to be OK.

Our school is certainly more progressive than some. The emphasis is absolutely on academic excellence and not secret handshakes and who your father is. Of course there is an element of that here. There is an element of the extremes in any of the places you go. And of course, for the most part, no one here knows what it is like to go without or worry about money. Home life tends to be more stable than it is for the average teenager. But we're all pretty decent and have all the same worries anyone else does.

This is an exciting place to be at school. There is immense community and team spirit. We take our sports – and winning them – very seriously. There are some brilliant minds here, students and teachers alike. It is genuinely exciting and fascinating to watch what everyone is doing and every student is encouraged to be excellent, original and unique. Watching our team at the debating championships was breathtaking. We have a possible future chess champion. The art department looks like a museum. Our school productions could be professional ones.

I am a school patriot, but I don't see anything wrong with that. What's wrong with loving your school and loving every moment there? We will never get a chance like this again after uni to play first and work second in such a nurturing environment.

Something has gone very, very wrong with the system that so many people hate their school days so much and get so little out of them.

REBECCA, 15, CANTERBURY

Attends a mixed comprehensive producing results significantly above the national average. The school is one of the most sought after in the area and has just received an 'outstanding' assessment from Ofsted. The school was particularly praised on its 'excellent pastoral system and support units for students within the school'. Rebecca has been the subject of a systematic bullying campaign for nearly a year now. She has been physically and verbally assaulted. She has been inappropriately touched by both boys and girls. She has been threatened online, including death threats. Her property has been stolen and ruined. She says she 'has no idea' why her entire year group has taken against her.

I never really fitted in that much at school. Dad says I'm unusual and he means that in a nice way. But unusual doesn't help you much at school. In fact it's one of the worst things you can be. The more popular girls didn't like me much from Year 8. Things were OK in Year 7 when everyone was a bit happier and nicer. But things started to go really wrong in Year 8, and Year 9 was hell. It's just been the summer holidays, but I'm so scared for next year. Things had got quieter, but I've started to receive the same things on Facebook, and this girl Monica, who really hates me, sent me a message telling me to 'watch my back'. I'm scared.

I don't know what happened to make them hate me. It started in lessons. I love the lessons at school and learning and I'm really good at English and history especially, but most of my classes I'm good in. Several of my teachers say I'm on track to get an A*.

Every time I'd say something in class, this group of girls would start to laugh and mimic me. My English teacher is really nice and would tell them off, but that would make things worse. I won a prize for a Shakespeare essay I did, and these girls spread a rumour I copied it off the internet. Which I never would do. The deputy head called me in to ask me about it and I got really upset. They believed me and these girls got into trouble and their parents got called. That's when things got awful.

The next day I found my coat in a muddy puddle. It was a beautiful coat my mum gave me for my birthday and it was ruined. I told my mum I left it on a bus and got grounded. The next day my PE kit was in the toilet and somebody had weed on it. I started to cry, and the PE teacher who is the type who loves the loud, popular kids and sort of sucks up to them, yelled at me. Everybody was laughing at me and called me 'Piss Girl'.

Then everyone spread the rumour I was a slag and there were all these rumours that I'd had sex with these two boys in the year above in the park. I don't even go to the park. All these boys were passing me in the corridor and making these horrible noises at me and some lads made me watch a porn film on their phones whilst this girl stood behind me so I couldn't leave. A few days later some girls stood at the door of the toilets and these boys came into the toilets. I was so scared, I got hysterical, so they all ran away. The school nurse, Julia, suspected something was seriously wrong but I was too scared to tell her.

It's been like this for a year now. I get abused on the way to school and on the way home from school. People are too scared to be nice to me or stick up for me because then horrible things happen to them too. This really nice group of boys in my class told Monica to stop being such a bitch and she threw an absolute fit and told the class teacher I was getting boys to bully her. They made up all these lies about me.

On the last day of term, someone left a petition in my locker telling me to kill myself and suggesting ways to do it. More than half the year had signed it. I could understand it more if I'd done anything bad, but I promise I haven't. I really haven't. Maybe I'm just a bad person, and I haven't realised it.

BONNIE, 16, OXFORD

Attends a grammar school with results well above the national average, which has been assessed twice in the last eight years as 'outstanding' by Ofsted. She describes herself as a 'reformed bully'. After the attempted suicide of a classmate – Chloe – she admits to have 'bullied terribly', she is now a campaigner for anti-bullying charities. She wants to be a filmmaker and is currently making her first feature film about bullying from the point of view of the victims. She thinks bullying is still a 'very misunderstood' topic and the negative impacts of it are 'massively underestimated by adults'.

It's a weird thing. I don't think anyone would ever say, 'Yeah, I'm a bully, I bully other kids'. But bullying is such a big problem and so common – there is no school without it – it's like a silent majority. Not minority. If people were honest, they all know they've bullied someone at some point. I bet even the Dalai Lama slagged someone off behind their back or something once. Maybe that's the problem. Not people coming forward to say they are being bullied. People saying they are doing the bullying. And actually, thinking about this, I think there might be something in that. There is something a bit addictive about it. Isn't there? Like that sense of power over someone. The pack mentality. That feeling that if it's happening to someone else, it's less likely to happen to you.

It's horrible enough to talk about this, so there's no other way to say this – but school has always been easy for me. I'm good at lessons, good at sport. The other girls always said me and this other girl were the prettiest in the school. I've never worried about my weight and I don't have to starve myself to be thin. The kids in the lower years liked me and I was always voted sports captain or class captain.

I don't know where it went wrong. You would think having all those things would just be nice and being well liked and lucky would mean I would pass on those things. But that movie *Mean Girls* is like a mirror to real school social life. You sort of forget to be nice because you don't have to work for it and then you start to be horrible. And then people start to get scared of you and you take that for granted, too. I can't really explain it.

I think my first real bullying was in Year 8. There was this Asian girl and she wore long skirts with no tights. She had really dark hair on her legs and she didn't wax or shave. One day I was like, 'Eurgh, do you share DNA with a gorilla?' I mean not just horrible, but a bit racist, right? But everyone started giggling and making noises. This girl got shit for weeks – mostly led by me. And a few weeks later she came in with waxed legs. And really red eyes. We didn't stop teasing her and one day she asked me why I was doing this to her. I think I actually said, 'It's for your own good, you ugly, hairy bitch.' Or something along those lines.

Of course looking back, I didn't have any real friends. More, er, *frenemies* who were scared of me. No one wanted to get on the wrong side of me. My God, the things I did and said. Even to my so-called friends. The things we all did to each other. But I don't think that's *all that* unusual. I don't think there are many girls who haven't said something really bitchy about even a really good friend if they are being really honest. Girls' friendships are pretty weird. There is always going to be competition.

So anyway, this new girl Chloe got on my nerves straight away. I just felt this really immediate dislike of her. Why? Because she was very pretty and sort of unusual and she was clever. And not like any of the other girls. She had this quality that annoyed us. We told ourselves it was because she was up herself and in love with herself, but I know now that isn't true. The bottom line was, I was jealous of her. And so we hounded her. Well, we did everything. And I knew we should have stopped when she seemed to stop eating. One day she was a normal size, even though we all called her fat, and then suddenly she just seemed to lose half her body weight. It didn't even occur to us that maybe it was the stress of what we were doing. So we all started calling her an 'anorexic bitch'. But by that time, people were quite worried about her and seemed less willing to be awful about her, which made me furious.

The weird thing is, I don't remember what I said that last time but she turned on me and said in this really hoarse but really, like, *menacing* voice, 'I hope you drop dead, you fucking bitch' and then she walked out of geography in floods – I mean *hysterical* tears. The class was stunned. A couple of people giggled, but you could tell everyone was really uncomfortable. I tried to laugh it off and our teacher was so dopey, he barely knew what was going on. He called after her, but let her go. I spent the whole lesson saying how I was going to get even with her for saying that, but I could tell people were worried and for once not agreeing with me. I know for a fact a few girls went to see the head of year after that lesson and there was a really weird atmosphere for the rest of the day.

I thought at worst there was going to be a bit of trouble, but I had no idea. The second I got into school the next day, I was fetched by the deputy head and taken to his office. They had called my mum. Chloe had walked out of school and had gone straight home and taken an overdose. And not just a few pills like some of the girls sometimes did when overdosing sort of became fashionable for a while. Like a *lot*. She was in hospital. Not conscious. In a really bad way.

I knew the whole year was being taken in separately to give statements and I wasn't allowed to leave the deputy head's office except with a chaperone to use the toilet. By that time I was hysterical and when my mum turned up, the look on her face nearly killed me. She had always loved the fact that I'd been so popular – like she had been. At first she tried to argue my corner. But the more the deputy head told her what had happened and the more he told me – she got whiter and whiter. I tried to defend myself but loads of people had said loads of shit about me and I was in deep trouble. I'll never forget when the deputy head said to me, 'You are a bully. You have bullied another girl so badly, she has harmed herself and we all better hope not irreversibly.' I just went into hysterics. So did Mum.

I got suspended. The school were shit scared about the story reaching the press, but luckily Chloe's parents weren't really the type to do that. I think what saved me was the fact everyone had been in on it, although I was identified as one of the ringleaders. I think Chloe's parents were more angry at the school than me or any of the other girls. Chloe hadn't told them anything, although they were very worried about her weight and couldn't understand what was going on.

Luckily Chloe did get better, although she was in hospital for a while. I decided to go and visit her to say sorry. What else could I do? My mum went mad and told me not to, but I went anyway. Chloe's older brother was really abusive towards me but her mum was OK, and let me see her once Chloe said it was OK. We spent a lot of time talking that afternoon and I cried and said sorry a lot.

A lot has happened since then and our school did this massive anti-bullying awareness for all the girls. I was allowed back, but was put on a really strict contract that meant if I broke it once, I would be excluded permanently. I'm still on it over a year later and I think I've only just started to regain people's trust, which I understand.

Chloe is my good friend now and we're making this film

together. She is all better, but she will always have some damage to one of her kidneys from the overdose. We both have to live with that, but her more than me. I feel like it's my fault she is scarred for life inside.

Bullying is such an awful problem and I don't think adults realise how bad it is. It's like this dark, horrible secret that runs through all schools and, in all honesty, I don't think schools know how to properly tackle it. You ask any kid that's being bullied and they'd tell you as much. Bullied kids are not being helped and no one really knows what to do about the problem.

LEROY, 15, SOUTH LONDON

Attends a very large Ofsted-accredited 'good' school in South London with over 1,000 pupils attending. The school's exam results are about the national average. He would like to leave and attend a drama school full-time, but is completing ten GCSEs at his parents' request.

The thing that annoys me when you read about schools in the papers is the extremes. You know what I mean? Like you hear about the school where a kid nearly killed themselves because of bullying. Or the kid who sat fifteen GCSEs at age six and he has an even cleverer brother who is two. Or all the kids becoming Muslim terrorists because the headmaster told them to. Or . . . or that girl who ran off with her dopey teacher with his shit guitar music. Or that one with the really fit teacher who left her naked pictures all over the art studio. Actually that'd be sweet if that happened. But not with our art teacher. He's a gay man, I think, and kind of fat.

But my point is, everything you read makes school sound like it's all interesting and dramatic or something. I'll tell you what school is like for probably 90 per cent of kids. Trust . . . Are you ready? It's OK. It's not that exciting and it's not that terrible. You have good days and you have bad days. Things go up and down. Sometimes you love being there and sometimes you hate it and wish the place would fall down. There aren't really any truly awful teachers, but there are a lot of OK ones and some really safe ones. You do get the odd *really* safe one, who can inspire you. We had one like that, but I think he was drunk a lot of the time. He left recently on long-term illness.

School is mostly just a series of mediocre shit bumping into each other from the hours of 8.45 a.m. to 3.30 p.m. And that's the truth. That's why I wanna go to acting school. I'll tell you what happens most days. You meet your mates on the way to school. You cuss each other all the way to school. You buy Rockstar or Red Bull because you're knackered from staying up all night on Xbox and try to figure out how to hide it, because energy drinks are like the new cigarettes. You get *enough* shit for them. No one really smokes any more because it's cheaper to buy weed than it is cigarettes, so what's the point? My brother says once you've added together the cost of fags and weed, it's so expensive, you might as well buy cocaine. I wouldn't buy cocaine because it's a shit drug.

There's this boy – this right chav – in our year who was stealing, like, his mum's fags and selling them to all the chavs in the lower years. He went and bought this really shit coat on the proceeds and then he got mugged. He was lucky anyone even bothered to mug him, if you ask me.

But anyway, you get to school. The teachers make you choke yourself with your tie before you can go into school.

Somebody should bring that up with the UN. Then you go chat shit with your mates in the playground and look at YouTube videos on your phones until the bell goes. You then have registration or assembly where most people fall asleep and teachers have a go at you about something or other. The worst is when the head tries to do an uplifting assembly and all you want him to do is shut the fuck up, so you can pretend you are still in bed. Me and my mate Jonah have figured out the exact angle you can sit at in those chairs that sort of makes it feel like you are still lying down.

If you're lucky you'll get something nice first thing like geography or food technology. Geography is basically colouring in and in food tech the teacher is so insane you can talk her into giving you any grade. She's quite a sweet old lady. We baked cakes last week and my mate was a bit lean and so we ate all the cake mix before it went into the oven. We managed to tell her this was a sign it was delicious and she gave us an A. There's this boy in our class who thinks he's Jamie Oliver and we stole his quiche for our exams. He got really upset and so I 'fessed up. The teacher was so impressed by my honesty she gave me another A! To be honest, Jamie Oliver is OK. He shares his food with us he makes at break, and it's wicked. Lots of men are cooks now. It's not as gay as it used to be. No offence to gays.

On the really bad days, you get PE twice first thing. People always think black boys love PE, but I fucking hate it. Our PE teacher was blatantly kicked out the Army for being a pussy, so he's a massive bully and is always trying to humiliate the kids who aren't good at sports. I'm not terrible. I just don't give a shit. But all the fat kids and skinny kids, he'll all be yelling at them like some sort of shit drill instructor. I hate him. And he kisses up to all the sporty kids. Like we've got this one kid who is being looked at by all the professional football clubs. I'm not saying it because I'm jealous, because I'm not – I don't like football. But this kid is an absolute wanker and goes around like he's some superstar already. He's always boasting about all the girls he's fucked and how rich and famous he's going to be. Everybody kisses his arse, but especially the PE teachers. Whenever there's a football match and they read out the players, they're all like, 'Well, it goes without saying you're on, Dan,' and then they high-five him. (*Makes a vomit-inducing motion with his fingers.*)

Of course, the best lessons are drama and English. Drama and English teachers are always the best. Maths teachers are always weird – always stink of coffee. So are music teachers. You'd think they'd be cool, but they're not. They are always sort of mental. We have one who makes us listen to classical music and he closes his eyes and sways around to the music. It's very disturbing.

And then you go home again. And the cycle repeats itself the next day. I mean, it's not bad, is it? But that's pretty much it.

What would be my dream school? That's a good question. You know those films that girls love about the two people who are going for the big dance competition and he's like a bad boy and she's a good girl? I hate dancing, but something like that, if it was acting. I mean, in those films no teachers are ever hassling them about their homework. They watch them dance secretly with tears in their eyes. It's such bullshit. In my school, it'd be like, 'Stop free-styling and get to food tech, you little shit.' And then they'd confiscate your iPod.

LEKHIKA, 18, NORTH LONDON

Attended an Ofsted-rated 'good' primary state school and 'satisfactory' state secondary school. Her secondary school was ethnically diverse with over 90 per cent of the students having English as a second language and a large number of students speaking limited or no English on admission. Many of the students take GCSEs in language subjects such as Hindi, Gujarati and Polish, but these are not included in school examination data. She became deputy head girl, got 10 GCSEs at A–C and is now studying at UCL.*

Moving from India to the United Kingdom was horrific in a sense. I hated leaving my family, my friends and my country behind. In India, I had a whole family with whom I lived; cousins, grandparents, uncles and aunts, all under one massive roof. Birthday parties consisted of inviting every family member nearby and wondering if there was any space for friends. My cousins became my best friends and my parents were my inspiration. I was one of the youngest three children and we were ridiculously pampered, and I think this is why I struggled so much when I moved to the UK. I had to grow up quickly and realise that perhaps there is more to life than my books and my family.

I completed Years 5 and 6 at an amazing primary school, which my little sister is now attending. I loved some of my teachers and I still talk to them. It may have been ten years since they taught me, but they always remembered me as the girl who couldn't get enough knowledge. However, my first negative experience in the UK came from the children I studied with at that school. By Year 5, they had made groups of friends and were unwilling to admit a new person. Yet in my mind, they had no reason to be so mean and crass. I didn't give in so easily either; growing up with my cousins, brothers and sisters ensured that I had a thick skin, and so I ignored them for two whole years.

My move to my secondary school, where I spent five years of my life, was, and probably will remain, the best decision of my life. It may not have been the best school or my parent's first choice, but it was there that I flourished. I made friends and met some amazing teachers who changed my life forever.

In Year 8, I was given the chance to be a presenter on the BBC school report and I grabbed it with both hands. I loved the chance of presenting a report that I had researched. Around this time, my school gave me many more responsibilities, perhaps sensing that I would undertake them with vigour unknown to many.

My time there gave me many experiences, choices and opportunities which to this day open new doors for me. Unknowingly, every time I represented my school, I made new connections and that was an invaluable gift.

I have now spent a term at university, and I love it already! From the millions of classrooms, to the six floors of the library, it has become a place of never-ending knowledge for me. It was a massive shock from A levels to university, but I have managed and I know that the next three years will be amazing.

I miss India, yes, and it will always be my home country. I was born there! However, I now love England as my own as well. Now, I have found myself in this country and it has become a second home for me. This is just one chapter in my book, which will span many more chapters and many more volumes!

TOM, 17, BATH

Attended a large 'satisfactory'-rated comprehensive school in the heart of the city. Confesses to 'hating' school and 'never bothering', despite encouragement from his teachers. Left school with only two GCSEs at F grade – he didn't show up for his other examinations. Says he is 'already regretting' his failure at school.

When people say school is the best years of your life and you'll regret it forever if you don't work hard, you always think that's a load of shit. Like everyone does, don't they? I tell you, though, the second you open that envelope and see all those Us and Xs you do suddenly see what all those teachers were saying. Like, it's a weird feeling. One of those life-before-your-eyes moments. Every fucked test, bunked class, exam you missed, time you got kicked out ... you sort of thought it was funny at the time. You thought everyone was overreacting or talking shit – and then you get it. I'm not going to lie. When all these people in my class were all shrieking and jumping around and calling their parents with their results, I honestly wanted to cry. I just went home and got back into bed. My mum and dad just shrugged when I told them and said something like, 'How typical.'

The thing is, re-sitting is bullshit. Anyone who tells you different is lying. It's like turning up for a party that's over and everyone has gone somewhere better. Much better. That's the best way I can describe it. I tried re-sits for about six weeks and just gave up. The classes were at, like, 5 p.m. and the teacher obviously could barely be bothered and everyone there was a dickhead with zero motivation. I just couldn't face it. At school, no matter how much you hate a lesson, there's still sort of an atmosphere that gives you a sense of it being worth you being there. These were just depressing. I'd have to get high just to face it. It was also sort of embarrassing. Like everyone knew it was the class for dummies.

It's weird, but you hate school your whole school life and now it's gone, there is a big hole. And it's making me feel nervous. I wake up at midday, watch Jeremy Kyle or a decorating programme or *Come Dine with Me*, go on the internet, chat to mates, chirps a girl I'm trying to get with, make plans for later. But after a couple of months, it's starting to feel, like, not right. Like the same day, day after day. My parents are threatening to kick me out if I don't do something, so I'm looking at college courses. The trouble is, I don't know what to do. Don't know what I'm interested in. I've even been looking at the Army recently online, which is pretty desperate. And I'm completely skint.

When teachers say stuff about you wasting your life, it's actually true. I guess looking at it, I've wasted, like, twelve years. I've got nothing to show for it. I don't know what to do now. There is no lesson in school that teaches you how to deal with life after it.

MARY, RESHMA AND CHARLOTTE, ALL 15, LEEDS

All attend the same 'outstanding' comprehensive educating 800+ students. All three have experienced 'sexual bullying' – an increasingly widely reported and recognised problem in schools, with girls most commonly the target. Though the number of reports, expulsions and exclusions connected to sexual bullying is rising steadily, few schools have fixed policies or procedures in place to deal with the problem. The issue of sexual bullying is currently under review by the government and the Department for Education.

CHARLOTTE: The big problem isn't necessarily school. The big problem is the world. I think the treatment of girls has become so much about sex, it's almost unreal. When we went back after the summer holidays, no one was talking about the places they had been to or what they did. Every single boy was looking at the naked pictures of Jennifer Lawrence (*a website called 4Chan released stolen, private nude pictures of the actress Jennifer Lawrence in late August 2014*). I mean what sort of message did that send to the poor Year 7s just starting that day?

RESHMA: True. Phones and porn are such a big problem. The school is mad, you can't access all these websites on school computers but everyone has got a smartphone, pretty much. And the boys look at some nasty stuff all day. There was this one boy who is *really* weird in another form. He was acting all weird in history, like sweating and stuff. The teacher realised he was masturbating. He had on a porn film on his phone, which was sitting on his lap. It was *disgusting*.

CHARLOTTE: True. And nothing happened to him. Nothing. *We* were told we'd get in trouble if we mentioned it or spread it. But this boy the previous week had said in another class that all girls secretly wanted to be raped and he'd also touched up another girl in another year. And nothing happened to him. It isn't fair.

MARY: So true. Some boys ran into the girls' changing room when they were getting changed. There was barely an inquiry.

And this really awful boy was in a debate with this really clever girl. He was losing and told her to 'suck his cock'. He was back in class the next day. And that's so common. Like, all the stuff girls get called all day every day in school. I'm not saying it's just boys. Girls say it, too. *I've* said it, probably. But bitch, slag, tart, whore, ho, fat bitch, skinny bitch, cunt – so many bad words for girls meant to shame them. And the only thing bad you can say to a boy is call him a fag. Even though that's bad too. And girls get touched all the time. Like you'll be standing in line for lunch and someone will grab your butt and all the boys are looking the other way and laughing. You know the only time something gets done? If another boy says something. Like, there's this boy in Year 11 (*they all sigh*) who always sticks up for girls. He calls other boys out and because he has a lot of respect, the other boys will listen. But they won't listen to girls. They'll barely listen to the teachers. This teacher tried to do all these 'respect' sessions. They were about boundaries and sex and saying no and all that. She's really pretty. The teacher. And the whole time the boys just laughed and made stupid noises. Every time she said the word 'sex' or something, one of the boys would make an 'uhhh' noise like you hear in porn films and everyone laughed. It was completely pointless and she got angry. The headmaster went and took them away, but aren't they just the type of boys who should have been there?

RESHMA: And our school isn't even bad. I know at least two schools near us where there have been much worse things. I've seen a film of a couple having sex in the art room at their school. And it's not fake. You can blatantly see it's a classroom.

CHARLOTTE: Some of it's total exaggeration, but I've also heard of sexual assaults in school. I've seen older boys bully the younger girls inappropriately and ask them things about sex they wouldn't know or make them look at things on their phones that are disgusting. I've told them to stop it and they'll just call you names. The thing is, I'm not saying all boys are bad at all. They're not. But when boys get together, they egg each other on. They can't resist showing off to each other and taking things too far. They often realise it after, but sometimes it's too late. The damage has been done.

TIMOTHY, 18, READING

About to start a place at Durham University reading education studies. On graduation he hopes to be accepted to the 'Teach First' programme which accelerates excellent graduates through the process of becoming a classroom teacher in more challenging schools.

I have to admit, I've been a little surprised and saddened by the general response to my ambition to become a teacher – and probably most of all by teachers themselves, which I've found a little disappointing. I absolutely loved school and went to a brilliant one. I've always loved learning and so teaching, to me, seems a natural thing to do. It'll be like staying at school in a fairly different way!

Part of the problem is certainly that it doesn't seem to have the cachet, particularly for blokes, that doing something like law or medicine does. If I told people I was going to work in Abercrombie & Fitch, they'd probably get more excited, which is mental. But teaching lacks glamour.

But mostly, it's just this huge whinge about schools, kids, the current state of the education system, Michael Gove of course. Everybody looks at you and goes, 'Oooh are you sure, mate?' and then starts listing all the reasons I shouldn't be a teacher: bad pay, you'll get stabbed by a kid, seventy-hour weeks and only getting paid for half, kids who can't read at age fifteen. The list goes on. And it's even worse because I got really good A-level results and actually turned down a place at Cambridge in favour of Durham, so they see my opting to go into teaching as a waste. Like something you do as a last resort. Is it surprising schools are bad, kids are getting taught badly and England is sinking lower and lower in the global league tables?

There needs to be a rethink. Private schools take pride in themselves because it's seen as a privilege to go there. Which it is. An expensive one. But I really think if kids were taught to take much greater pride in all their schools, learning and education, than the whole system would improve. I hope I can help bring that about. I can't wait to become a teacher.

DAWN, 16, HAMPSHIRE

*Attends an 'outstanding' co-educational grammar school for 700+ pupils. Has recently achieved seven A*s, three As and a B at GCSE. She is about to go and study four A levels at the sixth form attached to her school. Ninety-nine per cent of the Year 11 students applied for places at the school's heavily oversubscribed sixth form. They accepted about 80 per cent with the best grades.*

I've absolutely loved pretty much every second of school. I started here in Year 7 and I will stay on until Year 13. I will be absolutely devastated to leave. It really has been the best years of my life so far. I hope uni can match up to it. Some of the parents – although not mine or any of my friends' parents – have 'we don't have to pay for private school' parties. Our school is that good. They will all drink really expensive champagne and buy each other presents. They can because we are getting the same quality of education that anyone is getting at, say, Harrow or Benenden. And those schools cost £30,000 a year! And that's just the fees.

My dad is in politics – though as an advisor – and he says the best thing that could happen to education is to get rid of the private and state system altogether and bring back the grammar and modern comprehensive system. That way, your education isn't contingent on how much money you have, but how academically able you are. I think he calls it a meritocracy. I know some people still would suffer in that system, but it's a hell of a lot fairer than the current one. I don't agree with private education really, but so many schools are so bad and so overcrowded, it's not really a wonder people are choosing it.

My family aren't poor but we definitely aren't rich either. We could never afford the fees of the really expensive private schools or even the mid-level ones. There are three of us. So even though my parents earn probably about £80,000 between them a year, that's nothing like enough to cover three of us. And though we are all pretty clever, none of us are in the academic league to get scholarships or poor enough to get financial aid. It sounds awful, but we're sort of in that middle where you can't complain, but things aren't as easy as people think they might be.

My mum literally realised from our births that our best hope was a really good grammar school for all of us. We moved in the vicinity of this school, and also a good primary one, years ago when we were tiny to improve our chances. I know she has kind of hothoused us to be more appealing to the place, so we've not just had extra coaching since the age of five, but music lessons – we all play two musical instruments – language lessons – I've been learning ancient Greek for eight years now – drama classes, cookery classes, sport clubs, ballet lessons, horse riding. You name it. But it was worth it.

This school isn't just brilliant academically; it's brilliant on so many other levels. The teachers are amazing. We have several doctors in their subjects who have taught at world-class universities. One of our sports instructors is an ex-Olympic athlete. Our headmistress is a genius at raising money, so we have a state-of-the-art theatre for performances and an amazing sports centre with a swimming pool attached to the school.

And it's not just academics. The school really, really cares about the students' well-being. They have a junior council which is really influential in deciding everything from teacher appointments to how to tackle bullying. There is very little bullying as it is not tolerated by the students and the older students will often arrange a sort of intervention where they make the younger ones talk through the problem. All the Year 7s get a Year 9 buddy not just for the first week, but for the entire year. It is a proper mentoring system. All sixth-form students are expected to be attached to a form and do weekly charity work. I'm going to be a tea girl for a very old lady who lives near the school. Her husband died a long time ago and she's very lonely and frail. The school have been helping her for about six years now with our sixth-form students. We have about sixty elderly people in the scheme.

The point is, our school doesn't have anything like the resources or money of a private school. There are still twenty-five to thirty students in each class. There are kids across the class divide attending. But we've all worked incredibly hard to make this a community. We're incredibly proud of our school. Everybody works hard and plays hard. If somebody is struggling or in trouble, students *and* teachers all come together to help. We are always very sorry to lose a teacher and there is a very low teacher turnover, which is a good sign. In fact a few of the teachers here are ex-pupils. I don't see why more schools can't be like ours and I think my dad is right. One of the first steps towards a fairer system is getting rid of fee-paying schools and giving everyone a chance.

ROSIE, 16, HASTINGS

Her father died when she was twelve in a motoring accident and her mother, by her own admission, has 'struggled to cope' ever since, which has made home life challenging for her and her two brothers. She has attended an Ofsted-rated 'outstanding' comprehensive school and left school with 10 GCSEs A–G. She is now studying for a BTEC in management at the school's sixth form. She 'wouldn't have even considered' going anywhere else for her tertiary education.*

School saved me. You don't realise it at the time. When you are younger and all pissed off, you give your teachers enough shit. I was an absolute bitch to mine throughout Years 8 and 9 and then you start to realise that they are on your side more than anyone else in the world. I've cried on my teachers, screamed at them, sworn at them, told them to fuck off, thrown things not actually at them but sort of in their direction, walked out of school. I've been suspended three times but they never gave up on me.

I think I started to realise that they weren't going to give up on me in Year 10. I got arrested for shoplifting and the deputy head came to the police station to get me. It was on a Saturday and he was with his wife and baby. But he came anyway. He properly yelled at me, but I deserved it. He's such a nice man. He cares so much for his students.

Another teacher, who is our PSHE teacher and has been my form teacher since Year 7, has been my rock. Me and Mum row all the time, sometimes properly, properly badly. She has been the referee for enough rows between me and my mum. If I've had a bad row with Mum, the school will support it and we get what they call a mediator from outside the school. She's sort of like a therapist. Mum says the school has been like free therapy.

I used to hate all my lessons, especially the ones I found hard. The deputy head really worked to get me into the options I liked, even though I was flopping at everything in Year 9. I love history and most of all PE because I'm really sporty. I got an A in those two subjects. I don't think I've ever seen Mum look so happy.

I want to go to uni to study management and then I want to open a chain of girl-only gyms. A lot of my friends won't go to the gyms or play sports, because they feel self-conscious in front of boys. My friend was on the running machine last week and some boys just stood there in a row blatantly watching her and saying gross things until the manager said something. Girls are definitely getting less fit and fatter, so I think this could work. Without school, I never would have realised my dream or had the confidence to go for it. My business studies teacher is even helping me write a business plan.

Race

LEROY, 15, SOUTH LONDON

Born in England, and describes himself as 'proudly English-Jamaican'. His father was born in Jamaica and his mother was born in England with Jamaican parents. He describes their family as 'very modern and very British with some strong Jamaican influences'. He loves 'everything about Jamaica except some of the weird attitudes there'. When he is older he would like to move to the United States to pursue his acting career.

I have to be a bit careful here as my mum is very strict about how we talk about race. She's strict about everything, to be fair. She says it's very important to be mindful of your race and be proud of your race. But she also thinks a lot of black people have sunk into too much of a victim mentality where race is concerned. Like they blame everything that goes wrong in their life or isn't easy on the colour of their skin. She says it's allowing people not to take responsibility for their own lives. Which is dangerous. I can see her point. But at the same time, there are a lot of problems that I, as a young black boy – well, man actually – face as a result of the colour of my skin. I mean when was the last time you, a white woman, was followed around and around and around a shop? I just couldn't find the fucking batteries! I wasn't stealing. But that was the assumption.

If I'm honest, I don't think racism is dead at all. It's still a big conversation. Like, no one is saying smoking is really good for you. It's an accepted thing. People still smoke, but they do it guiltily, do you know what I mean? I think racism is a bit like that. People will say, 'Oh, yeah, yeah, racism is terrible and bad,' but it still goes on. A lot. And often the more vocal the person . . . I don't know. Like, it's hard for young brothers to relate to the struggles of brothers in the Martin Luther King days. But not that hard. I mean we choose to be at the back of the bus now instead of being told, but the line is still there, do you know what I mean?

And so many places are still so white. I want to go to acting school. Very white. I looked at several recently and it's really noticeable. We went to Oxford University on a school trip. I didn't see one black person there except this guy who was showing us around. And how many black faces do you see in, like, the Houses of Parliament on TV? None. Only one of my teachers is black. And yet after school how many of the cleaners do you think are black? All of them. Except this one Polish guy we all call Gunther. Even though he tells us that isn't even a Polish name and we are being ignorant. He's OK. He lets us steal his mop.

And then you go to our school and every face there is non-white, except Eastern Europeans, who are poor and keep themselves to themselves. But my point is, a city like London *does* have segregation. You see it everywhere. In Brixton it's a sea of black faces, in Southall everyone is brown and you go, like, Chelsea and everyone there is white. TV and adverts are the same. My dad says TV is geared to showing people how white is associated with stuff like wealth and beauty and that.

And that's another thing. My mum is really light-skinned. And my dad is dark. People are always saying to my mum, 'Oh you are so lucky, you have beautiful, light skin.' All the black girls at school want light skin if they're honest so they look like

Beyoncé, or Rihanna. But let's be honest. Those girls look pretty far away from any kind of African. They dye their hair blonde and straighten it. They have light skin. It's like black women are only pretty if they look a little bit white. My dad says that's advertising. My friend went out with this girl. She was really pretty. But she was really dark. He got cussed by a lot of people for that. And black people! I think that's a bit sad. And look at Kanye West. He's dating a white woman. I don't care how big her ass is, she's white. That sends a pretty strong message.

I've gone on a lot, haven't I? I haven't even told you about all the interracial racism. Like how bad people are to Somalians. Or how the police treat us. Or how I was the best in this audition for this (*well-known*) theatre company, but I don't think I got it because I was black. I get what my mum says. You can't play the victim or sit around and feel sorry for yourself, but anyone who says racism doesn't exist is a fool. And probably white, with money and reads the *Guardian*, which is probably whiter than the *Sun*.

JACK, 16, SOLIHULL

Born in England. Has two English parents, an older brother and two younger sisters. His father is an electrician and his mother is a stay-at-home mum. His mother votes UKIP. Says she has 'absolutely no problem with anyone of any race, but is sick of the way this country is abused by non-British people'. His father and brother both voted for the BNP at the last local election and hope to at the general election. This causes friction in the household as Jack's mum thinks 'they are a party of idiots run by a thug'.

Jack's father remains committed to his political and social views and wants to encourage his children to adopt similar views. They are all avid supporters of a London football club.

There is like some big thing about supporting the BNP. My mum says we should keep it quiet at school and with the neighbours, but fuck that. It's not a crime, is it? She gets well fucked off with my dad about how open he is about voting and they have rows about it. My kid sister, Ellie, came home recently saying she had a new boyfriend. You know how kids do, like I'm gonna marry so and so? Turned out the lad was a Paki. My dad went off his head at her and my mum went mad at him. To be fair, I could see her point. Ellie is only seven. But she was lucky they didn't tell John, my older brother. He's even more into it than my dad. He goes on marches and rallies and everything. I'm going on EDL march thing with John next week. I'm well excited.

Round here there's loads of support definitely for UKIP. And people are being pushed to it because of all the dirty immigrants. I know loads of people that would be voting for BNP if they could. It's not our fault. It's the country's fault. It's become a total fucking piss-take. My nan has paid her taxes her whole life. She worked for the country in the war in a factory. My granddad fought – and he was only seventeen – because he thought Hitler was a bastard. He's dead now, but he believed in our country and all it stood for. My nan couldn't get a hospital bed and died because of the shit care, because they gave the bed to some fucking African or East European. You go to the hospital and it's full of them with their filthy fucking children, all trying to get aspirin on a fucking prescription because they don't want to pay for it. It makes me sick.

None of my cousins could get into their local primary schools because of the fucking Romanians here and they're all a bunch of dirty thieves. Two of them followed my fourteen-year-old cousin home and told her they wanted to rape her and shit. It's disgusting. Just because they marry off their kids at twelve. If we see them again, we are going to fucking do them.

My brother John wanted to be a fireman. They told him – and this is no lie – that he wasn't eligible because he was a white bloke and he'd fall really far down the list. What sort of shit is that? So if he was black or Paki, he's all right, but because he's a white lad with a white girlfriend, fuck off. That's discrimination there. We are being discriminated against in our own fucking country. Am I allowed to go to some towel head's country and take their jobs? I don't think so. If we went there and threatened their women, they'd probably cut your head off, but it's OK for them to do it to our girls? It makes me sick.

But the worst is definitely the Muslims. They are disgusting. Near here they are all standing outside their mosques telling white people it's a 'Muslim zone' and not to drink and calling the girls slags and whores and stuff. My mate got set upon by a bunch, but luckily he's well hard so they realised they'd picked on the wrong person. But they're total fucking cowards. They pick on girls by themselves or young lads but won't try it with people like me.

They need to fuck off back to their country and leave us British people in peace. I know some top lads who are Asian. Born here and work their knackers off. I was having a laugh with one of them the other day in the shop and he was saying he might join the EDL! To be honest, he'd be welcome. It just goes to show, people don't want to be racist, but this country is forcing us all to become that. We need to protect our own. I think more and more people my own age feel like I do. I know hundreds. The government needs to watch out. People are well fucked off.

CARL, 16, MANCHESTER

British-born with Jamaican parents. Is an award-winning mathematics student and an all-round high academic achiever. Plays on the school's basketball and football teams and has been encouraged by his teachers to apply to be head boy this year. Has never committed a crime. Since the age of twelve, he has been stopped and searched by the police forty-one times.

The experience of being stopped and searched has varied massively. They are sometimes really nice to you. Especially the female police officers. They'll be quite apologetic and have a bit of a laugh with you. Especially when you are super polite to them and are clearly clean. I don't mind that. They're doing their job, I suppose.

But I've had some horrible experiences. When I was twelve, I was riding my bike to school. I was a lot smaller then. This policeman literally grabbed me as I rode past and pulled me off my bike. He really hurt my neck and I tripped and cut my knee. I was stunned. He got in my face and was like, 'Where did you steal that bike from, son?' in a really aggressive way. I was so frightened, I ran away crying, leaving my bike. When I got to school the head teacher was amazing when I told him what happened. They called the police instantly and complained. The police said I'd been behaving aggressively towards the police officer and taunting him and then because I'd run away, I looked suspicious! My mum turned up and asked to make a formal complaint and it was such bullshit, the stuff they came out with. I mean, as hard as it is to believe now, I was about five foot then and all by myself. What sort of threat would I have been? The police were so aggressive, indifferent and rude with my mum and me, we had to give up pursuing it. Now, looking back, I think there were probably veiled threats. Like, 'take this further and we could make things very difficult for you' and that sort of bullshit.

As I've grown taller and grown this Afro, things have got much, much worse. I get stopped literally all the time. As I said, some are really great and polite, but some have been arseholes. Just a few weeks ago I was in a big hurry because I was on my way to a job interview at Waitrose for a Saturday job. I asked the police if they could hurry it as I was on my way to an interview. He kept me for ages. I missed the interview and lost the job, which I really, really wanted. Luckily, I spoke to the manager of that section. I'm not saying it totally made a difference, but he's black too. I showed him the stop and search receipt and told him what happened. He was really sympathetic. He's got me another interview next week and this time I'll get my mum to drop me off.

I'm sorry, but are you trying to tell me that none of this is because I'm a big, black boy with an Afro? But what pisses me off is how wrong they are! I don't deal drugs. I've never even smoked weed except once when I was thirteen and puked all over this girl I liked. I didn't do it again. I'm polite to shopkeepers, women, bus drivers, the police – even though they aren't always polite to me. I don't wear my trousers round my knees mostly because I like to look crisp and I think that just looks stupid. But I should be able to if I want to, without people making assumptions about me.

I've never stolen a thing in my life except when I was six, I stole some sweets. I felt so bad, I took them back when I told my mum. The shopkeeper laughed so hard and gave me a massive bag of sweets, which worked out pretty well.

I have aspirations, you know? And this stuff wears you down. I watched the London riots. I'm watching what's going on in Ferguson at the moment (*the site of riots in America, triggered by the multiple shooting of an unarmed black boy by the police*). You see all these injustices you are just supposed to take. I don't agree with rioting and looting and robbing and that, but you push people far enough, they break. I sometimes wonder if that's the aim, so it perpetuates this idea of black people being unlawful, uncivilised animals and justifies all the stops and searches and that. It's shit.

The biggest joke is that if you're rich and white, you can break laws as you like. Look at that thing with Jimmy Savile and the politicians that has been covered up. And they're worried about some black kid carrying a bit of weed? It makes me so angry. And this is the fucking twenty-first century, do you know what I mean?

CHARLIE AND CAWO, BOTH 17, SUSSEX AND NORTH LONDON

Charlie is British and white with two British parents. Cawo is Somali and moved to the UK when she was seven. They have been dating for over a year and met via friends at a music festival in London. Charlie wants to study engineering and Cawo is interested in pursuing a career in modelling. She has just been scouted by a top model agent in London, but is worried her parents will forbid it.

CHARLIE: To be honest, I never really thought that much about the colour of people's skin before I started dating Cawo. If I'm honest I had always dated white girls previously – and I definitely had a type. I liked waifish, pale brunettes. But I had loads of black, Asian and Chinese mates. I grew up in a fairly white part of London and I guess there is a much higher proportion of white people that went to my school. But I never really thought about it. People often think I'm Jewish because of my Jew-fro, but that's as far as any sort of issue I've ever had and even that's a big joke. It's not nasty. I guess some of my mates were a bit surprised when I was so interested in Cawo. But I don't think it was because she's black, it was because she's just not my normal type. But to me, she's just Cawo. She's really beautiful and clever and I'm really proud of her. I wish it was as simple as that, though.

CAWO: My family are fairly forward thinking, but there are two problems. Firstly, I am a Muslim. There's no getting around it. I am expected to marry a Muslim. I mean, my parents are OK. They're fine with a lot of stuff and they're fine with me hanging out with Charlie, but they would never allow him to be a boyfriend or a husband. Unless he converts, which is fairly unlikely. He's an atheist. But the bigger problem at the moment – because we're not talking about marriage or anything – is more the Somali community. Especially the guys. Charlie can't meet me anywhere near where I live. It's a fairly tight community. If we were seen together we would get threatened, spat at, called names, guys would want to fight Charlie. The Somali community can be quite protective and they consider it to be like a betrayal. Like I should be dating a good Muslim Somali boy and staying near the street I live. I've been called all sorts of things for just the clothes I wear. So God knows what would happen if I modelled or dated a white guy. I wish we could move to a more mixed part of London, but we can't afford to. London is so expensive.

CHARLIE: So what Cawo is saying is she doesn't tell people she's going out with me. She tells even her really good friends that I'm her gay best friend and I help her with styling! I don't know how I feel about that. But basically, the only people she tells are her white friends. Her sisters, brothers, cousins, best friend think I'm the gay friend. It cuts me up a bit, but I don't want her getting abuse – or worse – from her friends, family and community. I can't even discuss our relationship on Facebook in case her family find out I'm not some gay fashion director. And in turn, this has made my family quite negative about Cawo. It's not about her colour per se. More about her religion and culture. They worry about my safety. But after a few too many the other day, my mother pretty much asked why I couldn't go out with a nice, English white girl. This of course has caused rows and Cawo doesn't feel that comfortable coming round. Though it's nothing like as bad as it is for her. My mum is sort of icily polite. So, we've been driven underground by our parents!

CAWO: Luckily we have lots of friends already at uni, so we get to spend time together at their digs and that. We spend a lot of time at friends when we want to be together. It's like in some parts of London and with this generation, race seems to be less of an issue. But it's still a big issue in a lot of places.

We went properly into the country the other day. I got stared at so much. I was wearing these quite African-influenced clothes. But you'd think I arrived in a space ship. I didn't see a single non-white face.

CHARLIE: Yeah, and we get a lot of stares where I live. Particularly if we are holding hands or whatever. Interracial relationships don't seem to have filtered out of London much. A mate of mine who is black goes out with a white girl. They go to York University, so live up there. Apparently they receive open hostility. They got asked to leave a pub the other day. They are both nineteen and the pub owner made out like it was their age. He said twenty-one was 'discretionary'. But apparently there were kids there with their parents. He said it was like that really old film *An American Werewolf in London* when they go into the Slaughtered Lamb. They walked in hand in hand and the place went quiet. He half expected to be chased down the road by men in white hoods with pitchforks.

SERAFINA, 15, NORTH-WEST LONDON

Comes from a Polish family who moved here five years ago. Lives with her parents, grandmother and three younger siblings. Her father is a successful carpenter and is trying to start an independent company for Polish workers. Her mother is a stay-at-home mum.

If I could get a pound for every sex worker joke I've heard, we could all afford to move back to Poland forever and live like royalty. I've been openly asked if I'm a prostitute, if my mother is a prostitute, even if my grandmother is a prostitute!

In class at school, it has been said many times all Eastern European women – they class us all as Eastern Europeans – are whores. And the men are pimps and thieves. Or both. It is true, actually. Sex work is a big trade for Eastern European women. More stereotypes. Because we are beautiful and blonde and look like icy supermodels. Except me. But surely, this should be a shame for English men? They are the ones buying the prostitutes. So it is a terrible business. I do know girls from my town who came here and everyone knows what is going on. Not all of them become au pairs.

People are suspicious of immigrants. And because of that, they tend to live in group situations and remain private. So it becomes worse, you know? It is a difficult time because the generation of my parents' age is happy to only associate with other Poles, shop in Polish shops, live in Polish areas, speak in Polish. I tried to explain this isn't good and they should mix more, otherwise what was the point of coming here? After five years, my mother speaks almost no English and my grandmother none at all except 'yes', 'no' and 'biscuit'. The word makes her laugh.

The other trouble we get is to do with drinking. It is hard to get away from something if you respond to that suspicion. That's a bad way of putting it. But we *do* drink a lot. I guess it is a way of feeling that sense of being in Poland, because you all go to each other's houses and drink a lot and get very drunk. There is always a lot of singing and laughing and play-fighting that becomes serious, more often. There is domestic troubles too. My father is very good and would never hit us. But many of my mother's friends have very bad troubles with their husbands. Especially when drunk.

The trouble is, people know this. When I got here, my friend Marik told me black boys always chase Polish girls because they think they are easy because they are always drunk at parties and things. And because they are pretty. I laughed. But I have since been told that by many, many people – even my black friends at school. This has made me wary as there is this very cute boy at school called TJ, who is black, who likes me. But I'm worried why he likes me, even though he seems like a really nice guy and is respectful to me. Anyway, my dad would not like me seeing a black guy one little bit.

The other things people are always saying is Eastern Europeans are inbred and always fuck their cousins and their sisters and then marry them. I find this offensive, because imagine you said this about other races or countries? Like a film like *Borat* makes a big joke about Eastern Europe and how they are all animal-like pig farmers who fuck their prostitute sister. This film was a smash! Imagine if a similar film was made saying all black people were like that? Or Indian people? There would be riots. But being offensive to certain groups of people seems to be OK here. I don't get that for a country that seems to take racism quite seriously.

FARZANA, 19, SHEFFIELD

Both her parents are Iranian and moved here fifteen years ago because of her father's job: he works in the pharmaceutical industry and her mother is a teacher. Her parents gave her the option of wearing a headscarf – though both said they'd prefer it if she didn't. Farzana now campaigns against the wearing of headscarves and burkas for young Muslim women, believing they 'perpetuate female repression, hostility towards Muslims and an inability to integrate'. Her parents still live in London, where she grew up. She is at Sheffield University studying politics and economics.

It's a seriously shit time for the Muslim world at the moment. It's gone insane, hasn't it? It seems to have reached its kind of crusade period and the violence is just beginning. If I'm glad for anything ever, it's that I'm here with liberal parents, in the UK, largely out of the clutches of the Islamic state of any kind. I don't particularly practise my faith that much. Neither do my parents. We have a healthy respect for the Koran, I guess. But that's about it. How can you admire a religion that is bloody, brutal, primitive and hates just about everything with a violence. Including itself. And fears. The Islam world at the moment is very fearful and it reacts to this by creating fear.

I know race and religion aren't the same thing at all, but you can't separate them entirely. Of course you can't. Muslims are being placed under this big brown umbrella that is increasingly being seen as a bad thing by the rest of the world. And to be honest, they are at fault. I can think of no one I hate more than these pathetic, barbaric little men that are creating all this hatred for all of us.

When I was very little I sort of wanted to wear my scarf. I went to a pretty ethnically mixed school, although nothing like the diversity there is now. There were several girls in my class with a headscarf and they used to tease me about not wearing one. Luckily, my parents were sensible enough never to make a big thing of it and so I wore one sometimes, fashioned out of a scarf of my mum's, and other times I didn't. It just wasn't a big deal. My mum never has, but partly because she has such amazing hair! She told me later her real reasons.

The turning point was definitely the 7/7 bombings. I'm a bit young to clearly remember 9/11 and any of the effects. I was little at the time and really confused about the whole thing. My dad explained it to me really well, but I just couldn't understand why you'd want to destroy the country you live in. It didn't seem to make any sense. Like burning down your own house. After that, my mother wouldn't let me wear it at all. I think she was relieved to have the excuse. It is such a visible thing, and even in London, many of our friends were getting called 'suicide bombers', 'dirty fucking muzzers', 'sand niggers', everything. To their faces. A friend of my mum's got abused and glasses thrown at her walking past a pub. Another friend of the family had her headscarf pulled off her in public.

Things calmed down for a while, but it's all completely erupted again now. I'm not excusing it at all. Racist, abusive behaviour is inexcusable. But I think there is something very cowardly about headscarves and especially burkas. It is forcing the women to wear these symbols of the Islamic world, which say very clearly they are neither to be trusted, nor fit to be looked at. The ones who tell you it is because women are sacred are talking bullshit. They are the same types who say women shouldn't be educated or should have their clitorises removed.

I have tried on a burka and it makes you feel awful. Like a shroud. I nearly had a panic attack with one on. It says so much about how the Islamic world see women, but it also contributes to immigrant women never fitting into any Western society. Maybe this is what they want?

Of course I have experienced racism. Many times. But by wearing Western clothes and fitting in, you reduce this by a thousand times.

The most liberated I feel is at gigs. My boyfriend is in an indie-punk band. I met him when I was fifteen. He took me to gigs and to some festivals and I thought it was the coolest thing. I went to a drum and bass gig a while back and it was so aggressive. It was all nigger this and that and fights and people looking for trouble – and that was just the girls! I went to Glastonbury for the first time this summer, and it was so happy and free. Like a great big rainbow tribe. Maybe they should send ISIS to Glastonbury.

DUSHANE, KIERAN, 19, EDDIE, CARL, 17, AND ADAM, 16, WEST LONDON

All were born in the UK. Eddie and Carl have UK-born parents and Jamaican-born grandparents. Kieran and Adam (who are brothers) have Afro-Caribbean-born parents. Whilst they are all proud of their heritage, they all agree their race has had a negative impact on their lives. They would argue that being black and male leaves young men significantly more vulnerable to gang culture and crime. They also argue that being black negatively impacts on employment opportunities, the quality of education and access to resources. They also all strongly believe being black and male massively increases the likelihood of being given a jail sentence and for a longer length of time. Kieran has a nine-month-old son.

KIERAN: I can barely get down the street without getting hassled.

ADAM: Trust. The feds would have nothing to do if it weren't for black boys. Like I know this kid who is the whitest kid you ever saw. He's like the Milky Bar kid or something. And he wears glasses and these peak clothes. But it's all an act. He's actually OK. He goes and steals enough stuff from good shops in London and he uses our friend Mark as a decoy. Mark is black and wears all these gang colours and like the whole store is following him around whilst Milky Bar fills his pockets with enough stuff. Probably diamonds and shit. You get some shady-looking or even not shady-looking black man to walk into Ferrari and the white men could probably all leave in a car and no one notice. Especially if they were wearing a suit. A nigger wears a suit and people assume he's going to court.

Do you think you might be a target for the police because you have several criminal records?

KIERAN: I do know what you're saying. I do. I wish I hadn't gone down this road. All the road business, you know? But Eddie has never done a criminal thing in his life and he gets nearly as much shit as I do.
EDDIE: Believe.
KIERAN: Eddie doesn't talk much . . .
DUSHANE: He has verbal constipation. (*They all laugh.*)
KIERAN: Niggers, especially the young 'uns, chat enough shit. They can't keep their mouths shut. It's all, 'I'm gonna fuck up this person, rob that person, fuck this man's woman.' If someone commits a crime on another estate on a Wednesday, I've already heard about it on the Monday. You know what I'm saying? That's why I keep my business, my business. I keep my mouth shut. Dealings with the police and especially being in prison teaches you that. It's the only way to survive. The man who comes out of jail saying they were king is a liar. You keep your mouth shut and yourself to yourself.

What is your biggest regret?

KIERAN: So many. It's hard to pull out of a path, you know? I guess I wish I'd stayed in school and kept going. I'd like to be legit. I'd love to have done law. Life on the road is as stressful as shit. I'm not saying there isn't upsides. But there is a lot of down. A lot. It doesn't stop. You're on all the time.
CARL: I love weed. But I probably shouldn't have started smoking it. I left school with a GCSE in weed smoking.
DUSHANE: But the trouble is, school is shit. If you live in our area, all the schools are bad. You see on TV and that, all these schools that look like that Harry Potter place. Why the fuck aren't they building schools like that around here? I might stay in a place like that and work.
EDDIE: Because those are schools for rich white people. You get me? I'm not saying all like, it's everyone else's fault. You choose to sling and that's a choice. But we don't have that many choices. Like if I was born with a silver spoon and got to go to a school like that, you think I'd be on the road?
KIERAN: Exactly. Like at school, they used to give you all this Obama shit. You know, the President of the United States was a poor black boy. That's like one example in how many billion people live there? Maybe once upon a time, I thought crime was all about being a big man. But it's mostly about survival. We talked about this before, but I had responsibilities. I have more now. And no one is offering work to me. Even if I didn't have a criminal record, I wouldn't have a chance. Not in hell.
ADAM: True. I just finished my GCSEs. Not good. And nobody has a fucking idea what to do. You go to college maybe to get your mum off your back and end up skipping classes, smoking weed and then trying to make proper money. Like,

no offence, but I don't want to end up in McDonald's. And if you go legit, that's all that seems to be on offer.

EDDIE: Or Shoe Zone.

KIERAN: Fuck Shoe Zone. People put that in places to let you know you are poor. Nobody would even rob that place.

CARL: Romanians would. (*They all laugh.*)

KIERAN: Universities and the House of Commons, the City, are filled with white boys. You saying there's no race issue in this country? Like, I admit that I loved the (*2011*) riots. I stole some shit. And I'm not sorry that I did. But anyone who said – and I mean the government and all the fucking media – that it was just about robbing is full of shit. That was about rage, you know what I'm saying? I didn't know that Mark Duggan guy, but we all felt that. And I don't even think it was just a colour thing. It was a generation thing. That's for it all, man. People are losing hope. And it's happening all again. Where's that place in the States? (*He means Ferguson, Missouri.*) When is it not going to be OK for the police to shoot people just because they are black?

EDDIE: Preach.

CARL: Can you imagine, like, what's the most expensive school in England? Right, Eton. Can you imagine if some police just walked up to some kid at Eton and put seven bullets in him? As he was walking along, minding his own business? I mean, seriously? Can you imagine?

DUSHANE: Yeah, man! I never thought of that. That police would be seeing jail time.

CARL: Serious jail time. It wouldn't be just like, 'Oh well, sorry about that, peeps.' Or worse, cover it up.

KIERAN: Trust. And that's what disgusts me. This is a country of two laws. There's laws for rich people and there's laws for poor people. But if you get me, there's sub-laws. And they exist if you're black. You get caught doing a crime and you are poor and white, you are fucked. If you get caught doing a crime and you're poor and black, you are double fucked. It's hard sometimes to be in a system that is counting against you from the moment you are born in your skin.

MEGGIE, 14, NORFOLK

Both her parents and grandparents are British-born. She has always lived in a rural community with a small population. There is just one class for every year group in her school.

I've always lived here and I've never really travelled very far from here. I've never even been to Cambridge. When I'm a bit older I definitely will. But my dad (*who is a vet*) is very busy and my mum can't drive and hates taking trains. I think she might be a bit scared of leaving here.

I love it here. It's so much fun! Everyone knows everyone and there is so much to do. A lot of my life is about animals. Even though we don't, we practically live on a farm, there's so many of them at home. Dogs, cats, pigs; I have a horse, chickens. Everybody at school is fairly similar. I know everybody in my school and I've known them a long time. I love it that way. I can't imagine living in a big city where nobody knows anyone else. I'd hate that. There is no crime here, I don't think.

I don't feel bad that I don't have any friends who aren't white. There's nobody like that at our school, so how could I? I'm sure I will one day. But there just isn't anyone like that who lives here either. When my parents watch the news, it is so funny to see all those people who look so different. I think I'd be scared. Not because I don't like people of other colours, it would just be so different to what I'm used to. I don't think London looks or sounds like a nice place at all. I don't know why everyone talks about it like it's so great. I think it looks dirty, crowded and scary.

FARIAD, 17, COVENTRY

Moved to the UK from Afghanistan six years ago with his family, including his parents, grandparents and siblings. Thinks the UK 'is the greatest country in the world'.

Anyone who comes here and slates England is out of order, man. If you don't like it, piss off back home or stop complaining. I hear it all the time from immigrants and I don't get it. But to be fair, you hear it a lot less from Afghans. They all want to be here. They love the UK!

It's safe. Schools are good, hospitals are good. The houses are nice. I even don't mind the weather and all the rain. And you have so much freedom here. If you've lived in Afghanistan, you really know what having no freedom is. Do I miss home? No. But this is my home now. And I love English girls.

It's not all perfect. You get trouble all the time. Lots of groups hating on each other and it's all racial. I get called a freshie even still. But a lot of the hating has moved on from Afghans to the Eastern Europeans. They would snake their own grandma for some dollars. They're snakes, mostly.

I tell you about one time, though. My sister is eight and she has really, really bad diabetes. Like she needs to take these shots all the time or she could die. She's a good girl and does them herself now. She carries it in a little case with ponies or some shit on.

Anyway she'd gone to school in the morning and I'd been praying so I was wearing my prayer clothes. My mum calls me on my mobile all hysterical saying my sister was ill at school and she'd forgotten her medication and needed it. I'd smoked a bit that morning and was still sort of in prayer mode, and so I wasn't thinking that clearly. So I grabbed her school bag and ran out the house in the same clothes, which would look like a dress to you. Her school is three stops away on the train, so I ran like a madman to the train station and literally jumped on the train, sweating like fuck – I couldn't breathe. I should exercise more. I didn't realise how all these people were like moving away from me because I still couldn't catch my breath. Before I knew it, there was some police all around me. What sort of suicide bomber would carry a bomb in a pink bag covered in horses? Once I explained, it was OK and I didn't get arrested, luckily. But some Afghan-looking guy sweating like mad in a dress and clutching a backpack didn't go down so well. I just couldn't breathe because I smoke too much and everyone thought I was about to blow up London.

And anyway, terrorism is deep. I love this country. I wouldn't even graffiti here, let alone blow it up.

Gender

RAY, 15, SOUTH LONDON

Lives with mother, stepfather and a younger brother and older sister. Has a girlfriend of six months but says 'girls confuse the hell out of him'. Attends a 'really forward-thinking grammar school'. Defines himself as a supporter of gender equality but is 'totally confused' by feminism and what it stands for. Is a big supporter of gay rights.

To be honest, I think everyone is a bit confused at the moment about what they are supposed to think about gender. Like, back in the day – I mean my parents' day – it was more simple. There were men and there were women and they sort of had roles. Like women could work if they wanted to, but there was a bigger expectation on men to do more. I don't mean that in a sexist way, but men were probably expected *more* to look after the family. And women stayed more at home.

My mum worked on and off but mostly on. But I have to admit when my brother was born and my mum stayed at home for a few years with him until he went to school too, I loved it. I know you aren't supposed to say that because it might be taken the wrong way, but it was really nice coming home from school to Mum rather than getting picked up by the childminder or my sister walking home with her mates when I was a bit older. I really missed that again when she went back to work.

But that's part of the problem. I sometimes don't know what I'm allowed to say about girls. I told my sister that when Mum went back to work and she said I was being sexist. I wasn't. I just liked having Mum around at home. If Dad kept the house as nice as Mum and cooked like she did, I wouldn't mind if it was him around the house. But Dad can't even get the shopping together that well. He fucks ... messes it up every time. Last time he forgot all this stuff we really need and basically bought a load of steaks and wine and not much else. Mum went mental at him and had to go herself anyway. When they argue, she says he intentionally does things wrong so she doesn't ask him again. He just starts to laugh, so I think there might be some truth to that. Maybe I'll try that when I'm older.

My girlfriend and a lot of her friends have started talking about feminism a lot recently. And especially my sister. She's gone crazy for it. At first the boys in my year and my mates just ignored it. But it's suddenly started to piss a lot of people off and there's arguments about it in school. There's this guy in the year above who is well clever. He'll definitely go to Cambridge. He said feminism is really dangerous and it's a new form of sexism and it's forcing women to hate men. He had a massive row with my sister and it got pretty nasty. Now a lot of the boys in the year below her are calling her 'an ugly, hairy, feminist bitch'. I try to stay out of it, especially as she's definitely not any of those things. But the school had to have a big assembly on respecting rights. The classics teacher did a big talk on the history of feminism and it sounds all right, to be honest. I can't see what the big deal is.

But the one thing I don't get is my girlfriend, Julia, and all her girlfriends are all saying girls get a harsh deal and don't get respected as much as boys and only get judged by their looks and that. And then they all go and put all these pouty selfies on Instagram all looking really hot. If they don't want to be judged on their looks, why do they keep doing that? It makes no sense to me at all. You can't have both, can you? Or can you?

MARNIE, 18, ENFIELD

Describes herself as an 'ardent feminist', having got introduced via school and several current prolific feminist writers. Lives with her parents and two younger sisters and is attending Sheffield University after a gap year working with women's charities. Says her strong views have resulted in the break-up of one relationship and the breakdown of three friendships, including a 'lifelong female best friend'. Regularly gets subjected to abuse on social media for being a feminist.

Feminism has definitely become the sort of topic of the year, I think, which is great. Less great is the inevitable backlash. But that's just a sign it is working. That people who find the idea of women having power scary or distasteful is proof feminism is working and some men are worried about this. I know the big argument is that it's inverted sexism, and women are now just asking to be more powerful than men or special treatment or whatever, but that's just bullshit. And if it is being more aggressive than ever before, then so what? Nobody is going to give women anything if they politely ask for it. That hasn't worked – women being polite about things. We need to be more aggressive, I think. People say all the time that we live in an equal world and already have equality, but that's such shit.

One of the things the internet has shown us is how many men hate women. Not just indifferent or feeling a bit superior, but proper women-hating misogynistic stuff. Look at all the hate that high-profile – and even not high-profile – girls and women get. Every time there is a feminist article or debate, it's not just a few but hundreds or even thousands of men come out saying they are going to rape or maim you or kick your cunt in. The abuse I've had is unbelievable. And I'm not even famous yet. I think any woman in the public eye has to have seriously thick skin. And that's just wrong. Even fucking horrible men like Chris Brown don't get the abuse some female writer does for writing, say, about abortion or contraception.

I'm a bit young to know, but I think it might have come as a bit of a surprise to older women. Like, if you were a teenager before ... when was the internet invented ... say before 1998, or a woman doing something public, what was the worst that could happen? Someone could send you a nasty letter which your employer intercepted. Now everything is so open and easy to access and I think it has left women really vulnerable. I'm really proud of the way it hasn't worked, but why should it be happening at all?

Of course not all men hate women. Not by a long stretch. But I was talking to one of my best male friends the other day and he was saying feminism might become a real divide for our generation, maybe in the way politics used to before they were all fucking shit. Like, on one side there will be everyone pro-feminist and the other anti. And people's opinions on it are, like, really telling. It's like people who say they hate gays or are still racist. The joke is on them. They are the dickheads. It's like, get in the fucking twenty-first century, dude!

But I don't know. Things might be getting more extreme or maybe the more extreme feminism gets, the bigger the kick back from men, y'know? Threatened people act out. Do I think men's position in society is under threat? I'd say not. Their privilege is going to take more than a few years of hardcore feminism. But we should live in a world where people are judged equally. It would be nice if all the stupid people could be driven out and put on an island. Maybe then we'd all have a fair shot, because only really, really stupid people have a problem with feminism.

BILLY, 17, WEST SUSSEX

Lives with his parents and a younger brother. Says he has discovered what we agreed to call 'opportunistic feminism' and it's the 'best thing ever'. Attends sixth-form college because there 'isn't much else to do' but feels generally worried about the future and what he is going to do.

Can't believe I am admitting this. I didn't even think of gender much. Didn't give much of a shit. I mean, there's men and women. So what? I haven't got a problem with women being powerful. My mum earns more than my dad, I think, because my dad is currently self-employed and just starting up his own company.

I can't say I gave gender a second thought. I respect girls, I think. I've watched pornography. I like pretty girls. Especially Emma Watson, even though it feels like I've grown up with her, which can get a bit weird. I probably know some of my mates who don't entirely respect women. There's this big thing in gaming at the moment which just fucking pisses me off. It's a pretty sad dickhead who doesn't want a girl playing games with them online. I mean, how old are you? Eight? It's like when little kids don't want girls playing football with them in the playground. Whatever, man.

But it worked out pretty funny and I sort of started with feminism accidentally and it's been pretty all right and now I appreciate it. Basically, it went like this. I got advised to study sociology for A levels because I didn't know what else to do. I'm doing English and history and dropped French because it was too hard. I liked debating stuff and some of the issues, and was best at those sorts of subjects, so the head of sixth form advised me to take it because I need three subjects.

We had this new sociology teacher who started at the beginning of the year and she's really, like *really*, good. You know when you see films and there's that inspiring teacher who they will all follow around like he's Jesus and stand on desks and stuff? Well, she's like that. We don't stand on desks but she's really, really clever and makes you think a lot.

One of her big things is feminism and she's really into socialism and knows loads about civil rights. My parents always refer to politicians as 'what's-his-face' and 'thingamajig' so it's a bit different. So she organised this big debate on feminism because it's so big in the news at the moment and we were having these big arguments about it in class and to be honest, I think the class felt like it was splitting into boys versus girls on the issue.

None of the boys wanted to be on the pro-feminism side of the house so I said I'd do it. One thing is, I like public speaking and I like doing things properly. So I got really into it and did all this research and to be honest, I got quite into it. You women have had some properly bad shit and you still do.

So we had the debate, and I'm not gonna lie: I killed it. We *crucified* the other side and they were pretty pissed. They looked well stupid and it was partially because they hadn't done any work but also because they kept saying stupid things like, 'Well, men are physically stronger, so should rule society,' which doesn't make much sense if you think about it. If that were true, boxers would be in the House of Commons.

So it was all OK and felt really good and the headmistress was really complimentary. But it was a Friday and there was this big party that night. I do all right with girls, I suppose. But that night, it was like being Zac Efron or something. I was *surrounded* by girls all night and all the really pretty ones and they were all toasting me and calling me everything nice under the sun and complimenting me about how much I understand women.

It was a lightbulb moment. I asked the teacher that Monday if we should start a feminist society. She gave me a hug, she was so happy. I probably should mention Miss is *fit* as well as clever. It was total winning.

So I've ended up being the co-director of the feminist society. The more I get into it, the more I do think it's really important. The issues, I mean. But I also get to spend loads of time with all the girls, the nice female teachers like me, my mum is really proud of me. So I don't care about some of the stick I get. It just goes to prove girls just really wanted to be respected by boys. It's not really hard. Feminism is definitely nothing for boys to be worried about. I'm having a great time.

LEON, 17, EAST LONDON

Lives with his mum and younger sister and has been selected for an apprenticeship at a top UK football club. Says this is 'no guarantee' of making the first team and spends 'every waking moment' practising. His main goal is to be a national and international football star. Says he is loving the experience, but the pressure and competition to be the best makes him sometimes miss his old life of 'pissing around on FIFA with his mates and chatting up girls'.

I think the conversation about gender is really dishonest at the moment. I think for definite gay rights have really come on, which is good. I couldn't give a shit if someone is gay and I don't think every guy would have said that at my age fifteen years ago. Especially black guys. Who are, let's face it, still not always comfortable with the gay stuff, I'm not gonna lie. Being a racist just makes you look like a backwards motherfucker. Thank God.

But the whole sexism thing, I dunno. And if I'm honest, I think girls are a massive part of the problem. Well, some girls. I'm doing an apprenticeship at a very well-known football club. Scary times. You've got to keep the name of the football club and my name off record, all right?

OK, well, the conversation about the girls with my teammates and everyone I've played with is – well, I'd be well upset if my mum heard what we say. And I'd fucking kill anyone who spoke like that about my sister. I don't want to offend you, but it's pretty bad sometimes. But the thing is, being in this kind of world, football I mean, girls massively add to it – you know, facilitate. And I'm nowhere near professional yet. I might not even get there. But girls, loads of girls, just throw themselves at you and act so desperate. Like, they are so desperate to be with you because you might be a famous footballer. The things I've seen at the clubs with the proper, big names in football, you wouldn't believe. And you just think, 'Don't you have any respect for yourself, girl?' But at the end of the day, what are you going to do if it's just thrown in your face? Say no?

I don't think it's just footballers by a long shot. When boys get together, they talk about girls *enough* and it can get a bit out of hand. Like, if I was one on one with my real boys – my two best friends – the conversation might be real. Like, we might talk about feelings or real things. We were having a whole conversation the other day, and my mate admitted to me he'd rather go out with a smart girl than a pretty girl, because it's more real. I keep saying real, don't I? But in big groups, it blatantly wouldn't go like that. Girls are definitely objectified. Like this boy I know had anal sex with this girl, and he told us all in *detail,* but it was well bad because we all knew the girl. I felt kind of bad, but I didn't stop him.

The thing is, it's not just talk. I can say, hand on heart, I would never do anything to hurt or scare a girl. I might say stuff for a laugh, but I'd never hurt a girl. But I know loads of boys who hassle girls on the street way beyond the point of just chirpsing her. I definitely know boys who have pushed girls way beyond consent, especially when the girl is wasted. I'm not friends with them, but I've heard of boys I sort of know drugging girls, filming girls without their knowing and I've definitely heard of rape – even gang rape – in some circles I sort of know by default. It's not exactly a secret.

Boys chat about it – and I've heard first-hand like it's sort of a game. Funny, you know? Don't get me wrong, I'm not saying it's all boys *at all,* but I think it's way more common than people realise. But to be fair, girls need to fix up too and stop putting themselves in such a bad light and situations. I think they make themselves way too available, things get out of hand, and there's too much confusion.

All I know is, I'm locking my little sister up until she's eighteen. Believe.

MIKEY, 17, SOUTH LONDON

Has ambitions to be a doctor, although he is worried about gaining a place at medical school because it is so competitive to get in. Lives with his mum, who he describes as 'strong and clever', and sisters who he describes as 'lovely but deranged'. Once read The Female Eunuch *and thought it was 'weird but interesting'.*

I like smart girls. I love smart girls, *big time*. But girls have to fix up. They are making it so much worse for themselves than we ever could. Think about all the smart, amazing women in the world. And who do the girls all want to be? Kim Kardashian. Seriously?

I know women have had some seriously oppressive shit in history. But this generation is too much about playing the victim. Things are how they are. You either overcome it or succumb to it, you know what I'm saying? But girls seem to want to play into the hands of all these negative stereotypes about them. Shit, they create some of them, themselves.

Some of the smartest girls I know will actually pretend they are dumb so that boys like them. But then, you have to ask yourself the question where this all started which gets pretty philosophical. I go to a very competitive school. You have to be *smart* to go there. A lot of the girls will still play up dumb. I was talking to this girl who I am just mates with and she said guys don't like the really smart girls, which I think is *bullshit*. But then I gave it some thought. Who are the girls that are most fancied in the world? Models. I've already said Kim Kardashian. Nicki Minaj, who seems as dumb as her wigs. Even, I don't know, someone like Kate Middleton, who seems to be the poster girl for posh white girls – well, you never hear her talk, do you? Just walk around looking nice with a blank expression.

But then I thought further, and I said to my friend that what she was saying was that girls' biggest purpose in life is to be attractive to men and was that the case? And she was all like, 'Yeah. No girl wants to be the clever one, they all want to be the pretty one or the sexy one.' And maybe she's right. But only girls can change that, I think. They need to start playing up all their other qualities other than their looks. If every group that had ever been marginalised had just sat there taking it, we'd still have black people riding the back of buses. The weird thing about girls is they seem to enjoy lots of aspects of sexism without realising the bigger picture is negative. I might be wrong, but I think girls need to take a bigger stand before things get worse for them. I wouldn't want to raise my daughters in the atmosphere today. I massively want kids and especially girls, but I want them to have more Michelle Obamas and Hillary Clintons and less Rihannas and Mileys in their day.

ESTELLE, JANEY, FAYZA, ALL 16, NORTH LONDON

Attend a mixed comprehensive school together and describe themselves as 'into boys'. All have recently been introduced to the concept of feminism and are a bit confused by what it actually means. They are attending a big women's conference with their school in the spring and are looking forward to hearing some feminist figures speak on gender issues.

ESTELLE: To ask if there's sexism or gender inequality now is a complete fucking joke. There is loads. Absolutely loads and

I personally think it is getting worse. I don't think a day goes by when I don't receive some sort of hassle for being a girl or the kind of thing that boys wouldn't ever get.

FAYZA: Me too. I walked past a pub and these white men called me an 'Arab slut' and asked me if I liked it up the arse because that's what Arabs do. I was in my school uniform.

JANEY: Uniform is the worst. You get such perverts when you are in your school uniform. I went to Sainsbury's after school to get some food because I had orchestra practice for the school concert and we were going to be staying really late. These two guys followed me all round the shop until the security guard stopped them and told them to leave. But as I was leaving the shop, *he* told me I 'looked really sexy in my uniform'. I'm wearing a blazer and school skirt and tie. It's not some fucking sex uniform. Then the two guys were waiting for me outside and followed me all the way back to school and were hissing at me and saying stuff. It really scared me.

ESTELLE: It's because of porn. There are so many girls in uniforms and films being sold like 'dirty little schoolgirl takes on ten cocks' or whatever, it's made it so uncomfortable to wear uniforms. I actually think I feel safer in my own clothes.

FAYZA: Eurgh, porn. It's responsible for so much.

JANEY: Totally. Every single guy I know watches it. I get what the appeal is, in a sense. But it's made it impossible for boys to separate girls from sex, I think.

ESTELLE: Yeah. Or all girls fit into the 'slut' or 'nice girl' category and you are actually expected to live up to that. Like, you have to choose. And guys can be what they want to be.

FAYZA: I seriously think there needs to be a serious conversation about porn. Something needs to be done about it. I think it's messing up boys.

JANEY: But do you not think girls are watching it too? But in a different way. Which is as bad. Like watching it and thinking, 'I should look like that.' Or, 'I should be doing that.' You can't really avoid porn now, even if you want to. Like you'll be watching something and something will pop up that's really offensive. The problem is, I don't think *any* porn is made for women. It's like this thing made for men by men. And that's significant because it's like the objective is to humiliate women. I read some book, I can't remember what it is called, about the history of porn. And she was arguing that back in the day, like the Seventies, it probably *was* designed more for at least couples because it was just standard shagging. Like men and women shagging. And now, what you see is girls doing stuff that is actually so extreme it's dangerous for them. How can any girl watch that and be anything but uncomfortable? But I don't see how it's much different watching a girl just getting beaten up on screen.

FAYZA: I hadn't really thought about it. But, yeah, that makes total sense.

JANEY: Like, porn is hiding behind saying something is sexy. But it looks violent to me. And I know porn stars are all, like, consenting adults, except for the illegal stuff, but it just feels wrong. And apart from the sex, all the girls in the films are always getting called 'bitches' and 'sluts' and 'dirty little whores'. There's not insults like that for men.

ESTELLE: How much porn have you watched?

JANEY: Quite a lot. For research, though. (*They all laugh.*)

ESTELLE: But if you think about it, everything is as bad as porn. All people care about now is how women look. Like, it's all they talk about. Or care about. I feel like if a woman wins the Nobel Peace Prize, all anyone is going to be talking about is what she's wearing or how she looks.

FAYZA: Definitely. No one mentions what men are wearing or what they look like. Even the news. You have all these ugly guys reading the news and all the women look like models. Even on the news! Why should you have to be pretty or sexy to read the news?

JANEY: And there's whole articles on the fact, like Susanna Reid showed off some leg or something over your cornflakes. Who's a famous male newsreader?

FAYZA: Jon Snow? Krishnan Guru-Murthy?

JANEY: Yeah, either of them will do. Can you imagine anyone writing, like, 'Jon Snow gave a flash of his ample chest hair or endless legs'?

ESTELLE: Ew. I hope not.

JANEY: But that's the point. People expect it with women and not with men. My mum says, in her day, most female newsreaders looked normal. Frumpy even. And no one even cared, because it wasn't their job to look hot. Now it feels like that's the *only* job.

ESTELLE: That is so depressing. We've gone backwards.

DAVE, 17, ESSEX

Currently doing a BTEC in sports science at a sixth-form college. Is ardently opposed to feminists and the feminist movement and believes they have a 'man-hating agenda' and are asking for preferential treatment over men. Also believes several high-profile men have been 'witch-hunted' in the media and on social media due to the pressure and power of high-profile feminists and their 'dumb female sheep followers'. Would happily punch all men who describe themselves as feminists.

All this women's rights stuff is a total load of shit. Men are superior and that's that. There's so many examples of this and so it's well pointless banging on about women's rights. Girls are not as strong as men, or – and I'm sorry – as important as men. If they were, why is there the need for all this women's rights stuff? It would have just happened naturally. If you have to force something or press it, it's because it isn't right or natural. That's why I don't have a problem with gays. They didn't make themselves gay. And women, no matter how much they wish they could be, won't ever be men. They should give up and stop making themselves angry. Have you seen how angry most feminist women are? The girls at school into feminism are mental.

Give you some examples? OK. Football. It's one of the most important things in the world. It makes more money than probably any other sport and brings the whole planet together. Almost every country in the world loves footie on some level. No offence, but does anyone watch birds' football except as a sort of joke? Maybe when they're pissed. If the women's England side won the World Cup, I don't think there'd be parties on the street. It probably wouldn't make the news.

There's never been a female prime minister or president. (*I tell him there was one in the UK for eleven years.*) Is it? Well, you never hear about her. It's always Tony Blair or the war one with the cigar. But women don't matter in politics that much. All businesses are owned by men. All the important ones. The internet was started by men. Facebook, Apple, Lord Sugar, Mark Zuckerberg, the Army, Steve Jobs, Piers Morgan, footballers, it goes on forever. Where are the similar girls? No offence, but there aren't any.

There are some things that women do really well. And that's good. They should stick to that then. Like what? They write nice books for kids. The Harry Potter woman has done well. They're good at fashion. Most designers are women. I wanna say cooking, but actually all the top chefs are male. Another example. Women make good teachers. Obviously modelling. Not much else. There are a lot of female Indian doctors, I guess.

It's not that I hate women or mind them doing well. It's just that they don't or haven't yet, so how can they claim to be equal? It's like a school-level sprinter asking to be put on a level with Usain Bolt. You can wish it, but it doesn't make it true.

SEJAL, 15, BRADFORD

Currently studying for her GCSEs. Doesn't know any feminists but her father tells her feminism 'isn't ladylike'.

I don't like feminism or feminists. They are a bit scary. They shout a lot and hate all men. Emma Watson? Is she a feminist? Really? Oh. I didn't know that.

CHARLES, 17, SURREY

Is currently studying for five A levels but plans to drop physics next year. Says the issue of gender and feminism gives him a 'massive headache' and causes 'out-and-out rows' in every sociology and theology class he has. Agrees women should be considered equal, but thinks some traditions are good and should be held on to. Is ferociously against women being able to join the armed forces.

I'm going to come out and say it. I think gender has become a really fucked-up issue in this country and in a lot of the world. I think the massive drive towards equality in everything has messed everything up.

Take women's rights. No one is saying that women shouldn't have the right to vote or should be covered up in burkas or anything of the sort. But has women's rights really helped women that much and how often do they consider what this actually means and if they really want it? This notion of protecting women and providing for them – in theory that's anti women's rights, isn't it? Because if total equality wins, it removes that protection from women. So what has that produced? A big proportion of a generation where the father feels absolutely no sense of duty or responsibility to his child and so can just piss off. My dad walked out on us. And luckily he has money and so he financially provided for us, but apart from that, he does absolutely fuck all. My grandfather, who comes from a generation where a man stands by his duty, which includes his wife, was *horrified* at my dad. He pretty much plays the role of my dad in my family. But he thinks – and I agree – this has come from tampering with the natural way gender should be. Most single-parent families – and there are probably millions by now – the responsibility falls on the mother. I'm not saying women should be blamed for this, but I am saying it's because men don't have that sense of male duty now. And they should. It's their job.

I also question how much more respect women get nowadays and how much women respect themselves. I might be wrong, but it all looks worse to me. And sounds worse. I'm no different, but you should hear the way guys talk about girls. It isn't the sound of awe-filled respect or equality, I can tell you. And the stuff girls get online? I don't think it's romantic or unfair to say women didn't get called those names fifty years ago. Men were taught to respect and honour women. Just in a slightly different way.

Also, the way girls act – I think they are really confused by gender equality and what it looks like. It seems to me, in recent years, *more* not less women are getting famous for just getting their tits or arse out. What sort of joke is it that more girls see Kim Kardashian as a role model than, say ... well, anyone? Didn't she become famous for being thick and doing a sex tape? What does that really say about girls and their attitude to their own gender? All these women in the world and Kim Kardashian becomes a global superstar? It's sad. Equality for women hasn't made things better for women. It's made things worse for men and women. But particularly women.

WARREN AND SARAH, BOTH 15, SOUTH LONDON

Have been friends for a number of years and attend the same school. Sarah is 'unsure' about what she thinks of feminism and equality. Warren thinks that girls' internal relationships with each other are a bigger destructive force in their lives than a lack of gender equality. He likes girls very much but thinks they are all 'crazy'.

WARREN: I'm so confused about what girls want right now. One minute we are told to think of women as our equals. The next minute we are told to hold doors open for girls and not to be rude in front of them or say rude things about them. If you are my mate, a boy, I'm going to cuss you, call you every name under the sun and punch you in the head. Blatantly. But one of my boys got into bare trouble for hitting a girl. Because she's a girl! But that's what boys do to each other.

SARAH: That's *such* a dumb argument. And just such a typical one. Not punching someone in the head is not a sign you don't see them as equal. Physical strength is always used by boys in my class to prove girls aren't equal. Of course girls aren't as strong. Except Serena Williams. But girls are strong in other ways. Stronger than boys. But maybe it isn't about being strong. I think it's about being capable. I don't think girls should get more advantages, just the same as boys. And I think girls should be judged the same way as boys. If a girl does something with a boy, she gets so much abuse. If a girl dresses wrong, she gets abuse. Girls just get abused for nothing all the time.

WARREN: Nah. That's a load of shit. The people that give girls shit are girls. Do you remember that girl, Sonia, who brained those two guys after last year's prom and they filmed it or something and put it on Facebook? All the boys were kind of laughing about it. I'm not saying it wasn't bad that they put it on Facebook, but it would have probably blown over once everyone got threatened with suspension. But it was the girls that made it properly evil. So bad, she had to leave the school. They started this hate mail campaign against her, sent these pictures to her parents – you know, the ones of her doing the thing. She got bust up in the girls' changing rooms. I felt sorry for her, man. But you *know* it was the girls, not the boys. And it's the same with loads of stuff. Who's that girl who went out with Ricardo when he was seeing that other girl, Rachel? Yeah, Cecilia. She got *bare* shit and no one said *nothing* to Ricardo. And sorry to go on a bit, but that was all girls again. Boys don't give a shit about business like that.

SARAH: You're right, too. I think it's true. Girls definitely run the business of the school.

WARREN: Yeah, but it's a waste of time, man. They spend all their time bitching at each other and no time at all on serious business or having a laugh. Like boys have beef. For real. But it doesn't go on for an *eternity*. I know girls who have had arguments longer than a war. Any war in history. My girl still hates this girl who insulted her hair in Year 5. We're in Year 11 now. And another thing – that shitty thing that schools do, Mufti Day. I *hate* Mufti Day because every time it happens, I have my girl on the phone to me for, like, *two hours* the night before talking about what she's going to wear. And what the other girls are going to be wearing and if so and so is going to go designer and if so and so is going to look like a ho. And by the end I'm just 'aaaaaah'. I just switch her on speakerphone and go play Xbox or hang myself or whatever. She doesn't even notice. And then all day, they are all checking each other out like the clothes mafia and cussing each other's clothes and saying all kind of things about each other. And then at the end of the day, just when I think it's all over, she'll be on the phone *again* saying, 'Did you see what Nicole was wearing? No way was that real D&G. That was some market shit.' Or even scarier: 'Did you think Shona looked nice?' And you *know* there's no right answer to that question. You know the extent of boys' comments on the girls' clothes? She look fit.

Or she don't look fit. But we don't care that much. So don't tell me it's us boys causing the problems.

SARAH: Are you going to shut up now?

WARREN: NO! I gotta get this out of me. I'm traumatised. The only thing more scary than being a boy who has to deal with girls is being a girl who has to deal with girls. They are so bad to each other.

SARAH: Very true. (*They both laugh.*)

ANDREW, 15, STAFFORDSHIRE

Andrew was born Anna and has suffered with gender identity since he can remember and 'always felt like a boy'. He hastens to add that he does not feel this way simply because girls have a harder time than boys – though they do. Gender is understandably a difficult subject for him and he thinks the feminist movement has sometimes treated transgendered people 'really offensively'.

I don't want to be a girl any more, because I don't think I was ever a girl. I was born a boy. I have always felt this very deeply since I can remember. I actually don't really want to talk about my own personal experience too much, because I have spent thousands of hours talking about it. You don't just get to change the sex you were born with.

I get that it is a complex thing, but you wouldn't believe how much it revolves around talking to people about Barbies and footballs and willies and fannies and skirts and trousers and knickers and pants. It's like gender starts and stops with what you have between your legs. Maybe we need to stop thinking like this. It's such a binary way of looking at everything. Can we accept that maybe some people are not the right gender, and some people might be both genders, or neither gender, or some of each or a little of one and a lot of the other? Is that so hard to believe in the twenty-first century? Thank God, gay rights have come on so much. But gender is still so fucking set in the eighth century or whatever when they used to make freakshows of eunuchs. What they do to people who have gender reassignment or mess with gender or are confused is sick. How people are talking about them is horrible and scary if you are in the world. I'm part of this amazing support group. The stories are getting better. More uplifting. But there's more bad ones. I don't want to talk about them, because they're not my stories to tell. They are people's private truths.

But I don't see why we have to keep pushing gender as an agenda. Like, aside from the obvious, I don't think kids are even aware of gender as a *thing* until they're told. It's not just girls being given dolls and boys being given cars or kids being dressed in blue and pink, it's so much more. There are definitely ways you are taught to behave if you are a boy or a girl. I know a kid who is a boy and he just wants to dress like a girl and play with his older sister's oven. He's a kid of a close family friend, so I've heard all about it. He's just a fucking kid. And you would think he was torturing kittens or something, the way people talk about it in hushed tones. They're thinking of getting him an actual psychologist. I mean, *fuck off*. He likes dresses. He's four, for Christ's sake. What does it even matter, anyway? But his mum and dad are treating it like he has some sort of disease because he isn't interested in Mario Kart or whatever.

How are my parents taking my decision? Uhhh . . . OK. Not that well, really. They have good days and bad days. It's hard. I don't want to talk about it, that much. It's quite upsetting at times.

GUY, 17, BIRMINGHAM

Just thinks everyone should get on with the business of living and not complaining and doesn't want to say anything else on the matter.

I couldn't give a shit about gender. Male, female, other. Who cares? I just don't have much to say about it. I do wonder if people stopped chatting about it 24/7, maybe we could all just get on with life. Do you know what I mean?

Guys need to get on with the idea, or let go of the idea that they are boss. It's over. Forget about it. Done. Along with slavery and *The X Factor*. And I think girls need to stop telling everyone they are equal and just accept they are and get on with the job of being equal. It's like people who go around talking their business all the time, saying they are rich and have all this green and designer threads or something or they get loads of girls. The more you have to say it, the less true it seems. Like, do you think the Queen has to tell people she's rich? I doubt it. She doesn't have to. People just know. I don't know, I just feel that way about feminism and all the arguments around it. The more you talk about it, the worse it gets.

JANISHA AND EDEN, 17, SOUTH LONDON

Both girls are currently doing BTECs. They both think women's rights are often appropriated by women who have the 'least to complain about'. They both say they have bigger worries than whether feminism is working or whether they have equal rights to males.

JANISHA: I think feminism is a load of shit middle-class thing for people with nothing better to worry about. I'm not saying I don't see any point in it. I do. But it isn't a thing for me in my life or anybody I know. As I said, when there are so many things to worry about, I'm not losing sleep over how women look in newspapers or some rapper's video. And what pisses me off about that is if a woman is getting her tits out or shaking her booty in some video, how does all the feminists know her situation? She probably is doing it to pay the bills. She might have a kid to feed. Maybe she loves doing it. It's her business. But it so badly pisses me off that rich white women especially are, like, wagging their finger at other people's business that they know nothing about. If someone offered me ten G to shake my booty for some big rapper, I'd probably do it. I got bills to pay and shit to deal with and a younger brother and a mum who's regularly off her face.

EDEN: Innit. That's such a good point. Isn't women's rights about choices? Who says being a model or extra in a video isn't a choice? Why are only some choices seen as good choices? Like, we cuss down women in porn and say they are skanks and hos ...

JANISHA: They are skanks and hos ...

EDEN: But, yeah, but what if they actually want to do it?

You don't accidentally do a porn film or show your pussy in a magazine. And actresses show off their pussies and tits in films or whatever, but because it's Hollywood, it's OK.

JANISHA: I remember when I was still at school and we had this woman come visit us. She was a politician or something, I think. Or maybe a writer. I can't remember. I didn't have a clue who she was, but I think she might have been a big deal or something because there were newspapers and all the teachers seemed well excited. I'll text my girl to see if she can remember, if you like? This wasn't that long ago, but it seems *time* ago. I don't know what the fuck happens to time once you leave school. It feels like a million years ago. But I do remember she gave us a massive lecture about our rights as women, and respecting ourselves and not allowing boys to tell us they were better and how we could get any job we wanted and I just sat there thinking, 'What the *fuck* do you know about my life or anybody else's here? You really think any girl in this room wants to be treated like shit by a man? Or beaten up by her man? Or sell her ass on some street corner to feed her kids that she had well young instead of being head of a company or a lawyer or something?' You don't choose any of that shit. And I'm not talking about myself, but where I live, where I come from, I know enough girls in that situation. Do you know what I mean? And I bet all the girls or women who end up with some shitty situation, it's not like they wished for that. It's just fucked.

EDEN: Exactly! I wanna go to university and sit around and talk about women's rights too, but it's not going to happen any time soon unless I win the lottery or something. And I hate the expression 'keeping it real' but it's true to this situation. If you got real worries, some big struggle (*i.e. feminism*) you are supposed to care about seems less important. I know this lady who's got six kids, a son in prison, she's had bones broken by men more times than I can count because I've seen the evidence first-hand, money worries, social workers visiting and all that. You think she gives a shit about women in magazines? That sort of stuff is a joke to her. It isn't real life.

TAYLOR, 14, MANCHESTER

Feminism? I can't even. Ugh.

OSCAR AND THOMAS, BOTH 16, WINDSOR

Girls on top? WAHEYYYY.

JAMES AND WARREN, BOTH 15, SUSSEX

JAMES: What is feminism?
WARREN: It's this thing that women have to scare men.
JAMES: How?
WARREN: I don't know. It just does.

TILLY, 14, STOKE

Thinks feminism is a 'bit silly, but OK if it's the sort of thing you're into'. Runs an online Twilight *fan page and group. Can't see what all the fuss is about the* Twilight *books making girls look weak and subservient. Considers Edward Cullen to be her 'dream man' and the fictional relationship between Bella and Edward to be the 'dream relationship'. Isn't allowed to read the* 50 Shades *series until next year and says she 'can't wait to read them'. Her mum is an avid fan of both series and they talk about them 'all the time'.*

I think there isn't a more significant issue at the moment than gender. Seriously. Everyone is saying that females are making it all about them and it's a way to make them all-powerful and men not powerful or something, but that just isn't true. If people of colour just took racism, it probably wouldn't have stopped, would it?

But it's *so* not just about feminism and girls' rights. I think boys are really, really struggling too. I had a long talk with my best friend, who is a boy, the other night and he is just so depressed at the moment about just being a boy. I think it must be really confusing for them. I wish I could explain myself better, but I think boys are under too much pressure to be the stereotypes of boys everybody likes. Like, good at football, obsessed with sex, getting into fights and everything. But if you aren't that, what do you do? People call you gay for a starters, which I don't mean is bad or wrong, but boys definitely have this idea that it's one thing or gay. Aaaah. I'm explaining so badly! But say if a girl wants to be into football and dress like a tomboy, or if a girl is a really girly girl and loves dressing up and reading fashion magazines, or say a girl is really clever and is brilliant in all her subjects, or say a girl is into heavy metal and dresses up in black and wears those minging T-shirts all the time, there will be other girls like her. Or you can even be a bit of both. But with boys, there's just a certain type that is the best that all boys want to be.

Who is that? Good-looking, tall, good hair, athletic, good in his lessons but not a swot, bit cheeky to the teachers but not rude, amazing smile, funny, bit mysterious. I bet Robert Pattinson was like that in school.

CHARLIE, 17, BERKSHIRE

Thinks feminism is 'all right for girls' but 'completely stupid and fake' if you are a male – doesn't believe men can be feminists. Says his looks and personality make him 'irresistible' to girls. He has dated models and actresses. He regularly gets stopped on the streets and asked out by girls and gets 'hounded night and day' on social media by adoring girls.

I don't know that much about gender politics, but I think it's much, much harder being a girl.

Being a guy, there are a million ways to be interesting and attractive to the opposite sex. You have your thick but athletic type like David Beckham, weird poetry type like, say, Johnny Depp, old-school gentleman like Benedict Cumberbatch, girly boy like Harry Styles, cool guy like, say, Idris Elba, dangerous guy like, er, James Bond. I could go on forever. Some women even find Boris Johnson attractive. There's a man for all seasons, as it were. Some totally random friend of mine likes that tub of lard James Corden. Thinks he's as sexy as all that. Strange girl.

With small variations, the only thing that makes a girl really interesting is if she's slim and beautiful. Let's not bullshit. Men might have a preference for blondes or brunettes or redheads, or dark-skinned women, or light-skinned women, or a variation on slim. Men might go on record or say to the girls in their lives that personality matters or brains matter or being a good person matters, but those things are just bonuses. Men want a beautiful girlfriend that makes them look good. I feel bad for ugly girls or fat girls, especially if they are nice, but that's just the way it is. We want Keira Knightley not Adele.

Ugly guys do just fine if they are cool or smart or have a lot of women. Without a good face and body, women are screwed. That's the bottom line.

TANYA, 15, EXETER

Currently studying for her GCSEs. Was born with a harelip that has been 'improved a bit' by surgery. Says she is worried she will never get a boyfriend because she is 'so ugly'. Genuinely believes being beautiful is the most important thing in the world for a girl and would give 'almost anything' to change her appearance. Says her looks make her cry herself to sleep most nights. Her parents try to stop her reading fashion magazines, but she reads them on the bus anyway. They make her more depressed.

When I was little my dad used to read me all the princess stories and tell me I was a princess and I was the most beautiful girl in the world, and I believed him. I would watch all the

Disney films and look at all the books, and I really thought I looked like them.

I soon realised differently when I went to school. I was born with a harelip which they've done an OK job on, but it is still really noticeable. On my first day a boy told me it was 'ugly' and I went home crying. I'd like to say it was just kids being kids, but things have got worse pretty much every year since. I haven't been blessed with good looks at all. I hate my face and body. I have real trouble with my skin; I put on weight really easily even though I don't eat much; I'm taller than the other girls so I stand out even more. I don't feel pretty in any way. I'm so ugly it makes me cry every night. I've thought about suicide more times than I can count. I hate myself.

The thing is, though, I'd do anything to change the way I look. I've begged Mum for more plastic surgery but it just upsets her. But it's other people that make it so awful. If I'm not being teased, I'm just invisible. No one pays me any attention. I think I embarrass people about the way I look, so they look right through me. I watch all the pretty girls at school with beautiful faces and hair and figures. Their life is so different to mine. And it's just because they are pretty. They aren't nicer people or cleverer than me, I don't think. But just because they are pretty, they have friends, boyfriends, teachers are nicer to them, people in shops are nicer to them. They will probably even get better jobs than me, because people think nicer people deserve more.

I've never met a boy like me, but I know that all people care about if you are a girl is how pretty you are. I keep trying, but people don't like me because I'm so ugly.

RACHEL, PAULA, NICO, ALL 16, ESSEX

Will complete their GCSEs this summer. All the girls think that gender issues are getting worse and not better and that all people care about is if a girl is good-looking rather than clever or ambitious. None of them consider themselves to be good-looking and they often refer to themselves as 'ugly' and 'fat'.

RACHEL: Body is definitely the biggest struggle for girls. I think things are getting worse. The scrutiny on women's bodies is something else. Back fat, arm fat, thigh gaps, muffin tops, circle of shame, wobbly tummy, detoxes, bootcamps, fat-shaming, Photoshopping. I was telling my dad about this the other day. He's older as he had me when he was fifty-nine. He couldn't believe it. He drives a black cab and said it sounded more complicated than the Knowledge! He said there were only two types of girls in his day: pretty girls and homely girls. I'm not even sure what that means. Maybe kind and sort of motherly? But now there's millions of things to worry about. And that's before you even start thinking about periods or body hair or sex. Or getting pregnant. Or contraception. And we're lucky, I guess. Living in the West. At least we're allowed to ... Paula, tell her about your second cousin.

PAULA (*quietly*): She had FGM. When she was really little. I had no idea. We don't talk about it. She told me herself. It made me feel physically ill. Especially when I saw how much it had affected her. I was born here and my parents are very observant Muslims, but very much against this. It annoys me when everyone thinks all Muslims cut their daughters. Many are against the practice. But it is happening a lot in other parts of the world. Probably here, too. It is barbaric.

NICO: To be fair, a lot of boys get circumcised too. Don't Jewish boys all have it?

PAULA: I don't think it's the same, at all. There is a sort of medical reason for that. And to do with cleanness. Sorry, gross. But with girls ... there's no reason other than to remove a girl's ...

RACHEL: Sexuality?

PAULA: Yeah. I think it scars you for life, physically and mentally. If you don't die. It's such a big thing to talk about different attitudes to female bodies. But whether it's really serious like FGM or something less serious like all the disgusting jokes about periods or smelling 'fishy', you're always made to feel awkward as a girl. Or bad. My mum says you find peace with your body after having children. But that's a lot of years of feeling like shit.

NICO: But at least we don't look weird with something dangling between our legs. That'd be *so* gross.

ALL: Ugghhh.

PAULA: I don't think I'll ever want to see a boy's bits. Even if he pays me.

JAY, 16, STAINES

Is in a band and 'literally couldn't give a shit about gender issues'. He just thinks men should treat women better so that 'everyone would get laid more often and there wouldn't be all this suspicion and upset all the time'.

Girls whinge all the time about being girls. And I get that there is some shit that they have to deal with. But everyone loves girls. Especially teenage girls. Look how many porn films are made about them. All girls have to do is smile and they get served in the pub. The reason they never get arrested is because they are girls and probably cry and everyone feels sorry for them. They get jobs just because they are girls. They go out with older blokes who have cars and jobs and their own houses. That never happens to blokes our age. Some fit woman in her twenties or thirties isn't hanging around the school gate picking us up in her convertible. And everyone gets all het up when it happens to girls, saying they are being preyed upon by paedos or something! If some older woman preyed on us, we'd love it!

All I'm saying is, being a girl is wasted on girls. They moan about blokes fancying them or getting yelled at from vans or being given stuff by pervy shopkeepers. What's the problem? We'd love it if that stuff happened to us. But everyone treats teenage boys like they are scum. I'm gonna say it on behalf of boys to all women: feel free to take advantage of us or see us as sex objects. If it means in twenty years' time I get paid less, it'll be well worth it.

Technology

RYAN, 17, CHELMSFORD

Currently studying for a plumbing apprenticeship. Has an iPhone, iPad, laptop, family computer and two game consoles, but says he isn't 'obsessed with technology'. Said at first he used various technologies for twenty hours a week. On analysis this is closer to fifty hours a week.

I'm seventeen and I don't think technology even means as much to me as it does for, like, thirteen-year-olds. Actually, that might not be true, but relatively speaking, by the time they get to my age, say, they'll be even more immersed than we are in it. Like, every age thinks that they've reached the – oh, what's the fucking word? You know, the top. The zenith. And then, it does to the absolute max, you know? Like we were *pissing ourselves* with laughter the other day when we were watching this movie with some Atari shit in it. It was properly funny. And my dad said it was the height of technology then. But then, my mum has the first ever iPhone still and that even looks like an antique, because she's scared of change and never breaks things. It's mad how fast technology moves.

Technology is everything to kids these days. Maybe even more than it was to us. I have some mates who are mad into gaming, and will do it 24/7 if they could. At the weekends, I'll happily go get a little lean and stay up until 5 a.m. on these gaming nights. But that's a social thing. If I did that on a Friday, I'd go see my girlfriend on a Saturday. But to be fair, she loves gaming too, so I'd play all sorts of stuff just with her. It's part of why I like her. Her passion for Fifa (*laughs*).

I'm not that interested in Facebook or Instagram. That's for girls and kids. And Twitter is for utter wankers. Like people who want to be able to tell the world they just took a shit next to Ashley Cole in a club, or whatever. Who gives a shit? Literally. Twitter should be named 'Shitter' really with all the bullshit on it. My girlfriend loves Twitter and she gets some real weirdos trying to chat to her on it. But she does post pictures of herself in bikinis and in her knickers and that. What are they called that girls love? Yeah, selfies. What a load of shit that is.

I'm on my phone 24/7. But everyone is. The older lads in the company I'm training in still read the paper in the morning, but none of my mates do. Except if they're taking a dump. I probably should stop talking about shitting, shouldn't I? You just get the news on the phone, if you're interested. This bloke called Mario who I work with who's an old geezer – he's about forty – he keeps telling us that nothing on a laptop is ever going to be the old-school fun of Page 3 and porn mags, but we rip the piss out of him. Why would you pay to see some bird's half-covered tits and fanny, when you can watch girls getting up to anything you could want for free? I'm not mad on porn, really, but of course I watch it sometimes. But I prefer the real thing, and a lot of porn gets a bit weird. Some of my mates are *obsessed* with it. My mate John . . . well, the stories he has about porn. I'm like, 'You're fucking wrong, mate.' But it's there, y'know. On the internet. God knows what young lads are doing with their free time now (*laughs*).

There's this properly old geezer at work. A Jamaican fella. Properly nice geezer. Sort of quiet, but the shit he comes out with. We all call him Morpheus for a laugh, but it's a respectful thing, because he's all wise and stuff. But he says that technology – hold on, I've got to remember this, I can't remember exactly – but technology is taking, I think, the thought and beauty out of all things. Like, you don't read, because you Google stuff. Beautiful women are just there in every position. No mystery. You don't talk to people as much. Just chat to them online. And if you want to see the North Pole, no one goes any more. They look on Google Maps.

I don't think about technology all that much. I grew up with it. But could I live without it? No way. Not a chance. How did people find things before? And make plans to meet? And things like, if you wanted to see a film, how did you do it? I know people went to the cinema. I've never been to the cinema in my life. Why would you when there's illegal downloads and Netflix? And no, I've never bought a CD. I don't think I know anyone who has, either.

JARED, 16, SOUTHAMPTON

Admits to being an 'avid' user of internet pornography – sometimes watching porn films for up to four or five hours a day. Says he is 'very worried about this habit, but feels unable to stop'. He owns a laptop and a smartphone, though he wants to upgrade both to Apple products as he says they are 'way better'. He estimated he was on technological devices for about twenty-five hours a week. On analysis, it was closer to sixty hours.

I remember the first time I saw porn. I was probably about six. I went to a primary school that was attached to a high school and there were always older kids, mostly giving us shit.

But some were OK. This bunch of lads were like, 'Look at this, look at this,' and it was some porn film. I didn't know what it was, exactly. But I remember being really interested in it, and knowing it was probably bad. But in a good way.

I'd say by about nine, a lot of the boys at school were either interested in seeing porn, had seen some or were watching it a bit. You'd have to be pretty clueless to not be aware of it. I didn't get a mobile phone until I was eleven, when the obsession really started, because it was easy to access.

But I'd definitely seen a lot before then. A lot of my mates had mobiles and after football practice, we'd sometimes watch a bit on John's phone, who had this wicked phone with a really good screen even then. We'd all cuss each other down, saying, 'You've got an erection, you pervert,' and you would deny it. But . . . it's porn. Isn't that supposed to happen?

Once I got to secondary school, my parents bought me a laptop and a phone, because I needed one. They wouldn't get me an Apple, which is a shame, 'cos they have much better software. Luckily, my parents are clueless. I'm not sure what my dad does for a living. Something really boring. And my brother is disabled, so my mum spends a lot of time caring for him. It didn't really bother me, but they bought me a lot of stuff to make up for the fact I don't get much attention.

The first thing I did when I got my laptop for the first time – I got it about three months before my phone – was go up to my room and look for porn. It was exciting. Like a big sort of dirty, but mostly exciting, secret. The thing I couldn't believe was how much there was of it. It's like the more you look, the more you find and you can literally find anything. Some of it you have to pay for, but there is so much free it doesn't really matter.

At first I'd only watch a bit and then I'd slam the laptop shut and feel all scared. But then it was obvious – nobody cared and there wasn't going to be the porn police showing up to arrest you and tell your parents, so I kept watching more and more.

What porn do I like best? It changes. When I was a bit younger I liked all the lesbian stuff. You know, girls doing stuff with each other. Then there was the stupid stuff that everybody watched. The really fucking gross stuff that isn't really porn like *Two Girls, One Cup*. But you can just laugh at that with all your mates. As I got older I got more into hard stuff. I have watched the ones where the girls cry and act frightened and like they are in pain. I know that's probably not good.

I have got to the point now where porn has taken over my life a bit too much. I tried giving up for a while, but I couldn't. I just thought about it even more and I couldn't sleep.

Instead of hanging around with my mates at lunch, I'll go home and watch porn. I watch porn every night, sometimes straight from school. I just lock the door and put my headphones on. We went to Greece last summer and I was panicking I wouldn't be able to access porn, but luckily the hotel had a WiFi code and I could. But I had to be a bit more careful as we were sharing this apartment. I hated that holiday.

Do I think I'm addicted? I'm not sure you can be. Like, I read this article online about Russell Brand, I think, being a sex addict. Or something like that. He explained it really well. Like it was something comforting and exciting, but not as easy to control as you might think. I sort of can relate to that.

Do I think it has changed the way I see girls? Yeah. Sort of. I haven't had a girlfriend and it seems weird to think about the girls I know doing the stuff I watch. Like I do think about them in those . . . like, the porn scenes sometimes, you can't help it. But it's really hard to imagine doing it in real life. I don't know if real life will be as good as porn films. Why? Because some people say that girls are never as dirty in real life as they are in porn films. And, like, when you watch porn, you can sort of put yourself in the position of the man, and he's always the boss. I don't feel like that around girls in real life, so I don't think real-life sex can be as good. Also, no girls in school look like the girls in porn films, which is OK. But I love how the girls look in porn.

SALLY, 15, GLOUCESTER

*Says her 'entire social life' comprises her time and relationships on various different websites where she uses the internet pseudonym 'Frerard666'. She estimates she spends thirty hours a week in chat rooms and feels it gives her the connections with people she is unable to make in real life. Her teachers are already predicting she will get twelve A*s at GCSE.*

I know this isn't that much of an original idea. People have been doing it for years with online dating, but on the internet, you can be who you want to be. You can create this sort of character for yourself that is more appealing than your own. I think everyone does it to an extent. Even on Facebook. People post the best picture of themselves and make their lives sound so cool, and how is that different?

I'm not lying online. I say I'm fifteen and all the things I'm into. But online, I can be all the things I want to be: cool, clever and sexy. It also makes me feel closer to the people I love. The second I get up, and pretty much, like, every ten minutes, I'll check Gerard Way's (*singer and ex-frontman of the band My Chemical Romance*) Twitter. It makes me feel closer to him and better about all the other shit that is going wrong in my life. I have tweeted him loads and loads of time, but he hasn't tweeted back yet. That would be my absolute dream. I literally think I would die. I am so in love with him. But for now it is enough that he might see them and think of me, if only for a few seconds.

I did get into Ask FM for a while, but it gets so nasty on there, I stopped. You will get death threats, rape threats and jokes all the time. People constantly tell you on there to go and kill yourself, to go and self-harm because your life is worthless. I already feel like that, so I don't need to hear it all the time.

I try to stick to what is safe. For a long time I really loved this pro-ana website (*dedicated to and celebrating the disease anorexia*), but it kept getting shut down and moved. I was so pissed off about this. People were so negative about these and my mum went mad when she found out I'd been going on it and cried. But nobody on there was telling you to be anorexic. There were tips and stuff on how to hide it, how to keep yourself from feeling hungry, how to avoid situations where there would be food and stuff. But a lot of it was really supportive. There was this one angry girl on there who would, like, troll other girls because she was hardcore ana. You should have seen her pictures. Even I thought they were gross and I think the really skinny models have the perfect figure. I so wanna be really, really thin. Anyway, this girl would tell other girls on there they were too fat and not trying hard enough and the community banned her in the end. She kept coming back under a different name, but it was really obvious. She was mental.

Now I stick to the websites dedicated more to music and stuff. Especially My Chemical Romance. There is a cult dedicated to them that's really complex. Some people are hardcore pro-Frerard and some people are hardcore anti-Frerard. It gets pretty vicious sometimes. What's Frerard? It's basically this rumour about Gerard Way and Frank Iero really being in a relationship and in love with each other. There's loads of evidence for it, even though they are both married with kids. They kiss on stage really passionately all the time. Or they used to. Some of their fans want them to be in a relationship because it makes them more pure and some people – girls – are really anti it, because if they were gay, you have no chance with them. Actually, gay fanfiction is *massive* on the internet. My best friend is *obsessed* with the Dr Who fanfiction. She writes these really gross, detailed sex stories about the doctor. And also Sherlock Holmes. But they're kind of funny.

Do I think I spend too much time on the internet? No. I love the places I go on the internet. It makes me feel safe and like I'm part of something. I find it quite hard to cope in real social situations, because I'm so shy. I have more friends on the internet and I find it easier to make friends.

JULIA, 17, READING

Was an avid 'vlogger' and 'YouTuber' in her younger teenage years. After an experience of being groomed by a much older man over the internet, now avoids being online much except for basic email communication and shopping.

I do miss the internet. For all the crap that goes with it, there are parts of the internet that are great. The thing about it is, because it's a new thing, or new-ish, it's definitely *for* young people. It's their space, do you know what I mean? Older people get it, but they definitely aren't passionate about it. I think that might be part of the appeal, because I don't think they really get it, either, so it's like a secret world for teenagers. Like with texts and stuff, there's also an internet language, too. My dad literally can't understand a word of anything said on the net. A while back, I was watching a Drake video on YouTube and Dad was like, 'What the hell are they actually saying in the comments section beneath it?' I can see why teenagers like that. It's their own language they created.

My parents haven't stopped me using the internet. That's pretty much impossible to do. But they want to check on everything now and no computers in bedrooms. I think it's fair to say what you do on the internet is private, isn't it? How many people would be really happy admitting to everything they do and see on the internet? I also think that's why teenagers are so into it, because it's a secret world, a fantasy world, but also a private world. It's a bit like sex. You only want to share it with a few people and you want to be able to choose those people. I think that's what scares parents where kids and the internet are concerned, because it's a part of their kids' lives they have no control over.

I met Marcus in an InstaChatRoom. It was a music one, so nothing dodgy. If you go to, like, a dating one, things can get weird. And Tinder has created a whole other level of weird. But so many of my mates *love* it.

But anyway, Marcus seemed so cool. Said he was this music producer and was really knowledgeable about hip hop and the grime scene, which I was getting into. His life sounded so glamorous. All executive parties in LA and hanging out with celebrities and models. At first I couldn't believe he was chatting to me, but we chatted more and more. I ended up telling him all about me and my dreams and aspirations and that. He was such a good listener. Well, virtual listener. Eventually he started, like, asking me really personal questions and it seemed really natural to tell him. He asked me questions about my sex life – which was non-existent – my fantasies, my body. Even my periods, which seems weird and creepy now, but totally normal then. He said we needed to be totally open with each other.

He asked for my Facebook and he asked me to put up some pictures that would just be for him. Not like sexy ones, but say, if he asked me to wear a blue top, I'd post a picture that day of me wearing a blue top. Then he started to tell me what to eat, what to wear, how to cut my hair. He told me what friends of mine he approved of on Facebook and the ones he thought were 'trouble' and I should cut ties with. I know I sound like a total idiot now, but I was in really deep and this had been going on for months. I really trusted him. And he told me really personal details of his life – or what I thought were details.

He said Skyping was too risky for now and he didn't want to get me into trouble with my parents, so could I send him some pictures? Pictures just for him. At first they were fairly harmless. Like cute snaps in the mirror, but then he asked for more. Said it would be a sign of 'trust'. I refused and he told me he loved me. I was completely blown away and excited, so eventually I did. And then he wanted more. And videos. And I set up a webcam for him, because he asked me too. And things got worse and worse.

He looked at my Facebook page obsessively and he started asking if I'd bring a friend of mine – Melanie – to come round and talk to him. I knew it might not be just talking as Melanie is really pretty. I was completely panicked and also really jealous. He obviously fancied Melanie. But worse, I didn't want anyone finding out what I'd done. I knew it was wrong. I felt really ashamed. I said 'no' and he went fucking crazy. Said all kinds of things about me. And then he said he was going to post all my pictures online and that he was going to contact all my friends on Facebook and tell them I was a dirty slag and a prostitute. He then said he was sending my pictures and films to my mum and actually sent a screenshot of him writing my mum an email with the right email address and all these attachments.

I just panicked. He was sending, like, 300 emails to me an hour and as many texts. He was sending me 'reminders' of all the things I'd done for him. Told me he knew where I went to school and was going to stick up thousands of pictures of me naked all over the school. And he did know where I went to school. I'd told him many times. We'd talked about school. He even knew who my favourite teacher was. He'd asked if I'd ever had sexual fantasies about him. Which I hadn't.

He said it would all stop if I brought round Melanie. That I'd spoiled his trust and made him angry, but I could make it all better, if I showed him how much I loved him and did what he asked. I tried to reason with him. I mean, Melanie wasn't even that much of a good friend. There was no way I could explain it to her. But he just wouldn't listen. He said I had a day to make it happen or everyone I knew was going to find out who I was. That he was going to fuck me up forever.

I can't really describe how I felt that night. It was like all of life and all the things I'd done were filling up my lungs and

I couldn't breathe. I could barely hold a knife and fork at dinner I was shaking so much. Mum and Dad could see something was wrong, but I just told them I was feeling ill. That night, I turned everything off. Phone, computer, camera. Everything. It was like turning off a life-support machine. Massive relief. And awful. And then I decided I was going to kill myself. My life was over anyway. And I took a fairly big overdose of everything in the medicine cabinet. Even vitamin C (*laughs*).

I don't remember anything until I woke up in the hospital the next day with all my family around me, my best friend, my form teacher and two policemen. Well, actually one of them was a woman.

Of course whilst I'd been having my stomach pumped and all those awful things and been unconscious for the best part of twenty-four hours, they'd pretty much pieced together what had happened. My friend knew the password on my phone as we had each other's, as we were always grabbing each other's phones to take selfies and that. I hadn't even thought about that. I hadn't been thinking about anything but Marcus for six months. Not friends, school, parents, my sister, my interests – especially netball, which I'd been really good at. My whole world existed in that computer and in that fucking webcam and with him.

Telling everyone everything was the biggest relief ever. I can't tell you on record too much about what's going to happen next, because I've been told not to. But put it this way, he was *none* of who he said he was. Just some random guy in his thirties. And he was doing the same thing to a lot of girls my age. I haven't got my head round it all yet. I have nightmares about it most nights. What he saw. Who he is. Is this a sex crime? It has caused terrible stress in my family. Especially with my dad, who I know just wants to kill the guy.

The counselling has helped a bit. The lady who sees me a lot has focused on blame and sometimes I see it isn't my fault and sometimes I don't. I'm not an idiot. What kind of big producer who hangs out with models in LA talks to a fifteen-year-old girl avidly on the internet? I should have known. I should have.

If I could give advice to anyone it would obviously be: don't talk to strangers on the internet. Especially anyone who asks you weird things, no matter how nice or cool they seem. But also, don't make the internet your life. So many teenagers, including my friends, don't have any interests any more outside the web. If they go to dinner, they have to Instagram it. Any funny thought they have, they have to tweet it. I don't think it's healthy. We are definitely a generation completely dependent on the internet. Addicted. I don't think any addiction is good, is it?

DEANA, 16, EAST LONDON

Uses the internet 'obsessively' and estimates she spends around forty hours a week online. 'Hates' Twitter, but is passionate about Instagram, blogging, vlogging, Snapchat, Keek, Ask FM and various apps. Says 'Facebook is over because so many old people are on it. Especially teachers and parents.' Was the victim of some very personal photos going viral after a 'boyfriend' passed them on to a couple of his friends. Despite this, she continues to post information of a personal nature, but is now 'much more careful'.

Daniel is a fucking little prick. But he got his head busted in for what he did to me and he cried and pissed himself, so revenge is sweet. He'll be looking over his shoulder for a long time now, believe. I don't forget things easily. His day isn't over and he is *definitely* a dog.

Everyone puts shit on the internet – texts and shit, email, you name it – that they shouldn't. Don't get me wrong, I was *foolish* trusting that man – well, I say man, but he ain't no man – but what I sent him wasn't even that bad. I've known other girls send much, much worse stuff. Look at Tulisa (*a singer and TV personality whose ex-boyfriend released an unauthorised sex video that went viral*).

I do try to brazen it out, if I'm honest. I was really humiliated by that. Words can't describe how I felt then and how I feel now. It wasn't anything like me giving a man head. But it was me in different poses, some in my underwear, some half naked, one naked. There were nine pictures in all. To be fair, we'd been dating quite a while and sleeping together and that. I trusted him. One evening, I sent him, like, a funny, cute little picture of my cleavage from when I was watching TV in my PJ's and things got out of hand. As soon as I'd done it, I had this weird feeling. Like, something was going to happen. But what can you say? I thought he loved me and I thought I loved him. And we had trust. He swore on his mum and Jesus's life that he wouldn't show anyone, which shows what a piece of shit he is.

That morning was the *worst* day of my life, I'm not gonna lie. My phone was vibrating next to my head and I thought I was dreaming. My friend Lulu was all hysterical and saying all this shit. To be honest, she freaks out over bare shit, so I wasn't that worried. She once had a meltdown that she'd lost her tampon inside, you know, but then realised she hadn't even used one that day. But as soon as she said 'naked pictures' my heart just stopped.

Daniel had sent my pictures to two of his boys. He tried to make out like it was an accident, but it wasn't no accident. And I swear on my life, it was like when we watched this film about germs spreading in food technology. My phone was going mad, with texts, people slating me, I was getting messages from people I didn't even know, I was getting my own pictures sent back to me. You cannot imagine how that feels. I've never been so scared as anything as I was by Snapchat that day.

I started screaming and my mum came in to see. She went fucking crazy at me later, but she was OK that day. Left my baby brother with my older brother who was still in bed, because he works nights, and he was all standing there in his boxer shorts, with his hair all mash up going, 'What the fuck is going on?' and I'm all screaming and crying. He went mad later on, too. Mum went into school and by all accounts stirred up bare shit. Lulu told me you could hear her in the economics room, which is two corridors away from our form room.

I don't like my school that much, but they were pretty all right about it. They got the police in and they scared everyone by telling them that passing on the pictures was sharing child pornography because I was under eighteen, and they were committing some crime. That scared people, I think. Some people were more sympathetic than you might think. Others were as bad as you might think. And worse.

I took two weeks off school. I was in a really bad way, and I had to be given these tablets to calm me down. There was a lot of involvement from the school and the police. I had to see this social worker and this counsellor who was a fool. Kept asking me to do all these pointless questions, which weren't going to change the fact that most of the school had seen my tits.

Luckily, word got around about what happened to Daniel. The police came to ask us about it, especially Mitchell, my older brother, but he'd been at work all night (*smiles*). I know violence isn't good, praise Jesus, but I feel no badness about that at all. He deserved it.

It did die down. But it doesn't go away. It comes up all the time and I'm scared that it might come up in the future at a job interview, or at college next year or any time. I definitely had to grow pretty thick skin and if anyone says shit, I just front it and they usually back down or shut the fuck up.

RAJ, 16, ABDI, AND JAWAD, 15, NORTH LONDON

All admit they have never read a book for pleasure, and the only books they have read have been at school. The only book they all liked was Holes *by Louis Sachar, although they found* Romeo and Juliet *'sort of OK'. When we calculate, they accrue over 250 hours a week between them online: gaming, on tablets and on mobile phones. However, they also point out that they 'almost never' watch the traditional television set and so this also includes all television and film watching.*

ABDI: Do you know what I found out the other day? That the internet used to not exist. I didn't know. My mind was all, da fuck?

RAJ: You're such a fool. Of course it didn't use to exist. Mobile phones used to not exist. That's jokes, man. Can you imagine no mobile phones? How would you even talk to people?

ABDI: With your mouth. But nah, man, the world would be so shit without all the stuff we have. Like, a lot of our teachers are all negative about it and say it is sucking our brains out. But that's bullshit. I was gaming with this sick guy in Columbia last night. He told me all this shit about Columbia that I didn't know from geography. That's educational. And he told me he'd gangbang my mum and sisters. But that's just gaming talk. You cuss each other to the max. It's psychological banter, innit? You wanna get them all pissed off with you, so they lose.

JAWAD: Gaming is so sick, but the problem is, you lose *hours*. You look and the sun be coming up. And you're like *shiiit*, I gotta go to school in an hour. I'm always late for school. My form teacher thinks I'm on drugs.

RAJ: My mum stopped me gaming. Said it was polluting my brain. To be fair, she was worried for ages that I was talking to myself and, like, insulting myself. She was glad I wasn't that disease where you have two personalities. But then she went mad that I was talking like that to strangers. Said it would bring dishonour to our family. I was all, 'Mum, they can't even see you. They don't even know your name.' But she just couldn't get her head round it and threw my headset in the dishwasher and turned it on. I was pissed.

ABDI: Your mum is scary. She always asks me how my studies are going like she's really saying she wants to kill me. And she has these crazy eyes.

RAJ: Shut up, man. And least she isn't Tank Woman.

JAWAD: But that's the best thing about technology and shit. Parents don't know shit. Like, I've sent my mum emails from an account I opened with the email address containing the words 'Secretary' and the name of my school saying school is going to be closed tomorrow. And she believes them. My dad knows even less. He grew up without electricity.

RAJ: That's a sick idea. It wouldn't work for me, because my brother would snake me and then my mum would bash my head in.

JAWAD: I hate your brother. He's such a dickhead. Do you remember when we caught him watching porn? With his hand around his dick? That was proper jokes.

ABDI: The other good thing is all the free films. YouTube, Videoweed, Project Free. You can watch stuff when it's out at the cinema. I've never been to the cinema. It's too expensive. Especially when it's free (*on the internet*).

JAWAD: The cinema is sick. Especially the IMAX cinema in London. I went to see the *Batman* movie there about six times. It was siiiick.

RAJ: Batman is sick. If I could be anyone, I'd be Batman.

ABDI: Yeah, but his women are all ugly. That woman in *The Dark Knight* looked like a hamster. He's Batman. He could have Kim Kardashian and Nicki Minaj. And Beyoncé. Even though she's *old,* she's still fit. Better than Rihanna who looks like my uncle.

JAWAD: Yeah, but they're not actors, you idiot. Batman isn't real.

ABDI: I know. But if I was *playing* Batman, I would choose my own women. I'd have them line up and show me their asses.

RAJ: True 'dat.

ABDI: You're never going to be asked to play Batman. More like the Somali Mr Bean.

SIMRAN, 15, CHARLIE, AND SCARLETT, 14, SCARBOROUGH

All three girls confess to being 'hardcore Directioners': they spend all their free time and money on the band One Direction. It is, however, technology that facilitates their obsession. Through a network of online fans, Twitter, Instagram, etc. they reckon they 'know the movements of the group at any given moment about 80 per cent of the time'.

SIMRAN: I like Zayn.

CHARLIE: Niall.

SCARLETT: Some days Harry. But mostly Liam. That's why we're such good friends. It'd be hard to share the same guy. Really hard. I stopped talking to my best friend for good when she started to like Liam. He's mine.

SIMRAN: Totally. My brother said Zayn was gay. So I punched him in the face. Nearly broke his nose.

CHARLIE: I didn't do that. But this boy sitting next to me in class was talking shit about the boys so I stabbed him with a compass. And hit him in the balls. I got suspended but it was worth it. Luckily, my mum is a *huge* Directioner too. She's basically Granny Directioner. That's what we call her. She's wicked, though, because she drives us everywhere we need to go like concerts and their hotels and stuff. She's pretty great for a mum.

SIMRAN: She is. I sometimes think she's more obsessed than we are! She has the boys' pictures up all over her office. It drives Charlie's dad mad. But more than anything, I can't imagine how anyone was a fan of bands in the olden days.

SCARLETT: It *is* quite complicated how it works. But the number of Direction fans really helps. Here, look at this list (*she shows me a list of about 100 names*). These are all the people it's my job to monitor on Twitter, Instagram, Facebook, Pinterest, Keek, YouTube to a lesser extent, any fan pages, their official website – although that isn't actually that helpful – and loads of other things. There's four of us in the group. Ella couldn't be here. And basically, the people we monitor are anyone connected to the group. The boys' mums, their hairdressers, friends, personal assistants, wardrobe designers. You name it. You can pick up so much about the band from all those things. Like if somebody spots Harry's PA in, for example, Manchester, the likelihood is, he's in Manchester. This info will go out and then you start watching all those people associated with the band in that area. We know in just about any place in the world where all the band members' favourite bars, salons, clubs, gyms, hotels, hairdressers and everything else. I know more about Liam's life than I do about my own brother.

CHARLIE: And we are all constantly connected by our phones. I probably send and receive about 5,000 band-related texts, tweets, updates, emails, pictures and that a day. Me and Simran were going to come up with this plot that Simran was dying of cancer and shave her head and tweet the band about it, but we decided that might be a bit extreme. Especially after that nice boy died. And the other problem is if they respond. Cancer is quite a hard disease to keep up with, you know. But you know, I've known loads of girls who have tried that. There's this crazy girl I know who tweets Zayn about ten times a day to tell him she's been raped. I mean, at least make it believable. Who gets raped ten times a day?

SIMRAN: Yeah, some fans are stupidly obsessive. Especially on Twitter.

CHARLIE: I could just eat Niall. I'd literally sell everything I own to just get him on his own. What do I want to do with him? Hang out. Make out.

Do you want to have sex with the boys in the band you like?

SIMRAN: No! Zayn's not like that. He's a strict Muslim. I think it would be quite traditional with him, which I like. It's never going to last with Perrie (*Edwards, from the band Little Mix*). She looks all used up. But we're not as lucky as Scarlett. She got retweeted by Liam. We screamed so much, her next-door neighbour called the police.

SCARLETT: That was the best day of my life. Apart from when I meet Liam and obviously when we start dating. Getting retweeted by him will never be matched by anything. Not when I get married, have a baby. Ever. Unless it's to Liam. In which case, Twitter will be less important because I'll be able to text him.

CHARLIE: And have sex with him.

SCARLETT: Well, obviously. But wouldn't it just be the best thing ever to have his number? Other girls would hate you so much. You could rent it to them for proper money.

SIMRAN: I don't think that's what a wife would do. You wouldn't need the money. You'd be rich if you were married to Liam.

SCARLETT: Oh, yeah. He's the *best*.

JOHN, 18, GREAT YARMOUTH

Unemployed but received a substantial medical negligence payout when he was a child due to an operation that went wrong, which he mostly lives off along with state benefits. Says he 'lives for technology and especially Apple'. Will travel to London and queue for every new Apple product released. Spends most of his money on the newest tech gadgets and spends 'every hour I am awake' hooked up to technology. Also admits to 'really enjoying' trolling as a pastime, targeting celebrities on Twitter and individuals in chat rooms, social media and news sites.

Technology is my life. I could tell you detailed information about every single gadget on the market. Good points. Bad points. Function. I'm like *Rain Man* when it comes to Apple, especially. I've been really pissed off with all the HTC vs Apple debate recently. All these HTC fans have been acting like they invented the wheel. Apple was there first, and will always be the best. You can't just take the vision and drive of Apple and claim it as your own. But HTC users get well shitty when you challenge them online, because they know they are inferior. Apple is king. Apple will always be king. Steve Jobs is God to me.

Why do I queue for Apple stuff? It's the thrill of being first to hold that new product in your hand, before everyone else. To leave with that new product in your hand, and everyone else is looking at you from the sidelines all jealous, like. I love being able to be one of the first people to get on the review sites and tell the people all about it. My thoughts and feelings. These products matter to everyone. There is no one, but old people, who don't care about their mobile phone or whatever. It's a part of you. I don't feel quite as passionately about my laptop and tablet as I do about my phones. Phones are my real passion. I have all my phones displayed in a glass case that I've had all lit up. It looks sick. It's the one place I won't let my mum clean.

How would I feel if I lost my phone? I can't describe it. It's never happened to me. People who lose them are just stupid and irresponsible. You wouldn't lose your kid, would you? Well, people spend as much time with their mobile phones, don't they?

It's one of the things I'm most excited about in the future. To see what they come out with. I keep sending my CV to Apple, but they haven't got back to me yet. It's their loss. I would be their greatest asset.

I'm not saying I troll a lot. I wouldn't even call it trolling as I'd never make a death threat or anything like that. That's horrible. I do it more for a laugh. Especially when I'm well bored. I think a lot of celebrities deserve it, because they are so up themselves. I wouldn't bother with big celebrities like Pharrell or the Kardashians because I don't reckon they even do their own Twitter accounts. But right muppets from, like, *TOWIE* or silly slag WAGS and a lot of footballers and those types do. And they react. I often call Lauren Goodger (*a reality TV star*) a dirty, fat whale and that, because I know she'll see it and it'll upset her. I've had some wicked online arguments with celebrities. They deserve it. I'm always trying to wind up Gary Lineker. He hasn't responded yet, but he will. He is such a mouthy prick who loves himself. How do I know this? It's obvious. Just look at the shit he comes out with. It's like, mate, you're a footballer, not fucking Einstein, you know what I'm saying?

Ask FM is wicked for a row. You get all these silly cunts,

especially girls, who are definitely up themselves and just digging for compliments. They just want everyone to tell them they are all gorgeous and perfect. So somebody says, 'You are fat and ugly and should kill yourself and your mum for that ugly face,' they just meltdown. It's well funny. And there's nothing anyone can do. All this policing the internet chat is total shit. It'd be harder than policing the entire universe and sea. That's how big it is.

My goals are definitely to work for Apple and Google. I'd be like the Willy Wonka of phones. I've got all these mad, wicked creative ideas for their products. I'm very secretive about them, because intellectual property theft is a growing crime. My mum looked at them once and I went spare at her. I love my mum, but she's not having my ideas either. I'm going to be the next Steve Jobs for sure.

RITA, 15, BRISTOL

A long-term illness has kept her off school for long stretches throughout her childhood. She says the internet has kept her 'sane and feeling connected to the outside world'. Two years ago she developed an interest in eBay. She realised that there was a high demand for unusual, rare and vintage Barbie and Sindy dolls and products. With the permission of her dad, she started buying and selling these products. She is now so successful, this hobby can make her hundreds of pounds a month and she is about to launch herself as a sole trader with the help of her parents and older brother.

I know the internet has downsides, but it's been a help to me all my life. Do I have to tell you about my illness? – because I find it embarrassing, but it leaves me very poorly a lot of the time.

When I can't be at school, I can FaceTime, text and Skype with my friends. Sometimes they'll even Skype whole lessons for me, so I can watch them. Sounds crazy but I miss lessons and school so much when I can't be there. I have a tutor, but it's not the same. School is an experience you can't just fake. It's even worse now, because everyone has started their GCSEs and I'm so sad about how much I'm missing.

Both to cheer me up and to help me with my school work, Dad bought me an Apple Mac three years ago. Before that I had a crappy laptop. This is brilliant.

I've always had a real interest in business and numbers. And I love fashion even more. I excel at business and textiles at school. And I've always loved dolls. Not so much in a girly way but in a high fashion way. Both Barbie and, to a lesser extent, Sindy have had a very important impact on fashion over the years. Barbie really is the original supermodel, but she doesn't age! She's perfect.

I was watching the *Antiques Roadshow* really sick one day with Mum and they were talking about the value of classic toys and especially dolls. The next day I started looking at eBay. There was so much stuff on there, and because I have a good eye, I could just tell what was good and what wasn't. And besides I don't want to give away too many tricks of the trade (*laughs*).

My dad and I agreed a limit and worked out a profit and loss margin. The first thing I sold, I made £60 profit. Just like that. Now, I know everything there is to know about the doll business. I know all the good online auction houses, especially the more fringe ones.

When I'm well, I go to junk shops, charity shops, markets, car boot sales, jumble sales. You name it. The best thing I got yet was this proper 1960s Barbie Dreamhouse for £4. Me and Dad are just having it fixed up and I expect I'll be able to sell it for a *lot* online. This business is a gold mine. I want to go into other toys and become an online millionaire by the time I'm nineteen.

Class

MILLIE, 15, NORTH-EAST LONDON

Lives with her mother, (occasionally) her father, three brothers and half-sister. Her family lives on state benefits, though her two older brothers will supplement this with 'other business'. Money remains extremely tight and she has always qualified for free school meals. She has never been abroad or on a plane, or to a festival, live gig or art gallery. She has been to the theatre several times with her school, which she 'loved, especially the Globe'. Her favourite music artist is Drake.

I was watching *Made in Chelsea* the other day, which I know is a load of shit. But it is entertaining. But I suddenly realised how rich their life is because they are so rich. You know what I'm saying? I know it is TV and stuff and exaggerated, but their London is so different from the one I know. Most of London isn't available to you, if you don't have money. And that's the truth.

Being mixed race, I do struggle a bit with identity. Not really in the sense of experiencing racism or anything like that. This is London. But I do think somewhere inside of me, there are two people trying to get out. There are definite big differences in the identities of black girls and white girls. And even more so, with boys. I like the grime scene, but I find it too intense. Or tense. When you go there, there is so much tension. Things can erupt any time. People are always carrying. Weapons and shit. The girls can be even worse. But it's still fun. Especially the music. But then, two years ago, we went to see this play at the Globe where Shakespeare performed. It was a really warm night and it was early evening. We went with our drama class, which is small, and all the teachers on that trip were so safe. It was, like, one of the best nights of my life. There were people of all kinds. And everyone was just laughing and having a really good time. The play was amazing. I *love* that part of London. All lit up on the river. It's a world away from where I come from. I want to live there one day. Definitely. It's my goal.

There is a romantic ideal attached to estate life, in films and TV, for real. Most of it is bullshit. Like, yeah, you do know a lot of people and from time to time people look out for each other and stuff. But mostly it's people fighting more than bringing each other cakes. What do people expect? It's thousands of people living on top of each other. Almost all of them are panicking about money 24/7. You see bailiffs around here a *lot*. There's a lot of gangs, violence, a *lot* of drugs. People aren't all putting their paddling pools together and having pool parties in the summertime. It's mostly a fairly shitty place to live. If you open your window at night, especially if it isn't cold, you can hear arguments, fighting, cars getting jacked, people cursing, especially the boys, what I call junkie sounds, you know, like moaning and stuff. I've heard gunfire enough times, though it's mostly boys trying to be gangster. Or I hope so.

I have mixed feelings about drugs. My mum has struggled a lot with addictions. She's definitely not a full-blown addict, but she's *way* too keen on bad drugs. She dabbles sometimes with drugs, but her and Dad will go on terrible binges sometimes when he comes home. I don't really want to go into too much detail, but horrible things have happened as a result. Neighbours have called social services and the police.

She can't really afford it, but if it's on offer, she'd take coke 24/7. When my dad comes home, it's usually if he's either completely run out of money and needs somewhere to stay or has suddenly made a whole load of money and wants to bring us presents. The presents are nice, but he will always bring shitloads of drugs with him. Coke, weed, booze, you name it. They'll get smashed for two days straight and then there is always this blazing row when they run out and one of them will get all paranoid and something bad will happen. Dad threatened to stab the next-door neighbour last month when they complained about the noise and the police were called. It was horrible. We were panicking about social services, because Mum and Dad were in such a state and that. But so many people around here are in the same boat, I think it's hard for social services to do anything.

My eldest brother is safe. He's my rock. Every single man around here wants to be a DJ, but he actually makes legit money out of it, doing parties and raves. I got really upset when I saw him last. He has promised to help me more and I told him how much I wanted to go to Venice. We did this massive project at school about the Venetian balls. And I saw it on *Made in Chelsea*. It was one of the most beautiful things I ever saw in my life. I know it's a small dream and you have to dream big. But I just want to see these for real, *so bad*.

He has promised me he is going to save some money from his next gigs and take me. To actual Venice! We're going in 2015! Just me and him. I cannot *wait*.

KATHERINE, 16, KENT

Comes from a 'very wealthy' family. Was born in South Africa and has also lived in France and the United States. Attends a £30,000-a-year school. Is 'obsessed' with sports, particularly athletics, and is 'semi-obsessed' with music, attending many music festivals. Has never taken drugs of any kind as she thinks they are 'vile'.

This whole notion that very wealthy kids are all attending the opera every night and going to polo matches is absolute crap. There is some of that, of course, but cultural sophistication is dying fast in the upper classes. Like everything else in England, it is about getting wasted and being seen with celebs. I could tell you some absolute horror stories about so-called culture amongst the really rich. I hate it. There's loads of talk about council-estate kids acting antisocially or what have you. Like the girl giving head to all those blokes in Magaluf, was it? The same things happen in Muscat. Rich kids are just as badly behaved. Or worse. Not all of them. But a lot of them. They make those absolute twats in *Made in Chelsea* seem tame.

One of the big problems, and there's no getting around this, is all the new money. The HUGE new money. Particularly the Russians – the Chinese are very conservative. They are so moneyed, they make my family look poor. They have *billions*. Not millions, but *billions*. They want their sons to be playboys and their daughters to be these kind of trophy wives. That might be OK in your twenties, but it just doesn't work at school. These guys are coming into school and on free week-ends, when we can go home, they throw these totally lavish parties at their penthouse flats in places like Knightsbridge and Chelsea. I've been invited to a few and I stopped going because they are so awful. They are absolutely full of cocaine and they hire *actual* hookers. I went to one, where they had a medical team in one of the bedrooms for anyone who got wasted and OD'd. I don't think anyone OD'd, but plenty went far, far, far too far. There were girls in my *classes* and the year above getting naked, French kissing each other for the guys. It was completely gross. And then we have to all go back to school on Monday and face each other. It's fucking hideous.

I haven't spoken to one of my best friends since one of those, she behaved so awfully. I still can't look her in the eye. But she was off her face on coke that one of the Russian upper sixth plied her with. She was fifteen at the time.

If you're wealthy, everything is always about charity. Charity polo matches, galas, dinners. But you just know people don't give a toss about the causes a lot of the time. I know several girls that will go to any event that Prince Harry might be at. He is pretty much the Holy Grail to these girls. I'd detest being married to a royal. Don't get me wrong, I do think charity is really good. I climbed Mount Kilimanjaro last year for this charity expedition. But it is a bit hard to take these events seriously when people are there for the free champagne and doing coke in the toilets. My point is, drugs, bad behaviour, entitled behaviour: it's so universal. And has nothing to do with class. The upper classes are just as badly behaved. I know a lot of the focus has been on the behaviour of bankers, but a lot of this is started, encouraged even, in elite schools and universities. My older brother has two friends who are in the Bullingdon Club at Oxford, and when you hear the stories, you just think, 'And these people are going to run the country one day?' It's completely shocking.

My saviour is definitely sport. I'm obsessed with it. I get up to train every day at 5 a.m. and practise again after classes. It keeps my head really straight and I can't drink, really, and certainly never smoke. I'd say smoking is a thing that has definitely died with my generation. Almost no one my age smokes. Except the foreign kids.

Music is another huge love, although I think it is quite sad that you have to have money now to actively follow it. I've been to Glastonbury twice now and spent thousands both times. We went in the VIP bit and hired this totally cool Winnebago. My dad got us pretty much Access All Areas passes, so God knows how much they cost. Once you'd figured in clothes, food and alcohol, as well as the ticket price, it's a really expensive weekend. But it was *so* worth it. It was one of the best weekends of my life. I was a little bit young the year before and found the whole thing a bit intimidating.

My friend Mark who is in a band – one of my few friends who aren't wealthy – says music has gone against the very 'for the people' principle it once had. And that it's essentially now made by posh kids for posh kids. At first I didn't agree with this, but then you think about the price of gigs, the price of instruments even; I don't think many kids whose parents are on benefits could afford it. Which is just really sad.

MATTHEW, 18, MANCHESTER

*Comes from a single-parent family with 'absolutely fuck-all money'. At thirteen, he won a full scholarship to an elite private school. Despite achieving three A*s and one A grade in his*

A levels and having wide extracurricular interests, he was rejected from a top British university. He received several scholarship offers from American Ivy League universities and is starting at Harvard to study economics in the autumn.

Look, I'm not about to slag my school off at *all*. Winning that scholarship was one of the best things to ever happen to me. It has changed my life for the better. And I wasn't some Eliza Doolittle with a penis. It *was* a huge culture shock going there, from literally a shithole council estate in the shittiest part of Manchester, to an institution that has knocked out more prime ministers than my neighbourhood has criminals. But the school were great. A few of the people there obviously thought I belonged with the hired help. Or the teachers, which some kids would actually call the 'hired help'. But I'd say 90 per cent of the kids were great. And I made a big deal, like a lot of noise, about being a scholarship kid, because I never wanted to hide. I never wanted people to think I was ashamed of where I come from. Because I'm not.

But I *am* allowed to talk about class, because I've been at both ends of the table. And we need to have a very big conversation about class, because after religion, I think it is the most destructive thing in the UK and many parts of the world. People laugh about it being some British hang-up, but that's bullshit, man. How can it be, how should it be that by virtue of just how you were born gives you so much or so little in life?

The other thing I will readily say is my school were great to me. But upper-class kids are instilled with not just a privilege – which is one thing – but an idea they are just *better.* It's not really their fault. It's an economic trick. Debt and money worries make people more subservient. Anxious all the time.

Passive. Skint people don't go throwing themselves around the world going, 'Look at *me*!' They don't have the time. Being poor is fucking time-consuming and from a really young age, you totally assimilate that sort of behaviour. It's fucked up. But you don't notice it just in yourself, it's everywhere you live. It's bleak. I think kids from the poorest families start to lose that 'anything is possible' shine from the age of nine.

Rich people have problems for sure, but they don't have the weight of the problems of poor people, do you know what I mean? Once you've observed one and then the other, it is as obvious as obvious can be. How can poor people really rise up if they are that tired and hungry just from being poor? And I use hungry in a funny sense. Because there wasn't, and I'm not kidding, one fat kid at my new school. The food there was bland, totally nutritious and plenty of it, but not too much. Loads and loads of fruit and veg and lean meat and fish. It's one of the first things I really noticed the first summer I went home. How many overweight kids there are now who come from poor families. It is definitely a poor disease. It's also to do with how much sport you play. And listen, that's another reason my passion for football will never die and why it means so much to working-class kids. It's one of the things they feel is left for them. That they can aspire to even if they are some black kid from Moss Side who fucking hates school. I know football has its problems. But I definitely think it offers the working class hope still. And not just those who want to play it. You can point at all those players and know they aren't there because they went to the right school. In fact, very few did.

One of the things that was most important to me was keeping my accent. It definitely gets less noticeable in term time and I go back and all my mates call me 'the fishmonger'. I'm not sure why a fishmonger would be a Manc, but that's OK. It is meant by them affectionately. Quite a few of my best mates travelled back home with me and were, I think, genuinely moved by the poverty all around. And it isn't relative poverty, but actual poverty. These are people struggling to live, where I live. In the house I live in.

One of the big parts of the problem is the now total lack of mobility between classes. Even more so than at almost any point historically. At least they used to have us in their fucking houses working for them, though I very much doubt it was very *Downton Abbey*. I mean, even kids in the middle stick with kids in the middle. Yeah, it *is* like class inbreeding. And again, if everyone just experiences what they already are, how easy is it going to be for anyone to change? That's why I'm such a freak.

So when I decided to go for these universities and you don't have to be a genius to work out which one, my mentor suggested, even for the day, I drop my northern accent and try to sound a bit more southern, I guess. I know some people will say – what's the bloke who cut his own throat? – yeah, it was a Pyrrhic gesture, me not doing so, but I am who I am. I think my working-class, poor-as-hell roots should have made me more impressive. Nah. I know these things are designed to make you sweat a bit and challenge you. And I'm not being soft here, but both the people interviewing just went out to embarrass me. Made a huge thing about the fact I'd done so little travelling, that my language skills weren't up to it. Picked me up on my accent. Made some really crass joke about working men's clubs or something. I actually left that interview in tears because I was so angry. These are supposed to be about academics. Potential. Your ideas. One of them said he assumed I voted Labour but refused to expand on the point and wouldn't let me respond to it, either. Not surprisingly, I didn't get a place. Not even with my grades, my charity work, my music grades, my mentoring of kids in the community, the fact I spent all my holidays coaching kids back home.

So I've decided to study in America and have been offered really generous financial support. I've been told America *does* have class issues. Y'know, all the WASP and *Mayflower* stuff. But I feel like if I stay here, my background will limit me. Like I've definitely hit an academic glass ceiling and might find that in the places I want to work. I feel bad about it. Like I'm abandoning my roots, and people like me. But I'll come back. I'm studying economics at Harvard, so it's easier to blow off the glass ceiling from the inside than the outside.

ABDUL, 19, MANCHESTER

Was bought up as a 'fairly strict' Muslim in a first-generation immigrant family in Manchester, after moving to the UK when he was five. Said he was 'absolutely terrified of my father, my religion and all the important people in my mosque' where he spent so much of his childhood. When his father suddenly died from cancer when Abdul was aged sixteen, he said he was 'fucking overjoyed because Dad was a bastard'. Realising he had no faith, he asked his mother permission to give up Islam. She agreed provided he moved to London under the pretence of studying medicine. He now works in a bar and a restaurant owned by his good friend Lawrence. He continues to send money home to his family.

I still have dreams my dad is alive and when I wake up I feel nothing but relief that he is dead. I was so happy when he died. There wasn't any confusion. No mixed feelings. Nothing hidden. I hated him.

I don't really want to go into my problems with Islam. They are so many it is hard to count. Other people can explain them better than me. I'm not a scholar and I didn't do that well at school. I just want to give you my opinion on something I think is going very badly wrong that no one is noticing, because all the panic is over the religion.

But, yeah, my dad beat my mum ferociously. All the time. You create a religion where women have no power, no visibility, then you are creating a bad problem. Where can they go? You can't even see their bruises, because they are covered. I think my dad even saw that as a good excuse to beat my mum for any reason. He also beat me badly and my sister who is closest in age to me. He left my older brother alone, because he's scary. If I was scared of anyone more than Dad growing up, it was my older brother.

The biggest joke was that Dad was a huge drinker. He was definitely a functioning alcoholic and there were bottles hidden everywhere. In the garden, in the shed, in the fucking prayer room. My brother was the same. And he did drugs and was definitely having sex with white girls. As were all his mates. Even some of the Muslim ones. I still have some of the pictures on my phone of them skinning up and doing dumb stuff with massive joints. A couple of them definitely saw weed as a loophole. Muslims can't drink, so they get high instead. I could show you my Facebook page right now with loads of friends who are praising Allah one minute and talking about getting high or drunk the next in updates.

So here's the thing. My friend Lawrence who I work and live with is white. But he grew up almost the same as me. Poor; no money; violent, alcoholic father; beaten-up, scared mother; violent older brother. He grew up about twelve miles from me. Poor neighbourhood. Estate. Violence. Drugs. Poverty. Everything I saw, except I had the mosque and religion in my life, which was no comfort or escape for me. Just more fear.

And what happens to the boys or young men who grow up like that? They leave school. No qualifications. No job prospects. They get married young, have babies they can't afford. Claim benefits. Play violent video games. Take drugs, some weed, drink, get into trouble with the police. And a lot of them – maybe the better ones – join the Army. Lawrence says the Army recruit wherever there are poor kids.

And how do they think it is different for poor Muslims growing up in England? Believing in a religion doesn't pave the house in gold, or buy you a car, or make you able to afford a wife. It's all just still England and it's shit to be poor and there isn't much for any of us to do. Muslim boys have all the pressures that Western boys do. The lack of prospects, no money. I think this is where all the radical, extremist stuff starts to look appealing.

My dad died just as my friends were starting to think about that stuff and I already knew I had to go and leave. But these thoughts don't come from nowhere. There are callings, recruiting, talking-tos from those in positions of authority. I don't like Islam, but I want to say for the record, very few Muslims have any interest in becoming violent terrorists or extremists. But I don't think the problem is one of religion really but one of money and class. If you told a white boy from a shitty, violent background with no job prospects and whose only interest was smoking weed and video games that he could go somewhere, be someone important, rule over women, carry a gun, make some money, be in some sacred brotherhood, you think he wouldn't be interested?

I don't know. Maybe I'm wrong. But you take any white kid with a comfortable family who's going to Oxford University to study law and ask him to join the Army and go fight in Afghanistan, how interested do you think he's going to be? Not at all. Why would it be any different for Muslim boys? Immigrant families are still often very poor and have all the problems of the poor. It doesn't take a genius to work it out and yet nobody seems to have worked it out in this government at all.

You take a Muslim kid, stick him in Chelsea and give him a load of money, fast car and a pretty girlfriend. He's not going anywhere near Syria even if he's the most devout Muslim in the world. Trust me on this one.

NICK, 17, AND MATTY, 15, HULL

Nick lives with his parents and four siblings who are largely supported by state benefits and 'have been my whole life'. He wants to get on a plumbing course but the fact they are so oversubscribed, plus his admission that he's 'fucking disorganised', is making this more difficult than he realised. The fact he is under eighteen disqualifies him from any significant benefits at this time.

Matty lives with his stepdad and younger sister. He has an older brother currently serving time in prison for robbery. His mother 'isn't around at the moment'. He rarely attends school, except 'when social get involved and threaten fines'.

NICK: Girls are well lucky because if they need most stuff – a place, some money – they can just get pregnant. Loads do for that reason. Loads. I don't think it's all that bad, either. They give houses away for worse reasons. Why not for a baby?
MATTY: So get someone pregnant, you dickhead. You shag enough girls. I'm surprised it hasn't happened.
NICK: Nah. I'm more traditional than that. I actually want to get married and have a family with a girl I love. For the right reasons. My parents argue night and day. Proper screaming stand-up rows. But they got together in school when they were fourteen. My mum is older by eight months. She calls Dad her toyboy. I also think it's important to be able to support your family. It proper upsets my dad that he can't. He's one of the few around here always hustling for work and that. But there's nothing here. Nothing. But my parents definitely love each other. Especially when they're both pissed. It's one of the reasons I'm probably more on the straight and narrow. Loads of my mates are dealing, robbing and that. But Mum and Dad are all 'not under my roof'. I do bits on the quiet. But not anything like a lot of people around here. Look at Gary.
MATTY: Gary is such a wanker. He's my older brother. Serving three years. He robbed an off-licence and his getaway car wouldn't start. He hadn't put any petrol in it. Says it's all right inside, though. Less money worries. Bit like school, but better.
NICK: Yeah, I heard that. No one round here is that bothered by the law. Like, you're not going out to get lifted or anything, but everybody knows somebody's who's been inside. My

dad has. His mum and dad has. I nearly was, once, but got probation. It's hard to be legit when there's fuck-all to do and fuck-all money. I don't even think it's for crime a lot of the time, just for something to do. I nicked cars because it was cold outside and didn't feel like walking. And you see all the kids standing outside the same chippie night after night or down by the swings. They get bored. Act out. It's not like they've got money to go to the cinema. The kids here are a fucking pain in the arse. I'm sure they're worse than we were. Well foul-mouthed.

MATTY: I fucking hate school. Hate it.

NICK: I did too. Like, I definitely regret not working harder now. And there are some good kids round here going places. Who's that girl who's going to university? Some bloke who's a mate of my dad – his daughter is going to a really good university. To study something really weird to do with plants.

MATTY: Yeah, Sarah. Hopefully she can learn to make weed. She's as fit as. She's a lesbian, though.

NICK: No she's not.

MATTY: She is. My stepdad told me. Fuck knows how he knows. The pervert.

NICK: Your stepdad is just wrong, man. But anyway, there is no reason to stay in school. Especially with the lads. Nah, with everyone. I dunno why. I think it's 'cos we see our parents not get jobs and struggle with money. There's no for jobs for us. Crime seems to be the thing that pays. And benefits. I don't care what anyone says. If knocking out a kid and claiming dole gets you a better life, who's going to sweep streets or work in Morrisons? I did that for a month and it was shit. Dealing with proper wankers. If I could get some wicked job at, like, Xbox testing games or at the Playboy mansion, I'd do it, 24/7.

But I don't think there's any pride in stacking fucking shelves. And Mum and Dad can't say shit because they wouldn't do it either.

MATTY: Also, schools round here are shit. I mean the one I go to literally stinks of shit. All the teachers look like skagheads or like they're about to die. My sister, Rachel, cries when she has to go to school. She's six. Kids are supposed to love school at that age.

NICK: Even I loved school at that age.

MATTY: Yeah. It's just a bit shit, really. I can't stand school. I'm learning nothing. Just can't see the point. My stepdad has already started talking about the Army. I knew he would. I'm thinking about it. Maybe. I dunno.

NICK: You're mad. Prison would be better. Why go through all that just to defend a bunch of towel-heads who want you dead anyway? Bastards.

MATTY: Yeah, but I gotta do something. Just dunno what.

ALEXANDRA, 18, AND MAISIE, 17, OXFORD

Both describe themselves as 'middle class' without really seeming to know exactly what it means. Alexandra has just started her A levels at a sixth form attached to a heavily subscribed school near where she lives. Maisie up until last year was at a private school until her parents could no longer afford the fees after her father's business collapsed. She will be joining Alex at her sixth form. They have been best friends for twelve years.

ALEX: I've been told my whole life I'm middle class, so I guess I'm middle class. But I don't have a bloody clue what that means. Also isn't there lower, middle-middle and upper-middle? The whole thing is completely confusing. Both my parents are teachers. Actually my mum is a deputy head. I think middle is a fairly accurate description because we definitely can't afford private schools or fancy cars. We have a fairly nice house. I know my parents aren't up all night worrying about paying the bills. But at the same time, I don't think anyone is really rich now unless you're super rich. When I go to university, I'll have to take out huge loans. Which I don't think is fair. But it does make you think carefully about what you're going to do. No more media studies just for the hell of it, for us.

MAISIE: I agree. My brother is super clever. Got a First from Durham. Can't find a job for shit. It was in history. And no offence, Al, but he doesn't want to be a teacher. Which seems to be the only thing available to history grads at the moment. I think he had a vision of doing something Indiana Jonesy in the history world and writing a really cool book about it, which was a worldwide bestseller. Turns out, neither idea is a job and both are impossible. My uncle has spent eight years trying to get a book published. No dice. He's obsessed about it. Should just give up. And become a teacher, probably (*laughs*).

ALEX: That's totally what scares me. I don't expect life to be handed to me on a plate. But you hear more and more horror stories that aren't stories. They're real. I could tell you of at *least* ten friends – good degrees, good unis. There just aren't any jobs. It's like you either decide to be a dentist from about the age of two, or you're totally, totally screwed. I want to read English and I'm scared I'm going to end up in the same boat as Maisie's brother. Brilliant and unemployable.

MAISIE: I've told you. I think you should defer for a year and do an internship at a magazine or two. You might get offered some amazing job and there'll be no need. When you leave, you're going to have to spend about a year working for free, anyway. So why not do it now and save yourself about seventy grand? We're too rich for any help and not rich enough to be able to do university worry-free. My fear is I'll go to Manchester and spend most of those three years working at Costa and missing out on all the good stuff anyway. And then end up working in Costa afterwards.

ALEX: Are things still that bad?

MAISIE: Not great. My dad's consultancy firm went under finally three years ago. It had been doing really well and then it wasn't any more. Mum's a GP, which is fine, but there's four of us kids. Dad can't find a job. Doesn't know whether he'll be able to at nearly fifty. He's really down. I didn't mind the school. They hung on as long as they could. But we're going to have to sell our house too, which I'm really sad about. I grew up in that house.

ALEX: It is a great house. Even I'm sad about it. But Maisie's right. You feel like you can't complain. Especially when you see all those programmes like *Benefits Street*. But our generation feels so joyless. When you hear people talking about middle-class privilege and all that, it feels alien to me. I don't have a uni fund and a dad who can get me internships at *The Times*. And when you hear all the stories about our parents going to uni, and the whole three years being like Rag Week, whatever it was called, and renting a flat in Maida Vale for £30 a week with three other mates, it just sounds hilarious. Like another world.

MAISIE: Exactly. Especially now. We had a lot more money

when Dad's company was doing well. I think I could handle how much life has changed if we were still the same family. But we're not. And it shows how money is the basis of everything. My mum and dad used to get on brilliantly. Now they argue all the time. And not bickering. Really nasty, below the belt stuff. And Dad is all bitter and snappy. Everything you say to him, he takes personally and bites your head off. And he won't do anything. Just lies around doing crosswords on his iPad.

ALEX (*pats Maisie's hand*): Oh, babe.

MAISIE: And my little sister is acting like a total spoiled bitch. On one hand I get it. She had to leave a school she loved. She's on the waiting list for these three better ones, but everywhere good is packed to the rafters. She's going to this school she calls 'chavvy' and literally throws a fit every morning she has to go. Screams and cries. Threatens to stop eating. I just have a constant knot in my stomach that won't go away.

ALEX: I didn't know it was that bad.

MAISIE: It's horrible. I feel scared all the time. I'm not quite sure how things went so wrong, so quickly.

ALEX: It'll be all right. It seems like the entire world is going through a bad patch. We have no jobs, money, career prospects, hope or fun. But we'll be *fine*. (*They both laugh. Weakly.*)

PRITI, 17, NORTH-WEST LONDON

Moved to the UK from India when she was seven with her parents and younger sister. Her parents wanted them both educated in the British system. Her mother is a stay-at-home mum but has a degree in philosophy. Her father is a baggage handler at

Heathrow Airport. She attended a 'fairly rough' comprehensive school in London and gained a full scholarship to a private sixth form. She is going to attend Sussex University to study law.

I think people use their class and background and lack of money as too much of an excuse now. I went to a fairly rubbish school and all I ever heard was this self-pitying stuff about not being able to change anything, so why try? If everyone had that attitude, nothing is going to ever change.

My high school wasn't that good. It was OK and there were some very good teachers, but not that many. If you wanted to do well, you had to be really self-motivated. Seek out and do extra reading, go to the best teachers for tips and pointers. Do independent reading and projects. No way could my parents afford tuition, so I had to do it myself. My parents are very smart, but very busy. My dad works twelve-hour shifts and overtime, so it was all down to my mum for help. But I liked learning so much. It was such a gift, especially seeing real child poverty in India as a kid. So many kids dream of going to school there who can't.

The funny thing was, when I went to a much better, very middle-class, private sixth form, I realised these were exactly the skills they teach you and encourage. To think, to learn, to reason, to teach yourself. That isn't laziness, it's a lifelong gift. Most high schools aren't teaching you anything but how to pass your GCSEs. It's why so many people fall down on A levels. They are so different. My dad says it's like going from a pushbike to a speedcar. My dad has funny ideas.

But I think this is the problem. It's not just the school's fault, but they encourage kids to be scared and lazy. There's no focus on yourself. In good schools they make you do things. It is harder to learn an instrument than play on a PlayStation. It is more challenging to do a debating competition than to smoke drugs and lie about. Kids aren't leaving schools well rounded at all, and it is making them lazy and scared.

Everyone I went to school with I lived near. Many on the same street. We live in that kind of community. No one ventures very far and it is like a little bubble. A mostly poor bubble. I have friends my own age who live where I do and have never actually been to proper central London. Like the Tate Gallery, or the British Museum, or the West End. It is so stupid. And sad.

So do I think going to university is a middle- or upper-class thing? I do, yes. It doesn't have to be. But people who are born a certain way are too quick to accept this is where they have to be and I think this is very sad. I would think this would encourage people to work more. Some people even blame the government and say this is a conspiracy to keep the poor, poor. But no government is stopping you picking up a book and learning. That is free. Xboxes aren't. Poor people still have no trouble buying these, it would seem, and then they wonder why they aren't going anywhere.

My parents are very proud of me. A lot of my friends are pleased but scared for me that I am now going so far away to study. It isn't that far. The world is a big place. I want to see the world, become a lawyer and specialise maybe in immigration law or maybe in women's rights. I might come from nothing, but that doesn't mean I'll ever accept being nothing.

WILL, 18, 'LOTS OF PLACES'

Born into a 'very rich and titled' family and 'virtually forced to go to boarding school' by his dad, against the wishes of his mum. He hated boarding school and was expelled at age sixteen for drug-taking. Shortly after his mother died from breast cancer after a long struggle, he had a 'sort of moral epiphany' about his class status. He has now renounced the family wealth and traditions and is a very active member in a group dedicated to hardline class war, anti-politics and animal rights.

I know what everyone is going to think. That I'm a posh wanker who is having a living-in-a-squat phase before he goes to reclaim his millions and take his father's seat in the family business or whatever. And I could. I really could. But I'm not going to and here's why.

I was definitely a massive disappointment. My younger brother by just over a year – cunt that he is – had already pre-reserved all the good genes before he was even conceived. And he's pretty much been doing it ever since. You can almost take it, I guess, if your *older* brother is more handsome, taller, fitter, stronger, more athletic, more charismatic and a total hit with the girls. It's a hard pill to swallow then; I sympathise. I have friends who have to deal with that. But it sucks way worse if it's your younger brother, believe me.

I'm the weird, arty one. I'm not actually gay, but my dad was always calling me a 'fag', a 'silly little queer' and a 'wrong 'un'. And that was when he was in a good mood. The kicker is, Damian is also a dead nice guy. A bit bloody daft. But good-hearted. He got that from our mother, I think. It's also a bit humiliating if your younger brother has to defend you from your own dad. But he always did. From the time I was seven and he was about five. What a childhood.

I got sent to boarding school at aged nine. I was so distressed to be leaving home I couldn't breathe. I thought I was dying the whole journey. They'd probably put working-class parents in prison for distressing their kids that much, but if your parents have enough money, you can pay doctors to do pretty much anything. I've been exploiting it ever since. I've taken every prescription med going through the years. Our family doctor was always a generous man.

And my childhood was just this aching despair and longing for my mum and my home, which I loved. Dad was rarely there. Away doing all his evil corporate deeds. And I say that not just as the hippy I've become. There are few fabulously wealthy people that don't exploit an awful lot of people, often to death. Maybe none.

Me and Damian both just loved Mum. To this day, I have no idea why she married Dad. Damian loved school. Was brilliant at it. But I just spent hours and hours looking at the sky. I wrote her these long, pitiful emails and letters begging her to look at the same star or piece of sky and she'd send me endless presents: leaves from our garden, homemade biscuits, a scarf that smelled of her. I didn't want money and sweets and iPhones and gadgets like the other boys. I just wanted reminders of her. It was probably a good thing we were only allowed to Skype once a week when I was little, because I'd spend the whole twenty minutes sobbing, which would set her off and she'd have to whisper so my dad didn't hear and cut me off from her and yell at us both.

School continued like that until I was fifteen. To be fair, they did everything they could to engage me. When it was obvious I was completely shit at sports, they tried music. I was good at music but wouldn't try for them. I was and still am fairly academically gifted, but wouldn't lift a finger to try. I was just desperate – desperate to get kicked out. But again, Dad was a big enough donor to the school to ensure I virtually had to set fire to the headmaster before I got kicked out. Which eventually I did actually try.

It was a week before the Christmas holidays. I remember because they had pretty much forced me to be in the choir for the big production. It was just over two weeks before my birthday. Trust me to be born on fucking Christmas Day, so my birthday pretty much got ignored by everyone since day one. And you don't forget a day like that. I'd been called to the headmaster's office, which wasn't altogether unusual. He was always having me in for little pep talks and occasionally threat talks.

I went with the usual air of hostility and to my surprise Damian was also there in the waiting room next to the head's study looking entirely confused and fairly uneasy. It was his first year at the school and he was already shining.

To cut a long story short, we were being summoned home early, which ordinarily would have been cause for celebration. But not in this case. It turns out my mum was in the advanced stages of cancer, had been in swift decline since autumn and it was unlikely she was going to see Christmas. Dad had insisted we not be told as he didn't want it interfering with our studies and he 'didn't want the drama'.

She did make it past Christmas, but she died on New Year's Eve. Our main house is fairly far up in the north of England and it was snowing heavily from about 4 p.m. It was, to be fair, a picturesque day to die.

The cancer had turned her fairly far inside out by then. It

was pretty grotesque. But I spent hours and hours on her bed talking to her, playing Scrabble when she could and just looking at the snow. By six o'clock she was so weak she was whispering, and so I just held her hand and one of the last coherent things she said to me was to promise to be brave and stay different. She told me that she was proud of me and was glad I was born just the way I was. By eight she was in and out of consciousness. Damian just sat in the corner looking younger and smaller than he ever had. And at eleven, before all the fireworks, she died. I knew the second she died. I flew over to her and shouted, 'Wake up, Mum,' and Damian also started shouting, 'Wake up, Mummy, please.'

As this was all sinking in, all the fireworks started, but I never saw this as anything other than an insult.

I don't really remember the next few days. But on 3 January, Damian and I were sent back to school. There were still tears on Damian's cheeks when Dad waved us off in the car, on his fucking mobile phone. He cried all the way there, but braced himself as soon as we got near to the school. He'd already learned to do that at that age. He'll go far one day. Probably be PM.

I spent the next two weeks melting down in every way, and was of course sent to the head. I couldn't stand that look on his face as I sat down – part pity, part disgust. So I pulled out a joint and lit it in front of him and just sat there smoking it. The look on his face was impossible to describe. It was like when one of those huge chunks of ice fall off a glacier and explode. I was punishing the wrong person, but still. The icing on the cake was when I flicked the joint at him and it bounced on his desk in a shower of sparks.

They called Dad. Made him come, I think, because he rarely bothered. Mum came to most school engagements. He didn't say a word in the car on the way back home. Not a word. When we got home, he turned to me, tears in his eyes, and sort of half slapped and half punched me in the face. I've never been punched by anyone before, and certainly not by him. I actually don't really blame him. And then he just turned and walked away. I haven't seen him since that night.

I left for London to stay with some friends that night, in a right state. I'd love to say I don't have any class resentment. That I don't care. But I do. There is something wrong with a class that still encourages people to send their children away. It was my dad's sheer level of assholery that made him cruel enough not to let us be with our mum as she was dying and properly grieve. There is something wrong with a class that looks down on the poor, the weak, the sick, the bad at sports, the not-successful in business, or those who aren't beautiful or like the rest of their class.

A psychotherapist would probably tell me it is my father I hate and resent and they wouldn't be wrong. But he, for me, sums up all that is wrong with it. Which is why I want nothing further to do with the whole sorry lot of them. I'd rather be poor.

Crime

JAYDEN, 14, SOUTH LONDON

Studying for GCSEs. Has just been accepted into Mensa. Lives in a 'really cramped' flat with his mother and three siblings. He is particularly close to his older half-brother, Christopher, who he describes as his 'hero'. He worries every day about Christopher getting into 'bad stuff'.

We walk along the Southbank watching the various street performances. Jayden watches everything with a quiet curiosity, not really commenting on much. He has never been here before despite living so close to it. Eventually we pass a group of women with their arms in the air. All their armpits are unshaven. They are a campaigning group called Armpits 4 August.

Why are those women standing around with their arms in the air? They look really weird. I could understand it if it was a protest about something important, but it isn't. It's not like someone is holding a gun to their head with one hand and a razor in the other.

White people worry about weird things. If you stood around like that where I live, with your arms in the air, your biggest problem would be someone stealing the collection box. You wouldn't be worrying so much about your armpits.

Well, actually it's not a white and black thing. It's a rich and poor thing. If you can't afford razors, I doubt you sit around worrying about women's rights or whatever. My brother steals all that stuff from chemists because it's so expensive. At one point, we had to rely on our church for nappies for my baby sister. But sometimes when my mum isn't well and we don't go to church, we miss out on that stuff. I'm too embarrassed to go alone. So my brother steals it. My mum doesn't even ask questions because she knows he ain't buying them with money but she isn't that good at the moment, so she doesn't ask.

Things were really bad last month, so my brother had to steal food from Tesco and he got caught. He's going to court next month. Everyone on the estate knew, but everyone's got their own problems so no one really judges.

I get scared my brother is going to go further, though. Deal some drugs. Maybe make some proper money. Everybody knows if you want to make proper money, you don't make it stealing from chemist shops.

Everyone likes my brother. He's really funny, so people like to be with him. Even the police who arrested him said he was safe. They told my mum he was a really nice kid. He's really funny. He has really white teeth, like mine, and he is always smiling and chirpsing girls. And he always breaks up fights between people. Like one time this boy who lives near us had this argument with this other boy. It was stupid beef. Something to do with his mum's washing line or something. And everyone was getting tooled up and shit. Christopher talked everyone out of it and made everyone see it was up to the mums to sort it out. It would have been bad. I get sick of all the fighting but especially the knives and guns talk. People talk about them more, but I do see them all the time. I'm not sure he'd be the best gang member. I think they want people to be more aggressive than Christopher is. I don't think he could hurt anyone.

I watch out for him every day after school when I'm doing homework. I always worry if he's late. I can see him from a way off from my bedroom. It's easy to get in trouble, even if you are just minding your own business.

MARIANNE, 18, BRIGHTON

Unemployed and not in education. Last year, Marianne says she was raped at a party by two of her classmates. Three others filmed it and seven in total watched, although it wasn't put online. The boys claim Marianne was conscious and consensual. She claims she was not. There were no arrests made and no charges brought. Marianne was advised by the school that her position there was 'not really tenable' and was offered 'completely shit' external support in order to complete her exams. She did poorly in her GCSEs despite excellent predicted grades. Marianne previously lived in London. She has subsequently moved to stay with an aunt due to threats and a campaign of bullying. She now never goes online.

I definitely agree that boys are becoming more sexually aggressive. And what's that word? Entitled. Yes. I think a lot of boys think sex is their right and getting it is their right.

A long time before this happened, I would see loads of examples of this. There was a group of really popular boys and they would rate girls on Facebook according to looks and bra size, and then if they got with girls they would keep scores on how far they went, what they did, how well they did it and stuff.

They were so popular, if anything bad was said about the girls in our year – and a lot of stuff was said all the time – everyone turned against the girls. Or if they didn't, it's because the girls were part of their circle and were sort of their girlfriends and even though they would say stuff about them sometimes, no one would criticise them. Sexual bullying was a huge problem in our school. You just have to go there to see it. The popular and good-looking boys and their girlfriends run the show way more than the teachers.

I think a lot of the time, everyone else would put up with it because they thought they might get into their circle. They were all super popular and had everything going for them and everything at high school is about that. We live in a weird area. Or I did. Our school backed on to a really poor and really rich part of London. And because it has an amazing reputation academically, but isn't private, everyone was fighting to get into it. So they had this really uneasy mix of kids. Some who had nothing and some who probably thought they should be at private school and had money and some in the middle like me. And this often tended to keep everyone in three distinct groups.

Basically, everyone wanted to be with the richer kids. They seemed to be the best dressed, the sixth formers who had cars, the prettiest girls and did the best academically. Almost always about 80 per cent of the Oxbridge group being coached in Year 12 were made up of those types. I was really happy when I was told I was going to be put in that group in Year 11. I know it sounds bad, because I badly wanted to go to Cambridge, but I was most excited to be in that group with them. We had some initial meetings to talk about what was expected of us and that it was going to be really hard work. That's where I met Carl. The others sort of ignored me, but he was really nice and we started to hang around together a bit. He wasn't one of the really rich ones, sort of in the middle, but he was so good-looking and so clever, everyone liked him. Everyone liked him a *lot*. I was besotted. It sounds stupid, but when he friended me on Facebook, it was one of the happiest moments of my life. All the other girls in his immediate circle were really pissed off, but what could they do? I was sort of in by default. They had a lot of social scenes – parties, hangouts and stuff – and it was really different to what I knew.

My family is just sort of middling. Like nice. But quiet. My mum is a primary-school teacher. My dad works in industrial insurance. I have a younger sister. My parents aren't exactly shy about sex but it's not mentioned. I've never, ever seen either of my parents drunk. I've never seen them fight. They don't laugh all that much, but seemed pretty happy. This has really upset them, but they never yelled or cried or even fought.

But this lot were so different. I went to one party and the parents were there, giving us wine and letting everyone smoke on the patio. The mum even got a bit drunk and was laughing when she found everyone playing strip poker. Everyone was telling her to join in and I thought she seemed tempted, which was kind of gross, but in the end the girl whose mum it was told her to go away.

Carl's best friend, Daniel, was the really popular and really wild one. He was definitely the richest kid in school and everyone was intimidated by him, even the teachers. He used to properly flirt with the English and history teachers and they didn't seem to mind at all. They even seemed to like it.

He was always weird with me. He would say mean things to me in public and then be super lovely when it was just us. He'd hug me in kitchens at parties and then when people came in, he'd just start to be Daniel again.

He had a birthday party. His sixteenth. Everyone wanted to go. I wasn't having sex with Carl, then. I mean, we did stuff together, if you know what I mean, and he would tell me he loved me. But he said it was better for both of us if we didn't go public. Why? Because he said I had to wait to be fully accepted by the girls and he didn't want to cause me any hassle because some of the girls were jealous. He kept telling me to wait and wait even when I got upset. But it seemed OK, because everything was good when it was just us and he would tell me he loved me.

It's really hard to talk about that night and I don't remember some of it. But Daniel was really friendly straight away and was giving me these tequila and vodka drinks. I was really nervous and I was also upset because Carl was talking to this other girl, Denise, all night. I know Denise really liked him and she was like really, really pretty.

So I drank and drank and then things were a bit of a blur. I remember bits and pieces and then nothing. And then I woke up in a strange bed. Carl woke me up and said I needed to go home. He was acting really weird. Like . . . I can't really describe it. I'd been sick. And then Daniel's older sister came in and she helped me up and gave me some Pepsi to drink and said she'd rung a cab for me. I knew something was really wrong. I felt really wrong. Like, like wet and sore. I was crying now and asking what happened and Daniel's sister, I can't remember her name, said it was best I leave. That I'd already embarrassed myself enough and I should go before the parents got back. I was begging to see Carl again, but she said no and that it was probably best to go straight away. It's funny to think that's the last time I ever saw Carl again. My parents saw him once again with his parents at that last meeting at school with the head teacher. I couldn't face going to it.

Almost straight away the abuse started. On Facebook. I was called everything. A slut, whore, prostitute, gang-banger. And that was probably the best of it. The girls were the worst. I was so ill I just stayed in bed and watched the abuse get worse and worse. Everyone was saying it had been filmed and exchanging the film. That was a Sunday; I didn't know what to do. And then about 11.30 a.m., there was a knock on the door. One of the deputy heads had a daughter in the year above me and heard about what was going on. Luckily, that was just before everyone was on Twitter so it stayed relatively in the circle of school.

He was with someone, I think from social services. I had to tell them what happened in front of my parents. So then they had to call the police. A policewoman took my statement. I had to be physically examined. I thought that was the worst day of my life, but things got worse and worse.

I wasn't allowed to go to school that Monday, but I knew from a few of the friends that were still talking to me, everyone was told to remove absolutely all references to the party off all social media and if anyone was to show, share or discuss the films, there would be automatic expulsion. No one was allowed to contact me, supposedly. But they still managed to. I got hate mail in the post anonymously telling me stuff like to go and kill myself. People set up a Facebook page that got taken down called 'Marianne is a Dirty Whore' with hundreds of likes. My dad's car windows got smashed three times. Everyone was really nasty to my mum and she got asked to leave her bridge and book club by some other mums of the popular kids.

But the worst thing was everybody's story was against mine. It got to the point where I even wondered myself, but I'm telling you for definite, I was unconscious. I don't remember a thing. We spoke to a solicitor and they said we could press charges but a court case could be even worse for me than what I'd already been through. To be honest, I'm not even sure my parents entirely believe my side of the story.

Both Carl and Daniel got really good GCSE results and went on to do A levels at another really good sixth form together. And remained friends with everyone at our school. Last I heard, Carl got a conditional offer to Cambridge and Daniel got an unconditional offer to Loughborough because he is so good at sports.

I'm not sure what to do with the rest of my life. I feel like it's already over. I have thought about suicide, but I wouldn't do it.

LIPSY, 17, MELODY, EBONY, LAETITIA, 16, LEAH, ROCHELLE, AND KARIMA, 15, EAST LONDON

They are all members of a prolific all-girl gang. All girls admit to regularly using violence. They are a little more coy about their criminal activities. Melody is the undisputed leader of the group. They consider this to be both their home and their territory. All gangs are notoriously territorial and all the girls stick rigidly to what they consider 'safe areas'. They have all had brushes with the law, but all decline to go into detail about 'that business'.

EBONY: There are wifeys, girlfriends, skets and hood rats. We are called worse things, but let's not go into that. Wifeys and girlfriends are what you want to be. It means you're special to your man. You will get respect. If he is respected, no one will fuck with you. You also might get stuff. Good stuff. Presents and that.

MELODY: Yeah, but that's part of the reason we run our own crew. There's too much bullshit you are opening yourself to if it's all about your man. You need your own tings. Like we cross over, but no man tells me what to do. I run my own show. I've been on the road since I was nine. All that wifey stuff can go and get fucked. I'm nobody's bitch. I am the bitch.

ROCHELLE: And people are properly scared of us. Especially Melody. I don't think even boys would take us on. Definitely not when we're together.

MELODY: Road ain't much of a place for young 'uns. So you have to toughen up. I'm not saying the females are always any nicer or kinder. Some of the craziest people I know are bitches. Myself included (*she laughs*). And any notion anybody's got that we're all like maternal and look out for the young 'uns is bullshit. But you do look out for your crew and that's sort of why you join, y'know? Nobody – and I mean nobody – would last very long alone out here. (*They all nod.*)

EBONY: Innit. And that's the bottom line. Like you don't have beef with one of you, you have it with all of us.

MELODY: There are enough ways to deal with trouble. Deal with it, man. But physical stuff, you know . . . an eye for an eye. Like this younger girl we know was holding (*drugs*) and got robbed and all fucked up by these little hood rats. They were dealt with properly. It's all about the message and respect.

LAETITIA: There is no one ever who has been on the road that has never been in a fight and probably had a beat down. It's part of life, here. It's how you grow. How you learn to deal. And we've all seen some fucked-up things. Many, many fucked-up things.

LIPSY: Beatings, rape, robberies, murder ... you name it.

MELODY: Uh-huh. And there isn't any of that 'no violence against women' here either. I've seen enough man rough up women.

LIPSY: Some crews are really vicious. Like if they go after you, they go after everyone you care about. I knew a girl who had her baby brother—

MELODY: Shut up. Put it simply, you get what you give. I don't expect some *Wizard of Oz* life. But there are compensations. Lots of compensations.

What's the worst thing you've seen on the street?

MELODY: Gang rape. That's ... well, it happens.

LIPSY: Uh-huh. Probably the same. I've seen lots of stabbings. Loads. Shooting isn't as common as people make out. But that happens too.

EBONY: Rapes mostly happens to skets.

LAETITIA: No, it doesn't. We know lots of people it's happened to. And probably more who haven't said. But word gets out. Which you don't want. There has to be payback, so it goes on and on. Like a circle. A cycle.

ROCHELLE: I saw a nine-year-old kid stabbed once. That was a long time ago. It shook me up. His mum was a crackhead though so it wasn't surprising. Kids of crackheads ... shit sandwich.

MELODY: Yeah. Kids younger and younger rolling. Chump change. And it has a lot to do with drugs. And the fact there is no legit money. Lots of parents encourage the kids to bring money to the table any way necessary. Plus, you know kids are easier to slip under the radar and want to prove themselves younger and younger now. I'd say in a lot of ways, the violence is more severe with the young 'uns. Once you have your status, you keep it with your crew. But you don't need to prove yourself every five seconds, you know? But it's still a slippery ladder to climb. The person who has your back can as soon put a knife in your back, you know?

LIPSY: But as well as kids, I think it's definitely true girls are more violent than ever. We have to be—

LAETITIA (*interrupting*): Definitely! There's a double threat to us. Girls and boys. Beat downs, robbery, rape, gang rape, the law—

EBONY: YEAH, the law. We don't get no help. Feds hassle us and turn a blind eye if one of their own commits a crime against us…

MELODY (*interrupting*): Fuck the feds. You make your own laws. That's just our life.

MARNIE AND MAURICE, BOTH 13, YORKSHIRE

The day I meet these twins, they are collecting money with their Scout group for charity by washing cars and windows for people. Their dad is the local vicar and their mother is a trained music therapist. They both love their area and say they have never witnessed even a minor crime and have never met anyone who has committed one. One of the longest-serving local policemen is their godfather.

MARNIE: I think it's very important to be as active in your community as possible. Where we live still has a really nice small-town feel to it and every weekend there are different kinds of markets and in the summer there are fetes. My dad is a vicar in the local parish and he says a big part of today's problems is nobody looks after everybody just around them. If everybody looked out just for the people in their street, things would be much better. Like we hear in London how people are burgling their neighbours and setting fire to things and vandalising things. We were in primary school in the London riots and everyone was really scared it might come here.

MAURICE: I talked to my friend on Skype who moved to London and he hates it. He says it's so busy, people are on top of each other and always fighting. And how no one knows each other! He got his phone stolen at school and a girl got attacked in a park near him. That's bad.

MARNIE: It gets really snowy here in the winter, so people always check on each other, especially older people. I saw on the news that old people are really scared in London because their houses are getting robbed by people pretending to be the postman. I don't think any old people are scared here. I've never known anyone to get their house robbed. Especially by the postman. Ours is called Tim. He's been our postman since we were born.

MAURICE: Or their car stolen. My friend Jack, the one who moved to London, said their car got broken into because there was a shopping bag in it, and all there was in the bag was some bottles for recycling. But they had to break in and see anyway. That's how bad London is. Sometimes people say that London has so much crime because there are so many black people there, but I don't think that's true. Dad says it's definitely not true. He says that people rob and stuff because they are in pain and lost.

MARNIE: But not lost like you can't find your way home. Lost like you don't know where to go in life.
MAURICE: Definitely. That kind of lost. Probably because of all the drugs in London.

CHARLES, 19, SOUTH LONDON

Four years ago, Charles was involved in the attack of a schoolboy that resulted in grievous injury. Though not directly involved in the physical attack, he was one of the bystanders and one of the agitators of the rivalry between two different schools. He no longer has 'much contact other than on Facebook' with his old group of friends and hopes to become a barrister after university.

Schools are dangerous places now. Well, not all schools. Not the good ones, but most people don't get to go to those. You go to an average school in any city, but I guess especially London, and there is so much tension 24/7. School is not a place to relax and learn now for most kids. It's where you have to be on your guard at all times. I think if teachers knew what was being talked about and going on at all times, they would probably be more worried about working there.

It's everything, all day. I remember. You brush past someone in the corridor, look at someone funny in the canteen, even if you didn't look at them funny, you know what I'm saying? You're taking a piss and you have to be careful. You say something funny in class. You look at somebody else's girl the wrong way.

And all day, people are hanging around the gates. We had,

like, an on-site policewoman and some of those community police officers there at bell time, but there are a thousand kids in a school or more. You don't need a maths lesson to work that one out.

And like, if you have a beef – you know, like, words – with anyone, you might find they have their crew or cousins or older brothers or sisters come down to the school and wait to rush you or whatever. Actually, the girls were more up for bringing people down. Especially if they had boyfriends with a car. So, you call some girl a ho – which I never did – but suddenly you've got a car with her man after you.

And weapons. So many people bring knives to school. I knew some boy who said he had a grenade that he was going to bring into the school, but he was just full of shit, and we used to cuss him. I never saw a gun in school, but this boy in the year above got expelled and he used to hang around the school gates and the park near us if the school called the police on him. He used to show his gun and try to scare the little ones. There was something wrong with him. He wasn't right in the head.

But funnily enough, the few times everyone was, like, together, there was some unity against other schools. You ask any big school and I guarantee you, there is a rivalry with another school over something pretty stupid that seems important at the time.

We had a long, long-running rivalry with this school really close by. I don't know when it started, but it went right back to back in the day. My friend's older brother who's in his thirties said there were massive fights in the Nineties. But it was different then. You faced each other off if you met at, like, the bus stop or something. There still is a big McDonald's sort of between our schools and that was always a hot spot for trouble.

This was four years back, so it was well before Twitter was of interest to us; we were all about Facebook then, unlike now. But then, we were all about BBM (*BlackBerry Messenger*) and it was so easy to communicate with each other. Whenever there was trouble, it would go instantly viral in, like, seconds. And because everyone was linked, everybody taunted each other. If schools were like these places with boiling tension and stress, BBM or any kind of texting was like the match. You'd be getting all these texts in, like, some fucking maths class and you wanted to go mental and go fuck somebody up and everyone else was getting the same messages and everyone would, like, dash to the school fields to compare texts and discuss plans.

To be honest, I can't even remember, I don't even know what set it off that time. Maybe I never knew. Sometimes it was an argument over a girl. Usually a fight or a problem over money or thieving. Maybe someone just looked at someone else wrong or said something about their mum. But it was different that day.

It was really, really hot and had been all week and was quite near to the end of term, so everyone was fucked off and no one wanted to be there, including the teachers. All they did was put on DVDs or let us do what we wanted, provided we didn't bother them or fight.

Someone said that they were coming down that day all tooled up. Like a lot of them. The school went mental. Everyone was getting their hands on anything that could be used as a weapon. It was the only time most of us had ever taken an interest in school compasses (*laughs*). People were stealing forks from the canteens. The girls were getting together sewing shit from the textiles department, nail files, fucking sprays, you know, like deodorant. It was a mad day. But if I'm honest, it was good fun. We were all together and had a purpose.

But of course by lunchtime, the teachers had caught wind of what was going down. Word got out that we were going to be let out early and escorted home, but that never works because the school was massive. We also heard that they (*the other school*) were going to be let out late to stop us crossing paths. Texts were flying everywhere; girls were crying in the corridors, boys were comparing knives behind the stage in the hall. It was a mad day. At about 1 p.m. after lunch, the head has us all pulled in the hall a year at a time and says we were all going to be let out a year at a time. And that anyone who didn't go home would at worst be arrested and at best be suspended or expelled. Police had been informed; parents had been informed. But for a lot of us, our parents couldn't give a shit. As far as they were concerned, once we were at school, we weren't their problem. They were more fucked off we were being let out early. Initially, I think there were probably more complaints about that, than the fact their kid was walking around with a knife in his pants (*laughs*).

So I was in Year 10 and we got let out first. Year 11 had been gone by this point (*GCSEs finish in late June*) but they were well in and were all going to show up in solidarity. There was loads of police, but not as many as needed and loads of parents were waiting in cars. We made a show of walking home through the park, but the plan was to go back round and wait where we thought they would approach.

We were fucking humming. Like everyone was in the mood for a fight, y' know? It was a weird atmosphere. And it was so hot. A lot of people had tied their ties around their heads. More and more people started doing it. It was like our trademark. And normally everyone was *loud*, like on any normal day we'd all be swearing and cussing and yelling, but we were quiet.

We were walking up towards this train station where a lot of us caught the train. Walking out the station was a boy from that school. You know, you can tell immediately from the uniform? He took one look at us and just ran. It was such a stupid thing to do, because maybe if he hadn't or had gone back into the station, we might not have. And he ran to the dumbest place possible. Up over the bridge over the road. There was twelve of us. Maybe fifteen. It was no contest, really. When we got to him, we beat the shit out of him and he just dropped. I remember when I saw a boot go into his face – not mine – and it just sort of caved and blood spurted, I stopped watching. But by that time it was too late. Everyone had lost it. The last thing I remember is my friend pulling out a knife. He was definitely going to stab him. Thank God, and that's about the only thing I'm grateful for now, another mate of mine shouted something and pulled the knife back, really fucking up his hand and all cutting it and shit. It'd be a really different story, otherwise. There was blood everywhere and the boy was making this really horrible sound. We all just ran. In every different direction.

We all got arrested. The whole thing was on CCTV, because that bridge is a real hot spot for drug deals and a girl got raped there, I think.

He shouldn't have been at school that day. He'd already done his GCSEs. He was going in to drop a textbook off.

MELODY, 16, EAST LONDON

Gang member.

If you want to roll and be taken seriously, sooner or later, you have to do something hardcore to prove you are up to it. I had to organise the gang rape of a girl. Some bitch. No one important. What was the worst part? The sound isn't great. Almost always they scream. Then whimper. Then it goes quiet.

PAUL, 17, WOLVERHAMPTON

Left school with no GCSEs and no work experience, except a 'head full of criminal ambitions'. Started work at a warehouse for an internet supply chain, but hated the hours and lasted less than a week. He lives with his father and relations are strained. Has decided to join the Army after 'getting clean and fit'.

My old man found a load of drugs under my bed. Smack and coke. He knew I was dealing. Nowhere else to make money and I couldn't be bothered to steal cars and shit. Grew out of that and you can't much now anyway. There are no screwdrivers-in-the-ignition jobs any more.

He gave me a choice. He was either going to take me to the police or I had to enlist into the Army. I got in. I start next month. So I've stopped being a drug dealer and I'm going to learn to be a killer. Fucking great system, innit?

JOSEPH, AHMED AND JOYCE, ALL 17, MANCHESTER

Sixth-form students Joseph and Ahmed are a couple. Joyce is a good friend of theirs. Due to Ahmed's religion, his homosexuality is strictly prohibited. His family has no idea he is gay. Young gay couples still often receive negative attention and sometimes abuse and violence. Joseph and Ahmed think the fact they are an interracial gay couple increases the likelihood of this.

AHMED: Crime and violence are a huge part of every young person's life. I think in the past, parents worried more about their daughters. You know, sexual violence, rape and harassment. Which is a really big thing, of course. I feel so sorry for my sisters. They're not allowed to bloody do anything. My parents keep them virtual prisoners and it'll be that way until they marry. I mean, one of my sisters is eighteen!

But I think, especially in the last few years, there are as many threats to teenage boys. Part of being a man seems to be getting into fights and it seems to be worse than ever. Like, gang culture is really prolific here, and there is a double assault. Because they seem to be inherently violent for the sake of being violent, so they'll go round looking to beat someone half to death for fun, but also there's the element of robbing them. Mobile phones means there is likelihood you are carrying, like, a £400 device in your pocket, which makes everyone a target. If you get out of your teens without being mugged, you are a freak of nature.

JOSEPH: One of my mates was mugged by a bunch of eleven-year-olds last week. Insane. He didn't tell people that, though (*they all laugh*).

JOYCE: I don't know. The trouble is, sexual assault is still a massive threat to girls. From men. But girls are becoming more violent. I mean, my little sister who is ten is often telling me about little girls who are getting into fights. Girls are much louder than they used to be. Which might not be a bad thing. But with that comes violence. I'm not really explaining myself very well. But really loud girls seem to be the ones most likely to fight. Maybe. That's a really bad explanation.

AHMED: I know what she means. You see a big group who are talking quietly, you feel OK. You see a group being really loud; you know to cross the street. I mean, I'm reasonably small and look quite camp. Joseph is massive and with that comes two problems. People want to beat the shit out of me because I'm a 'queer Paki' – even though I'm not actually a Paki (*he laughs*). People want to take on Jo because he's massive, but usually in big groups. He got chased by a bunch of guys with fucking crowbars last summer. Can you imagine what would happen if we went around holding hands? We'd probably be killed eventually. Weirdly, people seem to have less of a problem with Jo and Joyce together and me as their little Asian hag fag. Everyone thinks they are together.

JOSEPH: I don't think that's entirely true. People in my experience seem to think that Asians can't be gay. There is this really horrible stereotype that Asian men are sexless. They think because I am black, I will fuck anything that moves, but if you are brown or wear a turban or whatever, sex isn't important. But he is right. We would be beaten senseless if we went around snogging. I can't come out. I'm sorry to say it but a lot of brothers are really homophobic and that's not going away. My ex-boyfriend who lives in London – who is also black – has been beaten up four times. He's really despondent about it. It's like two important parts of you fight to co-exist. There's not much you can do about your skin colour or who you like to fuck in terms of gender. Do I tell my teammates about being gay? No. Only two of my good mates know.

JOYCE: I think there is a lot of violence directed towards lesbians too. Last year in school, there was an actual discussion that went on in class that the teacher didn't even stop, basically saying that all lesbians needed a good fucking and they wouldn't be lesbians any more. You hear that a lot from dickhead boys our age.

JOSEPH: Yep. Before I got myself straight, and I mean realised I was gay, I was a nasty little prick. I think because I was trying to convince myself I wasn't gay so became extra macho. I was always making jokes about lesbians and rape with my friends. I can't believe the shit we used to say. Rape for a lot of boys is very, very funny and I think that it is encouraged. You see rape so much in porn, in mainstream films on the TV. Rape as an industry must make fucking loads. I don't think I know a single boy my age, younger or older, who hasn't watched a porn film with some sort of rape in it.

OSCAR, 15, WINDSOR

Oscar attends one of the most expensive and prestigious schools in the country. He comes from a titled and wealthy family. He hopes to attend Oxford University, as five generations of his family have. He is a member of the Conservative Party and has won several awards for his debating. He hopes one day to be prime minister.

In a nutshell, I think this country has become a bit of a joke where crime and our response to it are concerned. The penalties as they exist don't act as deterrents and the one thing criminals actually seem to learn is how to play the system. Additionally, it's a fairly well-documented fact that prison is a joke. Hours and hours of daytime television and you perhaps become a better pool player and certainly a better criminal. Nobody is afraid of prison here or being arrested. And the police are woefully disempowered.

I'd have a two strikes and prison policy for less serious crimes. People do make mistakes and sometimes deserve a second chance, but certainly not a third. If they do it a third time, they're going to do it again. I'd impose life sentences, mandatory, for drug dealing of any kind. Drugs are without a doubt one of the biggest causes of crime and misery. I'd impose a ten-year sentence, mandatory, for carrying a weapon of any kind. They want kids to stop stabbing and shooting each other? Scare them.

I'd increase police rights to stop and search. I'd make it an absolute law that unless you have an educational position or formal training and a fixed job or college place, you have no right to become a resident in this country. It's the elephant in the room that no one points out, but mass immigration *has* contributed to crime and violence on our streets.

I'd massively increase the Home Office's rights to have people deported for committing crime. You want to come here and spread hate or rape women or steal? Off you go. Don't pass Go. Don't collect £200.

And finally, and most importantly, for crimes of the type of things where the person is clearly evil, I'd bring back the death penalty. Who is a good example of someone recently who should have been given the death penalty? I don't think the world would have mourned much for the loss of that Ian Watkins chap (*the paedophile and former singer of Lostprophets*). And what a message that would have sent to people of his ilk.

MARTHA, 16, NORTHUMBERLAND

*Martha attends a state school in Northumberland. Her dad is a soldier and her mum is a hairdresser. Martha took thirteen GCSEs and has been predicted twelve A*s and one A. She was a 'bit disappointed' by this. She has just won a scholarship to study in the sixth form of one of the most academic schools in the country. She hopes to study PPE at Oxford University. She wants to be the youngest female prime minister ever in Britain. Her biggest role model is Tony Blair. She doesn't much care for Cherie Blair.*

Crime and violence is a big problem in this country, but saying it gets worse year on year is patently untrue – look at the statistics. Nonetheless, responding to the problem by making prison time harder and prison sentences longer is not the way forward.

People with money and access to really good education very rarely commit crime. This tells us a lot. So crime is a symptom of having little money and bad-quality education. So this suggests to me there needs to be much more money spent on the education of the poorest people, not the richest. I think private schools should have to pay a percentage into state schools. I don't really agree with private schools but I'm not sure abolishing them is the way forward. My dad says if there were no private schools, it would force up the state of all state schools because the richest in the country would want a really good place to send their children, which would also be available to poorer kids. That seems a lot fairer.

I also think if you commit a crime, unless you are seriously violent or a danger to society, it would be much better to send people who would go to prison to places sort of like a boarding school for adults where they learn some trades or get better educated. I don't see the value of locking someone up for twenty hours a day as a punishment.

My cousin went to prison. He got a heroin habit when he started smoking at age fourteen and he started stealing to keep on taking heroin. Loads of people have serious drug habits where I live. It's like an epidemic. Prison made him worse. It was only when he managed to get into a proper rehab facility that he actually got the help he needed. But he was lucky. Somebody paid for him to go, and he said almost everyone there were rich kids or from a rich family or independently wealthy. What person struggling on an estate has £70,000 to send their child to rehab? And it seems to me that drugs are having the worst effect on the poorest communities.

There needs to be much better education about drugs in the poorest communities and better, affordable facilities if people do get addicted to drugs. Drugs equal crime.

This country is so unfair. It gives the wealthy all the opportunities and then gives the wealthy all the help if they get into trouble. Who is helping the poor?

KIERAN, 17, NORTH LONDON

Kieran has been to a Young Offenders Institute twice since he was fourteen. He did a six-month stretch for robbery and a nine-month stretch for GBH. He continues to commit crime. On the basis of his Key Stage One, Two and Three SATs, Kieran was in the top 5 per cent bracket of his academic year. He gained a level 6+ in English, mathematics and science in Year 9, which meant he should have been on course for A–A at GCSE. He was also considered to be 'gifted and talented' in history and geography. He was offered a place in a youth scheme in one of the top football academies in the country but lost it due to his violent and antisocial behaviour.*

I was kicked out of school at age fourteen. They tried to put me in this unit, but I punched the tutor there, so got kicked out of there too and didn't go back. Same as that football thing. In all the preliminary matches where you were being looked at by scouts and shit, I was always getting into fights and I hit the referee once. He deserved it. Do I regret it? Yeah, I suppose so.

And to be fair, I think my high school did try to help. There was lots of interventions and counselling sessions and second and third chances and fourth chances. But eventually I punched a teacher and accidentally knocked over one of the lady teachers who was pregnant when I was in some fucking rage in a fight, so I got expelled.

Everyone was scared of me at school. In school it's easy to be the big man and life is very different. My parents didn't want me. My dad was in and out of prison. My mum was mentally not all there, which wasn't helped by the fact she took a lot of drugs. Crack, weed and alcohol mostly. I don't know if she's still on it. I haven't spoken to her in nearly two years. I don't know where my dad is. Knowing him he's either in prison or dead. Or both.

I lived with my grandma for a while but she found it difficult to cope. There was talk of getting me placed in foster care, so I just took off. I started to do some work with older boys, by which I mean stealing and dealing. We were mostly robbing houses. It's actually well easy for the most part, unless you are aiming for really rich houses, which have much better security on them. But even average houses in OK areas have enough riches. Even in estate houses you find wide screens, DVD players, phones, cash, gold, designer threads ... you name it.

Anyway, we got nicked on the job. Because probably it was like in a middle-class area, we got the book thrown straight at us. I just got six months because of my age. I'd just turned fifteen. The other boys got longer.

I'm not gonna lie. YO is shit. Fucking scary, scary place. I'm told it's way, way worse than actual prison because older man is more mellow or whatever and just wants to do their time and catch up on sleep and *Jeremy Kyle*, you know what I'm saying?

But you've seen what the school playground is like. It's like that to the power of ten billion. Everyone is spoiling for a fight every second of the day, just to prove they are the biggest man. Because if you don't, you're in big, big fucking trouble. I mean, that show *Oz* is a bit stylised, but that is probably the closest to the reality of YO than any other show on TV.

There are fights, stabbings, drugs, more drugs, suicide, sexual assaults, all kind of things, and I'm not exaggerating. And there's nowhere to go and no one to complain to. You snitch, you're dead.

And there is no friends to be had in there. You don't make friends. You spend every second of the day making sure you keep yourself to yourself, making sure no one thinks you're lightweight and making it through. A lot of people take drugs, you know, to ease it, but I've never been into drugs. I preferred the gym. I don't even smoke. I seen what drugs can do.

I had the shit kicked out of me enough times, believe. But you can't back down. (*He rolls up his shirt to show me a nasty scar on his stomach.*) Courtesy of the second time inside. But it was all right. I got five days in the infirmary (*laughs*).

But in all honesty, prison both hardens you and sucks you dry. You come out a bit of a shell, but the second time was much, much easier. The second time I didn't roll in trying to be top boy straight away. I was quieter, which seemed to worry people. But y'know, look at me. I'm a big boy and I'm very fit and strong. You go in physically weak and your life is over. Anyone who tried to get to me sexually, any faggot or bum boy, would have to kill me first, because I'd kill him. But, yeah. Dropping-the-soap stuff is sort of bullshit, but yeah, you got a bunch of horny, angry young men together and what do you expect? Plus rape is also about the absolute punishment. The biggest humiliation. I dunno. I kept myself to myself. I saw and heard awful things every single day, but I ain't helping no one. You keep yourself together and alive and get out. That's all. Every man for himself.

All this Barack Obama 'anyone can do it if they try' bullshit is just bullshit. You can't. There aren't any jobs for most people who have stayed at school, gone to university, done the right thing, stayed legit. Who's gonna employ a black boy with a criminal record and no GCSEs? I'm not really asking for sympathy. I know I fucked myself too and people did try for me. And I know I've fucked up a lot of opportunities I had. But you never see it at the time, do you? It's always too late. I . . . I don't have high hopes for me seeing my twenty-fifth birthday.

Looking to the Future and Advice for the Next Generation

MARK, 17, BERKSHIRE

I bet life will look well different for kids in ten years' time. Like you don't realise it because things happen quickly. But think of how much has changed in ten years. People didn't even have smartphones then. Now, they are one of the most obvious features of everyday life. You never see people read books or papers or chat on trains. Or even in restaurants. They are too busy looking at their phones.

Oh my days. I'll definitely be rich and have a good job by then. I'd like to have a waterside place near the Embankment with some mates. I don't want to live with a woman until I'm thirty-two, because so many people tell me living with your mates will be the best years of your life. I'd like to have a serious girlfriend by then who's well fit but really career-orientated too. Maybe a lawyer who was a model at university.

I bet people will have sick technology by then. Watches or maybe rings as mobile phones. I bet all cars will be electric and absolutely everything will be on remote control. I hope I won't be one of those sad adults asking them to program my laptop and stuff because I don't understand it.

But then I just had a bad thought. Everyone talks so much about how London prices have gone up in the last ten years, imagine what they'll be like in another ten. I'm beginning to wonder whether it's better to turn immigration on its head.

For us all to learn the languages, move out there and start businesses. I've heard Russia is sick. Maybe that's the way to go? I could start a law firm out there.

My advice to the next generation? Save money and learn the languages of the big upcoming countries like China and Russia. You're gonna need them.

LINDSAY, 16, NORFOLK

I don't know. I used to think a lot about the future and losing my brother made that weirder. I mean, he used to think about the future too, and it turns out he didn't have one. Death very close to you is so odd. I don't know whether it is better to live in the present and enjoy that or plan for the future.

I guess I'll have gone to university and will have a career. I thought for a long time I wanted to be a teacher, but I keep hearing terrible things about public sector careers. You know, they are all going to hell in a handcart. After Jase died, I had this idea I wanted to go into medicine for a bit, but you have to be seriously good to go into medicine now. I think all doctors in ten years' time will be Chinese and Indian geniuses who stole all the medical school places. I don't mean that in a racist way at all. But you keep hearing how shit our schools are compared to theirs and how dumb we are compared to them.

Wouldn't it be funny if, in ten years' time, we all owned all the corner shops and takeaways and Asian and Chinese people came in and were like, 'Give me some of your shit English food and twenty fags.' Although fags will probably be fifty quid a packet by then. Sorry. That's really bleak, isn't it? I'm having a bad day today. The future scares me a bit.

My advice would be to not think about the future too much. To live in, and enjoy, the present. You never know what is going to happen.

LEROY, 15, SOUTH LONDON

I'm outta here, boy. I will not stay in London beyond drama school for shit. I tell you why. Number one, obviously I'm going to Hollywood, LA, USA to be a superstar. But I will have an apartment in New York, for my New York bitches, obviously. Don't tell my mum I used the word 'bitches' or she'll beat down on my head. For real.

England is no place for black actors. The only things that do well here are *Downton Abbey* which don't have much use for brothers and shit like *Gogglebox* which are just shit. I think the future of British TV is really, really bad reality TV. We don't make good films or shows, ever, at all. I mean, people are all praising *Doctor Who* like it's the British *Sopranos*. It's a white guy running around in a phone box with a schoolgirl. And the monsters aren't scary. He should be put on the sex offenders register and get himself an iPhone.

But anyway, in ten years' time, British TV and film will be a shell. All we'll have is, like, reality TV and something like Netflix from America. I think it's going to be much worse for the next generation in terms of entertainment.

My advice to the next generation of kids? Don't stay in England. Especially if you're not white. You're gonna be the next slaves!

JOHN, 18, GREAT YARMOUTH

I think there's gonna be a new world order in the next ten years' time. Dunno about me, but there's shit going on. I've done loads of the reading and it blatantly started with 9/11. Ebola, ISIS, immigration, WikiLeaks, CCTV. We're all being watched and controlled every second of every day. I think about a third of the population is going to die in the next ten years. For definite. There's not enough to go round for everyone.

My advice to the next generation is plan, plan, plan. If you have money, knowledge, a place to go, an escape route, know lots of languages, know people in authority and are in good shape, they might have some use for you. Otherwise you aren't going to make it. You'll probably die from government-planted disease or be assassinated in a phony government war.

MARY, 15, LEEDS

Uh, time goes so quickly, doesn't it? It feels like only yesterday I was in primary school and I'm about to sit my GCSEs and I'm being asked to make all these big choices about my future and my career and all those things. I think things are going to get worse for the next generation – but my advice would be enjoy your childhood for as long as possible.

It doesn't matter how cool the future seems or how cool being grown-up seems, nothing is as cool as being little and having no worries. And especially to girls, completely ignore all the pressure to look older. There's no going back once you do. I can't decide now that I'd like to look nine, although it would be sometimes cool if I could.

And read. Read, read, read and study. I keep getting told all this scary stuff about us falling behind in the world. Reading and studying hard are good habits to get into like brushing your teeth or going to the gym. It's hard to go back and do it again. Does that all sound depressing? It should do. The world is becoming a much more depressing place. Much more.

MAYA, 15, LONDON

My advice to future generations, is, where possible, don't be a girl. Being female is awful and is going to get so much worse. I realise I'm not in a good place at the moment, as I'm in hospital again. (*Maya is currently being treated for anorexia.*) I know we keep getting told that feminism is on the rise and it's all awesome being a girl. But it isn't. And I think it's going to get worse than ever before. There's girls being attacked online for every possible thing and I think the internet will become even more powerful in our lives and it's going to bring women down more than ever before.

My advice to future girls is, if you want any chance of happiness, stay offline, don't read fashion magazines, don't talk to guys. Don't talk to anyone. Maybe become a nun. And boys? What do they have to worry about? They will all be fine and they know it.

JAWAD, 16, EAST LONDON

One of the things I've learned is that money and knowledge are the two most important things. And the third thing I've learned is that adults actually aren't talking shit. You think they are, but they're not. Most of the time, they are right. You don't believe it at the time, but you realise this to be the truth.

Like teachers, parents, mullahs, elders, priests, nuns ... whoever is in your life, right now, telling you all the stuff you think is a load of shit – it isn't. And believe, stay in school and work hard. The second you get that GCSE certificate with the bad grades you kept getting warned about, you realise everything they said was true. It's really hard to go back. And when you think school is actually at least twelve years of your life, straight off, that's a lot of time to waste.

RACHEL, 16, CAMBRIDGESHIRE

I haven't really figured out enough yet to give really useful advice. God knows what the world is going to be like in ten years' time from now. It's already so different from when I was little. I think kids need to start thinking of alternatives and pretty quickly. Our generation is fairly screwed because it was born at the birth of the internet. We're sort of left in its wake and have suffered with all the lost jobs, lost money and negative changes. There's no jobs left in media, newspapers, advertising, photography and all of those because of the internet. The replacement industries like website design or dot.com opportunities have gone because everyone knows how to do them, so who's going to pay? You can't get into the BBC, acting, business or politics unless your parents know the right people. We were born too late to think up alternatives to replace what has been lost in time, but the next generation hasn't. Think quickly or you are going to be as screwed as we are.

MATTHEW, 18, MANCHESTER

I think unless you are really, really good academically and are going to be something that is guaranteed a really good job, like being a doctor or surgeon or lawyer who can charge extortionate fees by the hour, use school to suit you. Work throughout it as much as you can.

At the moment kids are sleepwalking through school and blindly going to university to rack up a debt of eighty grand and then are not able to find a job. School is the one time adults will properly help you and you can stay debt-free. Use it to the max. Get internships, make contacts, write to MPs to get political experience, help on fashion shoots, volunteer in Africa, be a dental assistant. Whatever you can. Use your teenage school years to make yourself exceptional and stand out as much as possible. There isn't much time. The world is intensely competitive now, what do you think it's going to be like in ten years' time? It's going to be survival of the fittest, sink or swim, more than ever. Kids need to get ruthless if they want to survive the coming world. Trust me.

ARUN, 17, BRADFORD

Don't be a fat fuck. Can I leave it at that? OK, kids are getting fatter. Kids from all over. White kids, Asian kids, black kids. As a kid you should be skinny and there are less and less of them, which is not good. I started to get fat around the age of seven. So did loads of my mates. Eating is a big thing in Asian culture, but it's going beyond that now. There's always loads of sweets. But also crisps, snacks, fizzy drinks, chocolate. You name it. And we definitely bribe our mums to give us what we want by telling her so-and-so's mum gives *him* whatever he wants. It's all about keeping up with the family and the neighbours. It works to get you mobiles, game consoles and for food too. And then you sit around on your phone or your Xbox or whatever and eat junk food all day. It's a bad cycle and becoming normal.

By the age of ten I had rolls of fat. On my belly. I had those moob type things you see on so many boys. You know, they look a bit like girls' breasts. Bits of me wobbled when I moved. I got out of breath walking up the stairs. If I kept on that way, I was heading for being dead in my thirties. I sorted it out in time, after I got into a fight in my first week of high school. I didn't want to be weak and the fat kid. Now I'm training to become a personal trainer and I want to work with kids mostly. That's hilarious that any kid should need a trainer. A kid should be like a lean dog, constantly running and feeding healthily and then running more. But most of them aren't like that any more. It's well bad. They all need to be re-educated. I keep reading all these scare stories about childhood obesity. But it isn't a story. So my advice? Exercise every single day.

Don't eat crap. Eat fruit and vegetables and lots of them. Avoid McDonald's like you'd avoid crack and have some respect for yourself. You only get one body.

MICHAEL, 17, LOUGHBOROUGH

My advice? Play sport. Doesn't matter if you're no good at it. Play football, netball, hockey, ice hockey, rugby, cricket, even fucking golf. Even though we all know golf isn't a sport. I coach kids now I've got my life back together. It's not just good for them physically. I think kids are losing that ability to work as part of a team. It will probably get worse in the next ten years. I'm definitely seeing more of that 'all about me' mindset with kids.

I guess that sums up a lot of the problems I think the next generation of kids are going to face, in a nutshell. They all want to be the stars not the players. That's not a good thing at all for either people or society. I don't think sport can help with everything, but it can help with a lot of things. Obviously most top-level footballers are a bad example, because they are fucking pricks.

MAGGIE, 17, EXETER

Don't eat the yellow snow. My dad used to tell me that. I have no idea what it means. But I've never eaten yellow snow, either.

I guess my advice would be: definitely accept yourself for

who you are. I know that sounds a bit fluffy, but I see with both my little brothers and sisters this *obsession* with being someone who isn't realistic. Like all boys wanting to be sports stars and all girls wanting to be pop stars. Or models. It isn't going to happen. Or at least not except for 0.00001 per cent of the population. What happened to wanting to be a vet? All my mates want to be these ridiculous things and they look at me weirdly when I tell them I want to be a vet. I can't imagine what it will be like in the future. I can't tell you the number of my friends who are realising now that they aren't good enough or going to make what they had their heart set on. It's really messed a few of them up. Be realistic.

KEELEY, 17, EXETER

I disagree with Maggie. When you are a kid and a teenager, it's the time when you should have wild and crazy dreams. Aim for the stars. As the world gets more depressed, there are no jobs and everything is just getting worse, kids are going to need something to hang on to. Dream big. Dream HUGE. I stopped dreaming when I was eleven because someone told me it was a stupid ambition to be an actress and now I'm working in Asda on a Saturday when I could have got an internship at a big London theatre. My parents talked me out of it. I couldn't have afforded it, but I should have tried.

DAVID, 18, BRIGHTON

I only have one piece of advice. If you are gay, don't be frightened. And if you are not gay, if you are frightened of gays, you are a moron. Get into the twenty-first century, and beyond. One of my greatest wishes for the next generation is that being gay won't even be a thing. That all schools will pretty much be like *Glee*. God, I wish I'd gone to that school! But in all seriousness, it doesn't matter how much you tell yourself that you can change or that you can 'ungay' yourself: you won't. You are what you are and it's like trying to be tall if you are short. Accept it and be happy.

I know it's not easy and it's easy for me to say now, but telling people and coming out, or whatever the kids of tomorrow are going to call it, is like losing a big weight. And turning a light on. You have all these ideas about how it's going to be. I hope it doesn't even have to be a deal for you. That it'll be like telling people you are planning to get your ears pierced. But I hear fewer and fewer tragic coming-out stories and more and more brilliant ones. I hope in ten years, this advice seems really old-fashioned, but if it isn't, don't be afraid. Hopefully by then they'll have put all homophobes in a museum.

MAGGIE, 17, NORTH LONDON

I have nothing to offer but don't use fake tan. It lowers your IQ and makes you look like an Oompa Loompa.

RADHIKA, 16, PETERBOROUGH

This is going to make me sound well old, but my advice would be to keep things in perspective. Like, I think of all the things that mattered to me when I was twelve, thirteen or fourteen, things I would *literally* cry about for days and days and days, think the world was coming to an end and I was going to kill myself – I can't even remember what they were about now. All those arguments I was having with my girls at the time. All the boys I said I couldn't live without. Not only do you change but what matters now won't even matter in six months. Trust me on this.

NICK, 17, NORTH LONDON

Don't let your drunk mate who can't spell give you a tattoo. I've now got 'Chelsee FC' on my back forever or until I can afford that laser thing.

MATTY, 15, HULL

Honestly? I know this is a bit bad of me to say because I take them, but don't take drugs. You start and you think it's a really good time and it gets to the point where you think you need drugs to have a good time. Whenever we do anything, the first thing we ask is, will there be any drink and drugs? If there isn't, a lot of the time I don't want to bother going. I don't know how I got to that stage so fast.

I was arguing with my mate who is nineteen. He reckons kids are doing more drugs now than when he was my age. I think they are doing less or about the same. But my brother is a proper mess and in prison now, mostly from drugs. I don't think smoking weed definitely makes you do other harder drugs but maybe it's more likely. Like having sex once makes you do it with more girls. Having sex once isn't going to make you want to have a gangbang, but you are more likely to want more. Know what I mean?

So don't do drugs, future kids. And stay in school. And definitely don't do drugs in school. It freaks you out when the deputy head comes and talks to you and you have to pretend to be straight.

DEANA, 16, EAST LONDON

Technology is going to grow and grow in the next ten years. I think it's scary how much more kids are going to be dependent on it. Like, it's properly weird to think how much we use every minute of every day that wasn't even available five or ten years ago. Like the expression 'tweeting' would have applied to birds back in the day. I wonder what the kids of tomorrow will be doing?

But I'd say, be careful. I learnt that from bitter experience. The more time we spend online, on our phones and whatever technologies are coming, the more trouble we can get into. And stuff can come back to haunt you. I sent some pictures on my phone to someone I trusted well over a year ago, and people are still looking at them, finding them, asking me about them. I know they've been on websites. Don't do *anything* on the internet or phones or whatever you don't mind the world seeing. Believe me.

ADAM, 18, GLOUCESTER

If you get a hoverboard for your birthday, you little bastard, send it to me. I've wanted one of those a lot longer than you have.

OSHANE, 18, NORTH LONDON

This probably counts for boys and girls, but especially boys: don't let anyone with braces give you head.

SALLY, 17, HERTFORDSHIRE

Oh my gosh, there is so much I'd love to pass on about what I've learned. Where to even begin? First off, treasure your friends. Guys will come and go and make you cry all the time. But good friends will be there for you always. And – and I cannot stress this enough – don't let guys come between you. If you both like him, if you value your friendship, neither one should have him. If one of you does, even if the other says it's

OK – it never will be. I've seen awesome friendships of ten years destroyed by this scenario. So don't.

Oh, there's so much to pass on! I guess the other big piece of advice and this is to everyone, as I know guys are increasingly getting caught up in this, is: don't diet. Just don't start. Not even slightly. It messes with your metabolism and traps you in the dieting cycle forever. The two of my friends in our long-term group who didn't diet or do anything faddy are now easily the skinniest. Or not necessarily the skinniest, but have the best bodies and the best attitude. At least two of our friends have suffered from serious eating disorders and they wreck lives. But even on the less serious end of the scale, dieting messes up everyone. The bottom line is, eating sensibly and exercising are the only things that work.

And one more thing: whatever you are wearing now, you are going to look back on it and want to *die*. You don't look good right now. Not at all. You will look at pictures of yourself in five years' time and want to die.

OWEN, 18, CARDIFF

Don't have a wank in the home ec room. Because you will always be known as the guy who had a wank in the home ec room. This is obviously advice from a 'friend'.

ROISIN, 17, NORTHERN IRELAND

This is really hard advice to give because I know I never would have been able to take it. But we are all told as teenagers to be more serious about stuff and take stuff seriously. I'd like to suggest the opposite. Your childhood goes so quickly. I think kids should hang on to it more. Treasure it. I also wish I'd been able to laugh at things and myself more. When you are fourteen or fifteen, you take everything so personally. I still do, but less so. But I have two really good friends who can always find the comedy in a situation and especially in themselves. They are definitely the happiest people I know. So basically: be less serious and laugh a lot more.

DAVE, 15, NORTH LONDON

Don't cross girls. They are evil. And listen to your mum. She is even more evil and will fuck with your life given half a chance.

CHERRY, 19, BIRMINGHAM

Having lost my best friend in the world to suicide, I'd tell any kid or teenager who feels like they are alone or at the end of their tether that they are not alone. I'm in the last year of being teenager, and I know how different I feel now compared to when I was, say, thirteen or fourteen. You feel like the whole world is against you and doesn't understand you. You can also feel fat, ugly, friendless, confused and like you wish you could kill your parents all the time. The good news is: it does get better. The bad/good news is: it doesn't go away entirely. You just learn to manage it better.

But no pain, no horrible thing in the world is worth losing your life over. Suicide is a really complicated thing. It is the ultimate in desperate acts. But you can't get away from the fact that it ruins a lot of other people's lives too. It's not like a terrible accident or a disease, where other people feel terrible but know they couldn't have done anything. Suicide leaves everyone else feeling almost as bad as the person who committed suicide. It's indescribable. There are so many places to go for help: counsellors, therapists, teachers, parents, friends. Don't suffer alone. The thing that gives me nightmares about Abbie is: what if she had second thoughts? What if, in the last seconds before she died, she wanted to live and saw all the things she missed out on? Career, babies, boyfriends, uni, a whole life. You don't get a second chance.

DAVID, 17, LEEDS

Your parents getting divorced is sweet. You get shitloads of cash and they are so busy finding their lost youth or whatever, they don't give a shit when you come home smashed out your head at 4 a.m. covered in hickies. Parents divorcing is a pretty sick club. Enjoy.

CHARLOTTE, 16, SURREY

I read somewhere that sort of domestic violence – though I don't know if it counts as domestic violence if you don't live together – is rising really fast amongst teenagers. I was in an abusive relationship for three years and it got so bad, I had to get a restraining order and the police involved. You never would have believed it to look at him or me, either. He doesn't look like the crazy, abusive type and I don't look like some victim either. I don't think there is such a type. Definitely not now.

It seems so daft now because it started when we were just kids. I was thirteen and he was fifteen. But he would just sulk if he didn't get his way and I didn't do what he wanted. It started out with not sharing my pick 'n' mix and then progressed to sex. I didn't want to and he wanted to. So I gave in. And it just got worse. Then the hair pulling started, then the slapping, then the punching. It ended up with a knife at my throat.

So I guess to all girls *and* guys: if someone loves you, they don't threaten you, make you do stuff you don't want to or hurt you. That's the opposite of love.

MENAHIL, 17, BRADFORD

Don't date a guy who doesn't drive a car. You can be nice and go out with someone who goes on the bus if you want to, but you'll regret it and wish you hadn't. Life is too short for buses.

RAJ, 17, MANCHESTER

If you have a friend, male or female, who comes out to you as gay, don't judge them and listen to them. My biggest regret is losing my shit when my best mate told me he was gay. We still don't speak. I regret it and miss him every day.

ALISON, 18, SURREY

I'm going to be the boring one and come out and say it: don't have sex. Don't *never* have sex. But don't be in a rush. Because . . . well, mostly not for any big, moral reason. Because it's crap when you don't know what the hell you are doing and a huge disappointment. I don't know anyone, male or female, who had a good time or a particularly pleasurable time the first time. Or second. Or third.

The first guy I slept with didn't, like, properly *insert* it. And just sort of rubbed it between my thighs. It caused a big mess all over my stepdad's couch. The second one tried to put *everything* in. I didn't find a happy medium for a while. I guess sex is good for me now with my boyfriend, but it took time. I think the rule of thumb should be, if you are in a relationship where you can properly, really, really talk about it, then you might be ready. And just 'do you wanna do it?' doesn't count.

I have a lot of male friends, and in some ways the pressure is even worse for them. I also have a twin brother, which is weird because we talk quite openly about sex. More than most brothers and sisters do. He told me all the pressure and expectation takes all the fun out of it. The double standard in society still encourages girls to some extent to keep their virginity, but boys treat it like it's some sort of horrible disease. Something to be got rid of as quickly as possible. Which is a shame. When was anything you were just pressured into doing any fun at all?

GUY, 17, BIRMINGHAM

Sorry if this advice is a bit sexist. But no matter what happens in the future, girls are always going to sleep with guys in a band. Learn the guitar. Or better still, learn the guitar and sing. Even short blokes who aren't that good-looking get a *lot* of women. I guess that advice might work for girls, too.

CHARLIE, 17, LEEDS

I think our generation has massively missed out on a lot of opportunities. This is a bit hard to explain – but we aren't like, *defined* by anything. Which is a small window and that kind of depresses me. Like you read about hippies, punk, World War I, World War II, Vietnam, women burning bras. I love history so much because it looks like so much happened. Like, it was *exciting*.

What are we going to be known for? The generation that spent a shitload of time on social media? The generation that wished they were old enough to grow a hipster beard? And it's not like there isn't a lot to get done. A lot of problems to solve. And it just frustrates me, because no one seems bothered enough to do anything about it. People my age just complain a lot. I don't know. I guess the next generation should try to do all the things we didn't do enough of: join political parties, start magazines, start radio stations, start businesses, volunteer, join the Army for a couple of years because it's the right thing to do. I do a lot of stuff and I actually get laughed at by my friends. I think my generation is a boring one. And we didn't have to be.

TOM, 19, SOUTH LONDON

The one bit of advice I wish I'd been given is: don't be a dickhead. Or too much of one. You don't have to be. I think this is true for all teenagers but especially boys. Because they are naturally dickheads. A certain amount of dickheadery is to be expected, but a lot of it isn't.

Here is a list of acceptable dickheadery: rapping really badly in rap battles, calling your mates wankers, fancying your mate's mum, crying because a girl fancies your mate, fancying your art teacher, wondering what it would be like to have boobs, watching porn once in a while, putting on your Facebook profile 'Scarface' or 'International Gangster' as a job, considering auditioning for *X Factor*, having a man crush on someone cool, kissing your guns in the mirror, being too scared to actually go into a proper gym, trying on your sister's bra just to see, wanking yourself into a frenzy, overdoing being ill because it's nice to have your mum fuss over you, thinking everyone hates you. Because they probably do.

Here is a list of unacceptable dickheadery: being racist, telling your mates you had sex with a girl – even if you had sex with the girl; if you tell everyone, girls will stop having sex with you – being homophobic, taking the piss out of your mate if he's actually properly upset about something, fancying your physics teacher, actually auditioning for *X Factor*, fancying any of One Direction, trying to make anyone have sex with you who doesn't want to, calling girls 'slags, whores, hos or bitches', actually sleeping with any of your mate's mums, watching so much porn you forget what real girls are like, looking at your sister in the bath through the keyhole, bullying people smaller than you. Because someone in life is always going to be bigger than you.

If someone had given me that list aged thirteen, I would have been much happier. Pass it on.

CARLY, 16, NEWPORT

This next generation will hopefully get back to the idea that there are more important things in the world than being good-looking. It's like everyone has given up on the idea. No one seems to care about the fact that people are smart or funny or talented. Good looks seem to give people and especially girls the ticket to everything. And that's not right, is it?

AMY, 18, LIVERPOOL

Don't smoke or drink. I think those things are going to be illegal probably in the next twenty years. I know I sound right uptight and old, but I don't do either and when I see how much trouble it causes my friends who do, I feel like I've swerved cancer or something.

We all started university this year and because I'm a med student, I barely have time to sleep and eat, let alone go out on the lash. You'd think with all the stuff we see, other med students would be like me, but they're the worst of all. I think it might be the pressure. But alcohol mangles people both inside and out. Not everyone. But so many people. I honestly think it's one of the biggest diseases in our country. If you don't start, you'll never know what you're missing. And you won't regret it. I don't.

NICK, 17, HULL

Party your little bollocks off. You can drink all night and day with no consequences. We're living the dream. You'll be living the dream. No hangovers, man! It's why old people are so bitter. Shit, I'm going to be old by the time this lot are my age.

PARTH, 18, BRADFORD

I guess this is one for the nerds and the uncool kids: one day, all the kids who bullied you, the kids who were better-looking, the kids who had all those parties that you weren't invited to, they are going to work for you. They're going to wish they were *you*. Nerds, geniuses, eccentrics, kids with crap jumpers and bad haircuts turn out to be rulers of the universe. They get the most important jobs in the world and the best chicks. The one thing I will say, though, is I hope when this next generation rolls around, there is as many women on this list as men. I think this next generation of women are going to be crazy powerful. Think about it. Bill Gates, Steve Jobs, Boris Johnson, Barack Obama, Tony Blair, Angela Merkel, Mark Zuckerberg, Larry Page, Thom Yorke, Trey Parker, Matt Stone. Those are all my heroes when I was growing up. I was bullied in primary school and people took the piss out of me in high school. Now I'm going to Oxford to study PPE. I hate to be a snob, but the football captain of our school who every girl fancied is going to somewhere no one has ever heard of to study sports science or some shit. Who do you think is winning now, bitches?

And God knows what role models future nerds are going to have. But I do know one. Me!

LOUISE, 17, EAST LONDON

My grandmother passed this on to me. It was the best piece of advice I was ever given. She called it the 'One Thing Rule'.

Basically, fuck all this trying to know everything about everything and instead take one thing. Learn to cook one dish better than anyone else. Know one book like the absolute back of your hand. Learn to play one song perfectly on the piano. Know about the life, completely, of one important person. Learn how to speak one language perfectly. Most people don't. The list goes on, but I've done this and I can't tell you how much it has helped me. It's a different way of looking at things, but I think it's perfect.

CONNOR, 14, MACCLESFIELD

You're all going to die.

EBONY, 16, EAST LONDON

Embrace the shape you are. If you're skinny, be skinny. If you're fat, be fat. If you're in the middle, be in the middle. God made us the way we are for a reason. Fight another battle you are meant to fight and not yourself.

ANDREW, 18, HERTFORDSHIRE

Learn to love your penis. Even if it's not quite the size you want it to be. I guess the same goes for vaginas. Although I don't have a vagina, obviously.

ASSAD, 17, EAST LONDON

Don't commit crime, man. It's a loop, a slippery slope or whatever you want to call it. And it's a really hard one to get out of once you're in it. Whatever happens in the future, I think the prison system will stay the same. And whatever people say about prison being like a holiday camp where you get to play Xbox all day is a load of fucking shit. Your heart is in your mouth from the second you walk in there and it doesn't come out from the second you leave there. You think the road is bad, try prison. You don't have no brethren in there, no one watching your back. It's a dog's world and I saw some nasty, nasty shit in there. Believe. I think all governments think kids commit crime for fun or something, but that's bullshit. Power and money is like a drug. And they're both hard to give up. I can totally relate. I am in a scheme now, but it *is* hard to stay straight once you've seen the other side of it.

I can't get a lot of jobs now. A lot of people won't even look at me. I can't go to America now. Ever. And I have to live with a lot of shit in my head. No amount of drugs or praying or whatever takes away memory. There's a lot of stuff I wish I hadn't done. You can rehab a lot of stuff, but you can't rehab your soul. Or your mind. And I think it's gonna get worse for kids in the future. I don't think the future looks that great.

APRIL, 15, DORSET

If you fall off a horse, don't get back on it. I did and fell off eleven times more. The last time I fractured a vertebra, which really hurt. Horses suck.

DANNI, 16, MACCLESFIELD

The thing that's freaking me out is that one day our stuff is going to be considered old-fashioned and people might call our clothes vintage! Oh my God. That's so depressing. Do I have any good advice? Don't pluck your eyebrows. Big eyebrows are dead fashionable now and they weren't four years ago. All my mates were plucking their eyebrows and now they won't grow back and they're so depressed they want to kill themselves. I didn't pluck mine because I wasn't allowed and I can look like Cara Delevingne without even having to draw them in. I'm just so happy about that. God, I wonder what will happen to eyebrows in the future? Maybe they'll have an eyebrow app. That'd be well cool.

HANAD, 15, NORTH-WEST LONDON

I'm not sure I should say this, as I don't want it to be taken the wrong way. My faith is the most important thing in the world to me. Being devout and a good Muslim are the greatest priorities in my life. But I sometimes worry where religion is going and I hope the next generation of any religion can change this. I don't think people should die in the name of religion. I don't think people should go to war over religion. I don't think just because another person believes something else, they are lower than scum and should be wiped out. I don't think women's private parts should be mutilated for religion. I don't think you should look like this or that for religion and if you don't, you are a bad believer.

I'm scared because I feel like I can't say these things. In the last couple of years, things have gone crazy. It really feels like a war has started. I used to have Christian friends, Jewish friends, friends who are girls, non-believers. Everything. Now suddenly the talk is so deep. There's no tolerance of any other ways of life. And it's like that on all sides. You see these lines where there weren't before. What's that thing that happened to Nelson Mandela? Apartheid. There is apartheid in school, on the road, in the towns. It's scary, man. I feel scared.

I don't know where this is going, but hacking off people's heads in the name of Allah on Facebook or whatever surely can't be what He really wants? But if you say this, you feel like you are putting yourself in danger. Muslims in the middle who want peace are shutting up. It's probably the same in other religions, too. I hope the next generation learns from our mistake. We need to increase the peace.

JEREMY, 13, TYNESIDE

Don't borrow money. My parents keep borrowing money and then they owe more money. I've told them they have to stop. My mum keeps crying all the time and a few times we couldn't go to school because Dad said people were watching to see if we were in. I don't know why they don't make it illegal. I will never borrow money and nobody else should either.

CHLOE, 17, SWINDON

My advice is to save. My generation have been given no guidance whatsoever in anything to do with financial stuff. They *so* need to change that for the next generation. My parents were really young when they had me and they are so screwed financially. Me and my friend worked this out the other day. That if you saved £10 a week from the age of ten to the age of eighteen, that would be nearly five grand. I don't know much about interest and that, but I think it would make it a lot more. Five grand would pay off a lot of my parents' debts at the moment. Nobody saves. Nobody is telling us to save money and that's a small amount. That's the best advice I can give.

RYAN, 16, ST ALBANS

Oh my *God*. Can you imagine how amazing it's going to be for kids in the future? I can't even deal. They won't have any problems because everything, like cancer, wrinkles and bad teeth, will probably have been solved or whatever. Thank God.

My main advice is never wear white. No one can pull it off. Not even Beyoncé. You'll regret it when you look back at all your photos on whatever replaces Instagram. Hopefully they'll make it illegal for brides in the future. Why would they insist on a colour that makes everyone look fat for the biggest day of your life? It's criminal. I'll be wearing purple.

HAYLEY, 17, COUNTY DURHAM

I'm scared for the future. Especially the generations of kids. There's nothing they can do except not bother to vote. What's the point? Every government just after the other just makes things worse. Things are awful now; imagine what they are going to be like in ten or twenty years' time.

KELLY, 17, GLASGOW

I'm really excited for the future and for what kids might achieve. I was so disappointed with the result of the Scottish referendum. There was this massive sense of change everywhere and people felt really empowered by what was going on. Like they got to be participants in events rather than passively watch what was going on and get told afterwards. We were so pissed off with the result, but I'm really proud of the fact we showed everyone in the UK how it's done. That you don't have to settle for what you're given or blindly follow anything. And that together, you *can* make a difference. And a powerful difference. It scared the crap out of all the fat cats sitting in Westminster thinking they were entitled to rule over everything without anyone questioning them even once.

I think that's a good rule for lots of things. Nothing changes if you don't fight it. We're having a definite new wave for my generation of feminism. We read about how women were treated in the last generation and it sounds *better* than it was now. The internet has shown the world what a lot of people really think of women. I think it's been a real eye-opener. The hatred is just so obvious.

If the next generation want anything to get better, they *need* to keep doing everything they have in their power. Voting, protesting, organising, being political, having opinion. People who say only 'they' can change anything, so what does it matter, are the lowest of the low. It's what people in power who want to stay in power depend on.

ALBERT, 15, EAST LONDON

Don't act like a stereotype. I'm a black man. There are stereotypes about black men. All of which are negative. All stereotypes are negative. There's no such thing as a positive.

But the question is, how did the stereotype come to be in the first place? Were *you* part of the problem? Part of that labelling process? No one can sit around complaining about being labelled and then act like exactly what it says on the label. You have to tear the label off. You know what I'm saying?

JAMES, 16, SOUTH LONDON

Wear a belt. Somewhere along the line everyone started wearing trousers like they are falling off. Well, boys anyway. I'm gonna come out and say it: it's well uncomfortable. And annoying. I nearly flashed a coachload of grannies the other day. And look after your teeth. I've fucked mine with too much soft drink and that, and it's well annoying now. So yeah, brush and floss.

RITA, 17, NORTH-WEST LONDON

I don't think we can advise the next generation. There is literally nothing more annoying than listening to advice from people who don't have a clue.

What are our big challenges? So many. Few jobs, unaffordable housing, growing tension between races and religions, deciding what our relationship should be with the internet, anger at the government, poverty. All those things and more. Who knows what crosses the next generation will have to bear? And they're not going to want to hear it from us, no matter what we think now.

I don't know if things will be better or worse for the next generation, but they'll have to make their own way and pull through and survive just like we are. The thing is, most things do, sort of, work out OK in the end.

Appendix of Generation Z Terms

Aired	To be ignored.
Allow	To leave alone or to disagree.
Bae	Abbreviated term for baby or sweetie. Can refer to a friend as well as a lover.
Bait	When something is made obvious.
Balling	To be rich or winning at life.
Bant	Shortening of the word 'banter' which means joking or something that is enjoyable.
Bare	A term which can be used to describe a lot of something.
Batty	Gay.
Beef	A disagreement or altercation.
Blade	A knife.
Blessed	A term used to describe a situation that is desirable or good.
Boo	Usually refers to a boyfriend or girlfriend. Sometimes just an affectionate term for a person.
Brain	To perform oral sex on a male.
Brass	Usually used to describe something as bad or useless.
Butters	A derogatory term which means disgusting or ugly.
Chav	Derogatory term used to describe the working classes, particularly to imply that they are common or poor.
Chirpse	To chat up or flirt with someone to whom you are attracted.

Clapped	A derogatory term used to describe the physical appearance of someone you think is ugly.
Cold	To act callously or nastily.
Cotch	A word used to describe chilling or relaxing.
Creasing	Laughing.
Creps	Shoes or trainers.
Cuss	An insult, to insult someone.
Cut	To stab someone.
Dead	Something that is boring or lacks atmosphere.
Deep	Can be used in two different contexts: a harsh insult or action, or to describe something that is profound.
DPMO	Don't piss me off.
Dutty	Something that is dirty; also used to describe members of the opposite sex as ugly.
Dyke	Slang/derogatory term for lesbian.
EMO	Someone who enjoys emotional, lyrical rock music. Both male and female often wear black clothes, eye make-up and piercings.
Faggot	Derogatory word for a homosexual man.
Feds	Police.
Fit	Good-looking, in good shape.
Flop	To fail at something.
Fly	Good-looking, sexually attractive.
Freshie	Fresh off the boat. Usually refers to someone from another country or an immigrant and is meant offensively.

G	Shortened version of the word 'gangster' but more regularly used to describe a friend as a substitute for 'mate'.
Gaming	To play video games, usually in a group.
Gassed	To be overly excited or full of oneself.
Green	Money.
Heads	People.
High	To be under the influence of drugs.
Ho	A derogatory word used to describe a female who is easy or promiscuous.
JK	Just kidding.
LOL	Laugh out loud.
Long	A word used to describe something that requires a lot of effort, of which the reward is not worth it.
Lean	Under the influence of cannabis.
Moist	Horrible or bad.
Neck	To give oral sex.
Neek	A word made using a combination of the words 'nerd' and 'geek' with the same definition as those words.
Nigger	Very offensive term for a black person, particularly when used by white people. Often used by black people as a term of endearment, friendship or greeting.
On road	To be part of a street gang.
Par	A word used when someone has been insulted or when something generally bad happens.

Peak	Used to describe a situation or event that is extremely negative or undesirable.
Peng	The description of a person whom one finds very attractive.
Piff	Used to describe someone who is attractive or something that is good.
Pikey	Derogatory term for someone who looks or is poor. Sometimes refers to a traveller.
Pisshead	Alcoholic.
Pranging	To be paranoid or scared, usually as a result of the use of drugs or alcohol.
Roadman	Someone who spends most of their time on the streets. Usually a member of a gang.
Safe	Used in many different contexts but always to describe something that is good. Can be used as a greeting, as thanks, or to describe someone that you are on good terms with.
Savage	Bad. Distressing. A response to a negative situation or event.
Sexting	To send a text with partial or total nudity and/or sexual content.
Sick	Used to describe something that is good, it replaces the words 'good', 'great' or any other word with the same definition.
Sket	A derogatory term usually used when talking about females who are loose or easy. A more extreme version of 'ho.'
Sling	To sell drugs.
Slutting	To regularly engage in sexual acts with more than

	one partner. A term only used for girls.
SMH	Shakin' my head.
Snake	A snake in the grass. Used to describe someone who is deceiving and untrustworthy.
Squad	A group of friends who spend time with each other.
Swag	Expensive clothes or accessories.
Tooled up	Armed.
Wavey	Used to describe someone who is heavily intoxicated from the use of drugs or alcohol. Also used to describe items of clothing that are considered cool but unique.
WYS	'What you saying?' Term used for 'what are you doing?' or 'what's up?'

Acknowledgements

Thank you to all at Hutchinson who helped me so much, especially the wonderful Emma Mitchell, Tim Bainbridge and Lindsay Davies. Matthew Hamilton for being my agent and 'getting' my original vision. My amazing mum and dad for loving me all the way – and then some. Three Blackwell and Jo Bennett for loving my mum and dad respectively. Ella Combi-Deanus for being the best and bossiest older sister that ever did live! Joel Combi, our dear, quiet only boy in a sea of noisy girls. Steve Deanus, the wisest and kindest brother-in-law. Coralie Llucia How-Choong: the French-baking princess. Ed Dorrell, Michael Shaw and Gerard Kelly, the '*TES* crew' who helped begin my writing career – forever thank you. Dave Butt, who was always there when I most needed him. Sarah Griffin through the best and worst of work and personal times – love you, chick. Andrew Mueller for the black type pedantry. Sir Anthony Seldon for his kindness and support. Michele Litvak for all he's done for Write Club. Will Self for being encouraging about my earliest writing and telling me to work 'extremely hard'. Ray Lewis – truly a prince among men. Everyone who has taken the time to come to Write Club, especially Dan Llewlyn Hall who is now also a good friend. The unbelievably impressive Mark Rose, who is going to be one of life's successes, thank you for helping to compile the appendix of terms. The many people and places that facilitated the interviews – I'm grateful and you helped make this book.

And most of all to Edward Schneider, who taught me the world is a good place, and people are good and who I love so much – you made it all possible.